ISSUES IN THE FRENCH-SPEAKING WORLD

ISSUES IN THE FRENCH-SPEAKING WORLD

Michael B. Kline and Nancy C. Mellerski

Greenwood Press
Westport, Connecticut • London

Library of Congress Cataloging-in-Publication Data

Kline, Michael B.
  Issues in the French speaking world / Michael B. Kline and Nancy C. Mellerski.
      p. cm.
  Includes bibliographical references and index.
  ISBN 0–313–32154–X (alk. paper)
      1. Cultural awareness—France. 2. Globalization—Cultural aspects—French-
  speaking countries. 3. Globalization—Political aspects—French-speaking countries.
  4. French language—Social aspects—French-speaking countries. 5. Group identity—
  Political aspects—French-speaking countries. 6. France—Civilization. I. Mellerski,
  Nancy C. II. Title
  DC33.M4435   2004
  306'.0944—dc22   2004044219

British Library Cataloguing in Publication Data is available.

Library of Congress Catalog Card Number: 2004044219
ISBN: 0–313–32154–X

First published in 2004

Greenwood Press, 88 Post Road West, Westport, CT 06881
An imprint of Greenwood Publishing Group, Inc.
www.greenwood.com

Printed in the United States of America

The paper used in this book complies with the
Permanent Paper Standard issued by the National
Information Standards Organization (Z39.48–1984).

10 9 8 7 6 5 4 3 2 1

Contents

Acknowledgments   vii

Introduction   ix

Note to the Instructor   xiii

Part I: History and Memory   1

1   Jeanne d'Arc: The National Heroine at Issue   3

2   The Trial of Maurice Papon: Holding France
    Accountable   25

3   The Aussaresses Revelations: A Tortured Memory   45

Part II: Competing Voices   65

4   Regional Languages in France: The Return
    of the Repressed?   67

5   The Headscarf Affair: Multiculturalism in Debate   91

6   The Power of Language and Culture in Quebec   117

7   The Ghost of France in the Construction
    of Postcolonial Identities   145

Contents

Part III: Equality   171

8   The Parity Law of 2000: *Aux Armes, Citoyennes!*   173

9   Affirmative Action at Sciences Po:
     Leveling the Playing Field   193

Part IV: Globalization   211

10   French Cinema and the Cultural Exception:
     Holding Off Hollywood   213

11   Trouble Down on the Farm: Big Mac Attack   233

Index   257

Acknowledgments

We are indebted to our colleague Marc Papé, a native *Ivorien*, who wrote the body of the chapter on the Ivory Coast. We are grateful to our former colleague Marjorie A. Fitzpatrick for her willingness to share her expertise in all matters of *Québécois* society. We acknowledge as well Réjane Hugounenq and Philippe de Vreyer for their advice concerning the controversy at Sciences Po. Our thanks to Wendi Schnaufer at Greenwood Publishing and Suzie Wright at Shepherd Inc. for their help and patience in the editing process. And as always, more thanks than we can express to Becky and John.

Introduction

This book is intended to make students better readers of French-speaking cultures. As you increasingly move beyond their surface manifestations (simple knowledge of foods, holidays and festivals, important historical dates, and the like), you will encounter the issues that are important to those who live with them and with which they grapple as concerned citizens. This book will encourage you to explore in depth some of the problems French-speaking peoples face and how they attempt to solve them. In so doing, you will become less likely to generalize or stereotype, a risk that often comes with observing cultural practices different from our own. As you begin to better understand problems in the French-speaking world, you will of necessity be brought back to your own culture, because the study of a foreign civilization only makes sense when we can compare it to the culture that makes us Americans. Indeed, it is impossible to understand another culture without recourse to comparisons with your own.

How French-speaking societies tackle contemporary issues is important in and of itself. Any society that is dynamic and worth study is interesting because it constantly faces questions that define it at a given moment. This does not mean that within a society there will be agreement on issues of importance. Through concise introduction to the issues, contending perspectives on these contentious matters within French-speaking societies, and questions that we want you to explore in your classroom, we want to familiarize you with the kinds of perspectives and opinions that help us to better understand contemporary French-speaking cultures. Our approach encourages you to make sense of them in comparison to similar American issues.

We start with three chapters that highlight the link between history and memory, because history is not simply a compilation of past events. People relate meaningfully to history only when the memory of the past is shared within a culture. Nonetheless, history has not one but many versions, and they vary at any given moment. Therefore, the interpretation of history and historical figures will reflect competing perspectives and ideologies. For example, we treat Jeanne d'Arc as a problematic national heroine whose true story begins after her death as she is interpreted and reinterpreted in the light of disputes between church and state, secularists and believers, nationalists and internationalists. We treat contending views on the more recent French past by examining the trials of Maurice Papon and Paul Aussaresses in order to demonstrate how a reexamination of unpleasant but crucial periods in French history—the Vichy regime and the Algerian war—can allow new understandings to emerge.

Our second group of chapters looks at the way in which social cohesion within a culture is challenged by competing voices. Can one speak of a single national identity where France and the larger French-speaking world are concerned, or have ethnic communities begun to challenge monoculturalism? Thus, a study of France's regional languages reveals how linguistic cultural identity is being reasserted at a point where the transnational forces of the European Union and globalization are threatening ethnic diversity. The French republican tradition of centralization and homogeneity is at odds with France's Muslim community, which seeks to preserve its ethnic and religious identity in the face of French assimilationism, as represented in the headscarf affair. In this light, it is important for us to address the situation of Quebec. Although Canada's culture wars have abated for the moment, the question of linguistic and cultural identity within the Canadian federation has created a series of constitutional crises within recent memory. In the same vein, we include a chapter in which the conflict in the Ivory Coast, written from the perspective of a native Ivorian, Marc Papé, illustrates the continued dominating presence of France within the African community of *la Francophonie* (French speakers). The chapter raises questions about the role played by France's economic and political presence in the country, as well as the persistence of the French language as an instrument of control.

We take up the question of recent initiatives in France regarding the fulfillment of the Revolution's promise of equality (*égalité*) as the subject of our third group of chapters. We study how the dominant groups in French society seek to maintain their position, and how those who have traditionally been excluded have begun to seek a new inclusionary status. We address the issues of parity for women in the electoral process and the French version of affirmative action (*discrimination positive*) at the Institut d'Études Politiques, a prestigious institution in Paris for the study of the social sciences.

Finally, the effects of globalization and Americanization form the subject of our last group of chapters. Two specific issues are highlighted in order to illuminate the troubled relationship between traditional French values and their surrender to the powerful forces of American-led globalization that have affected consumer society, particularly since the end of the Cold War. We trace the history of Franco–American relations in the area of the cinema, as well as the protectionist strategies that France has adopted to counter the American offensive in popular culture. The same issue exists in a seemingly unrelated field, that of agricultural practices under the impact of the biotechnical revolution. The focus of the dispute over genetically modified foods is centered upon a popular French hero, José Bové. The ideological pressures that are revealed within both of these chapters have as their common denominator an abiding theme in contemporary Franco–American relations, the resistance to perceived American domination of world markets.

The topics we have chosen are not meant to provide an exhaustive inventory of current issues in France and French-speaking cultures. Rather, we have selected a number of substantive and controversial areas that lend themselves to fruitful discussion as well as comparison to American society and culture. It is for this reason that a distinctive feature of the book is a discussion summarizing arguments for and against the positions taken within each topic. We also supply a vocabulary list that may prove useful in writing about and discussing the subject. The issues in this volume point to important fault lines within French-speaking societies; in addition, because of their volatility, there are frequently further developments that can be explored inside and outside of class. Therefore, we have included a number of Web sites and other resources to enable readers of this book to go beyond each chapter and to keep up with the evolution of these topics. Similarly, a number of the questions and activities provided at the end of each chapter expand the topic to include reflection on cross-cultural associations and give further ideas for discussion and debate. You will find that many of these questions and activities purposely lead you into other disciplines such as history, sociology, anthropology, and politics. It is our belief that the study of French will take you into every area that affects the development of modern societies. Our hope is that the issues explored in this book will carry you into the kinds of meaningful content and discussions that make language study a portal to intercultural understanding.

Note to the Instructor

Having recently participated in a reappraisal and redrafting of the curriculum in a college French department, the authors are well aware of the changing nature of French and Francophone studies. These changes, coalescing in the mid-1990s, are reflected in two key documents, *Acquiring Cross-Cultural Competence*, published by the American Association of Teachers of French (AATF) in 1996, and the American Council on the Teaching of Foreign Languages (ACTFL) publication, *Standards for Foreign Language Learning in the 21st Century*, 1996 and 1999. Within these approaches to the teaching of French, we place the teaching of culture as the nodal point around which cultural competence and the relationship between the perspectives, practices, and products of a society revolve. Students need to work with significant and meaningful content in order to understand that, as one penetrates beyond the surface layers of a society, communication frequently engages the controversial or confrontational nature of cultural discourse. It is through the examination of important issue-oriented problems and themes within a society that we seek to bring students to a sense of the immediacy and relevance of the culture they are studying when they deal with French. It is the realization that French and Francophone issues are part of an important and evolving global conversation (or sometimes a clash) that facilitates understanding of how their French class relates to the weave of both intracultural and intercultural dialogue.

We know that culture is a matrix of meanings that has evolved over time and that is often expressed in symbolic forms. The texts or scripts of culture correspond to what Lawrence Kritzman refers to as "socially symbolic activity"[1] that manifests itself in images, symbols, collective memory, controversies and debates, events and festivals, points of stress, competing ideologies, and other social and political phenomena by which French and Francophone cultures constantly define and redefine themselves. This approach lends itself very naturally to the standards movement in the United States with its five interlocking Cs—communication, cultures, connections, comparisons, and communities—because culture texts react reciprocally with their context as repositories for the perspectives, norms, and ideologies of all social domains.

This book is intended to be a useful supplement for instructors who are teaching fourth- or fifth-year high school French, or for postsecondary teachers who, during the first two years of college work, wish to expose their students to issues in the French-speaking world that are both contemporary and contentious. The topics we have chosen to cover are necessarily complex because they lie at the heart of discussions or conflicts within the French-speaking societies we study. For this reason, the text is in English. We recognize that the linguistic capacity of students may not yet match the proficiency required to deal meaningfully with the topics in the original French. On the other hand, wherever possible we have suggested resources in French to enable qualified students to deal with the issues directly in the language. It is the instructor's choice as to the degree to which students will read the resource materials, answer the questions, and do the projects in French or English.

As French teachers, we are the experts in the culture of our subject area, and our students deserve to study it in its particulars with us. As a consequence, our approach encourages the necessity for students of French to develop cross-cultural competence in its broadest form by encouraging them to investigate topics that will lead them to the connections and comparisons mandated by the standards. In addition, the kinds of issues we deal with fit the Level 4 and Level 5 specifications for the AATF-sponsored National French Contest.

We hope that the chapters of this book can serve as models for instructors who wish to develop their own units on themes with which they have familiarity, for example, the PACS debate in France and the corresponding controversy about civil unions in the United

States; questions of development and economic opportunity in the Antilles and the distribution of wealth in the United States; the role of French interventionism in a multitude of African nations and the role undertaken by the United States in the "new world order." The list of culture texts in the broadest sense is inexhaustible because, if a society is evolving and dynamic, it will always direct students to the intersection of history and memory, competing voices and contending perspectives that they need to know about in the age when cultural particularism meets global homogeneity.

Note

1. Lawrence Kritzman, "Identity Crises: France, Culture and the Idea of the Idea of the Nation." *Sub-stance* 76/77 (1995): 3–8. Reprinted in *French Cultural Studies: Criticism at the Crossroads,* eds. Marie-Pierre Le Hir and Dana Strand (Albany: State University of New York Press, 2000): 11–27.

Part I

History and Memory

CHAPTER 1

Jeanne d'Arc: The National Heroine at Issue

Jeanne d'Arc is the undisputed French national heroine, but how is it possible that she could be at the same time a heroine of the left and the right, of freethinkers and of believers, of liberals and conservatives? The answer lies more in what the French have made of Jeanne since she was burned at the stake by the English on May 30, 1431, than in what she did during her altogether amazing career. Jeanne's transformations have made her a continuing issue in France. The French take their patrimony seriously, but the French cultural heritage is not monolithic; not only is it open to interpretation, but it is sometimes fabricated. Many learn the story of Jeanne d'Arc as an interesting medieval adventure, or they see action-packed films about this savior of France, but they do not have a sense of Jeanne as an ideological figure transformed by the issues of those who have used her for their own purposes. Indeed, that has been Jeanne's destiny almost from the beginning.

Background

Jeanne d'Arc was born in 1411 or 1412 in Domrémy, on the border between the regions of Champagne and Lorraine. Her humble origins as a spinner of cloth and a shepherdess guarding her father's flock, along with her simplicity and piety, are a matter of legend, but she also seems to have been well informed about politics and military affairs. Although we know her as Jeanne d'Arc, her name was probably Darc; she was in no way noble. In her thirteenth year, Jeanne professed to be commanded by God through the archangel Michael to save France. Later, she would have visions of Saints Catherine and Margaret.

But why did France need saving? In order to understand Jeanne's appeal, we must first understand her role within the Hundred Years War. When Jeanne was three years old, the French suffered their most crushing and humiliating military defeat of the Middle Ages at the battle of Azincourt (Agincourt, 1415) in Normandy, when a numerically smaller English army under the command of the young English king, Henry V, decimated the flower of French chivalry. For the French, this battle marked the darkest hour of the war, which had been going on intermittently since 1347 between the French Capetian dynasty and the English Plantagenet dynasty. After inflicting defeats on the French in Normandy at Crécy (1346), Calais (1347), and Poitiers (1356), the English had signed a peace treaty to end the first part of the war in 1389. This peace lasted until 1411.

By 1392 matters began to go downhill for the French again. The reigning French king, Charles VI, was affected by the mental illness that plagued him increasingly. The Burgundians (*les Bourguignons*), whose duchy occupied the east of France, were allied with the English against the French crown. The English monarchy already controlled the southwest part of France, known as la Guyenne, through marriage and inheritance rights. After the defeat at Azincourt, the Treaty of Troyes (1420) made Henry V the inheritor of the French crown. Upon the deaths of Henry V and Charles VI, both in 1422, the infant king of England, Henry VI, became the inheritor of both the kingdoms of England and of France. On the French side, the disinherited son of Charles VI, known as the dauphin, was left with very little. Caught between the English in the west and the Burgundians in the east, his capital was reduced to Bourges on the Cher river. Those loyal to him were known as the Armagnacs, but at this time, because he controlled only the southern portion of the country, he was derisively labeled the king of Bourges (*le roi de Bourges*). The English besieged Orléans, on the Loire river. Should Orléans have fallen, the way would have been open for the English conquest of what remained of the French kingdom. The future of France hung by a thread.

Enter Jeanne

Into this situation rode Jeanne d'Arc. In 1429 she somehow convinced Robert de Beaudricourt, who was defending the town of Vaucouleurs, to send her with an armed escort through enemy lines to meet the French dauphin. She had shaved her head and donned men's clothing. After a danger-filled ride of eleven days, she arrived at Chinon, in the Loire valley. Put to the test, she was able to detect the true heir to the French kingdom instead of an imposter who had been placed on the throne as a trap, whereupon she declared, "Very noble lord dauphin, I have come and have been sent by God to bring help to you and your kingdom" ("*Très noble seigneur dauphin, je suis venue et suis envoyée de par Dieu pour apporter du secours à vous et à votre royaume*"[1]). To convince him of her mission, Jeanne revealed a secret to the dauphin that remains a subject of speculation even to this day.[2] Also known as *la Pucelle* (the Maiden), Jeanne was verified by examination to be a virgin, an important element at the time in giving credence to her purity of intentions and her possible link with the divine, since it was believed that the devil could not have commerce with a virgin.

With French affairs having sunk into near hopelessness, Jeanne was outfitted in armor and given a company of men, with whom she proceeded to raise the siege of Orléans on May 8, 1429. On the ascendancy and gathering momentum, Jeanne led soldiers to further victories, climaxed by a decisive battle against the English at Patay on June 18, 1429. Jeanne then led the dauphin to Reims where, on July 17, 1429, he was crowned king in the cathedral, the traditional site for French coronations. Hope was reborn with the ascension of a legitimate king, now known as Charles VII. After Jeanne had ensured that France would have a crowned and anointed king, Charles VII began to follow his own political goals. Rather than continue the war, he sought peace and reconciliation with his enemy Philippe le Bon, duke of Burgundy.

Jeanne's brief military career came crashing down on May 23, 1430, when she was captured by the Burgundians at Compiègne. Jeanne's military bravery and selflessness held true until the end, however, when she purposefully positioned herself with her small rear guard to hold off the enemy. Just when she and her men were to ride behind the protective walls of the city, the gate was closed. The possible betrayal of Jeanne has been of interest to historians for years.

5

The Trial

A former rector of the University of Paris, Pierre Cauchon, now the bishop of Beauvais and a collaborator with the English, acted as intermediary for the purchase of Jeanne from the Burgundians. She was transferred to the English stronghold at Rouen. Almost immediately after her capture, the clerics of the school of theology of the University of Paris, whose sympathies lay with the English, requested that Jeanne be turned over to them to be questioned concerning heresy. Bishop Cauchon was named as Jeanne's chief judge by the Duke of Bedford, representative of the English crown in France.[3]

What is unusual about the trial is that there was never a formal indictment brought forth against Jeanne. From the outset, Cauchon's agents scoured the countryside, trying to find evidence of heresy against her, only to return empty-handed. Cauchon and his assistants had to rely only upon Jeanne's own words in the hope of indicting her.[4] A second unusual aspect of the trial is that, while Jeanne was kept imprisoned in an English jail under the guard of English soldiers, she was tried in an ecclesiastical court, which had its own prisons and jurisdictions, and in which those accused of heresy were normally kept. The political nature of the trial was thus clear. Jeanne was a military and political prisoner who was being tried by those in the French Church who were in league with the English claimants to the French throne. If Jeanne were convicted of heresy, her military and political exploits on behalf of the French crown would then be diminished.

Although Jeanne was extensively questioned, she was never allowed a lawyer, contrary to usual practice. Her responses, remarkable for a peasant girl uneducated in medieval ecclesiastical subtleties, were characterized by calm intelligence and wit. In answer to the question, "How did saint Michael appear to you? Was he naked?" (*"En quelle figure était saint Michel quand il vous est apparu . . . Était-il nu?"*), Jeanne replied, "Do you think that God doesn't have the means to clothe him?" (*"Pensez-vous que Dieu n'ait pas de quoi le vêtir?"*[5]). Her simple faith stood in contrast to the offenses against doctrine or canonical law with which the churchmen wanted to charge her.

Under considerable pressure by the court, Jeanne signed a Latin document on May 23, 1431, in which she abjured her errors. She promised to give up carrying arms and to cease shaving her head and wearing men's clothing, in exchange for which she would escape burning at the stake. She expected to be imprisoned in a church prison rather than an English military jail. Pierre Cauchon ordered that she be returned to the latter, which practically guaranteed that Jeanne would "relapse," given the fact that male attire may have been her only defense against rape. She did, in fact, begin wearing men's clothing several days later, citing broken promises to allow her to hear mass, to take communion, and to be freed of her chains.

Cauchon lost no time in announcing that Jeanne's insubordination to the church was evident in her refusal to wear women's clothing. On May 30, 1431, she was handed over to the secular authorities, who had hurriedly erected a stake on the place du Vieux-Marché in Rouen. She asked for a cross, which was given to her by an English soldier as the flames mounted. She invoked her saints' help. The last cry of this heroic nineteen-year-old girl was "*Jésus!*"

The Appropriation of the Past

One might say that the true story of Jeanne d'Arc begins after her death. Through a series of treaties and military victories, the French began to take back occupied lands such that, by 1453, the English were finished in France. A church inquiry into Jeanne's trial was opened in 1452, with the result that, in 1456, the original trial was declared null and void. In 1920, 489 years after her death, Pope Benedict XV canonized Jeanne d'Arc as a saint of the Catholic Church.

In the same way that Americans have heard the story of Washington crossing the Delaware, the French have grown up with Jeanne d'Arc. She has been memorialized by hundreds of historians, biographers, poets, dramatists, composers, and filmmakers. Jeanne represents the principle that France is one sovereign nation, that it is entitled to its own government invested with authority, and that it has the right to resist foreign intervention. Nevertheless, what makes Jeanne an issue in modern France is how those principles are interpreted. She is the problematic national heroine because the opposing ideas and ideologies that have characterized modern France are readily found in the ways people have chosen to read her.

During the three centuries following her death, Jeanne was more or less forgotten. The nineteenth and twentieth centuries brought about a resurgence of memory concerning the Maid of Orléans. One of the first to challenge the legendary status of Jeanne was Voltaire (1694–1778), one of the luminaries of the eighteenth-century Enlightenment. A deist and foe of revealed religion, Voltaire believed that in her naivety Jeanne was taken advantage of by the clerics who conspired against her. "No longer make of Jeanne d'Arc a divinely inspired individual, but rather a fearless idiot who thought herself divinely inspired; a local heroine who was made to play a grand role; a worthy girl whom inquisitors and doctors of theology had burned at the stake with the most cowardly cruelty" ("*Ne fais plus de Jeanne d'Arc une inspirée, mais une idiote hardie qui se croyait inspirée; une héroïne de village, à qui on fit jouer un grand rôle; une brave fille, que des inquisiteurs et des docteurs firent brûler avec la plus lâche cruauté*"6).

In Voltaire's satirical epic poem, *The Maid of Orleans* (*La Pucelle*, 1755), Jeanne becomes the object of the sexual desire of every soldier and mule-skinner in France. Her virginity is even tempted by a donkey in whose form Satan is hiding. In one scene, while saving nuns from rape and pillage by English soldiers, Jeanne must fight while naked in order to recover her stolen armor: "Joan was *en cuerpo* [naked], when a Briton's eyes, With look unblushing, greet the wished-for prize; He covets her, and thinks some maiden gay/Has sought the sisters to enjoy the fray; Then flies the fair to meet, and forthwith seeks/To taint her modesty with loathsome freaks" ("*Jeanne était nue; un Anglais impudent/Vers cet objet tourne soudain sa tête; Il la convoite: il pense fermement/Qu'elle venait pour être de la fête./Vers elle il court, et sur sa nudité/Il va cherchant la sale volupté*"7).

While Voltaire's treatment of Jeanne d'Arc represents the views of the Enlightenment on revealed religion, this attack on the savior of France is the opening salvo of a century and a half of efforts by French freethinkers and anticlerical republicans to denigrate Jeanne as the divinely inspired representative of conservative Catholic values.

The end of the nineteenth century marks the culminating battles between church and state in France (the separation became official in 1905). Wanting to cast doubt upon Jeanne as a messenger of God, freethinkers used psychiatric explanations to portray Jeanne's visions as hallucinations. Anatole France, the winner of the Nobel Prize for Literature in 1921, claimed in his two-volume biography of Jeanne that she had hallucinations of the senses, particularly of hearing. "She had visions, and these visions were neither pretend nor fake; she really believed she heard voices which were speaking to her and that did not come from human lips . . . What else is there to say than she had hallucinations of hearing, sight, touch and smell? In her, of all the senses, the most affected is that of hearing" (*"Elle eut des visions, et ces visions ne furent ni feintes ne contrefaites; elle crut réellement entendre des voix qui lui parlaient et qui ne sortaient pas d'une bouche humaine . . . Qu'est-ce à dire qu'elle avait des hallucinations de l'ouïe, de la vue, du toucher et de l'odorat? Chez elle, de tous les sens, le plus affecté c'est l'ouïe"*[8]). Citing advances in the new science of psychiatry, he invoked medical authority to interpret Jeanne's messages from God: "There are in all these hallucinations the same objective clearness, the same subjective certainty as in hallucinations induced by alcohol poisoning, and this sharpness, this certainty, could quite well, in Jeanne's case, cause one to think again of hysteria" (*"Il y a dans toutes ces hallucinations la même netteté objective, la même certitude subjective, que dans les hallucinations toxiques de l'alcool, et cette netteté, cette certitude peuvent bien, dans le cas de Jeanne, faire penser encore à l'hystérie"*[9]). The admiration of Anatole France for Jeanne's personal qualities, what he calls *"la beauté de son coeur"* (the beauty of her heart)[10] are nonetheless overridden by his skeptical demythologizing, thus reducing her to nonmystical stature.

For its part, the modern French Church was eager to distance itself from the medieval clerics who had condemned Jeanne. At the time canonization procedures were begun in 1894, Church apologists repudiated Bishop Cauchon as a sellout to the English, comparing him to Pilate and Judas and as a precursor to Voltaire: "Ah! We admit it," said the archbishop of Aix, "she was sent to her death by a bishop who was no longer French since he had sold out to the English. . . . But Pope Calixtus III avenged the Virgin of Domrémy. He ordered the revision of the trial: he overturned and vacated the sentence as the most monstrous since Pilate's. . . . Cauchon was the precursor of Voltaire, that profaner of our most dazzling and purest national glory" (*"Ah! nous l'avouons, elle fut envoyée à la mort par un évêque qui n'avait plus rien de français, puisqu'il s'était vendu aux Anglais. . . . Mais le Pape Calixte III a vengé la Vierge de Domrémy. Il a ordonné la révision du procès: il a cassé et annulé la sentence, comme la plus monstrueuse depuis celle de Pilate. . . . Cauchon fut le précurseur de Voltaire, ce profanateur de notre gloire nationale la plus éclatante et la plus pure"*[11]).

In the nineteenth century, concern in France with building a modern nation led to the identification of patriotic models. Jules Michelet (1798–1874), the great historian of the century, described Jeanne's adventure with full lyricism, but he was also careful to rationalize her faith in terms of its historical background: "A twelve-year-old child, a very young girl, confusing the voice of her heart with that of heaven, gets the strange, improbable, if you will, absurd idea . . . to save her country" ("*Une enfant de douze ans, une toute jeune fille, confondant la voix de son coeur avec la voix du ciel, conçoit l'idée étrange, improbable, absurde, si l'on veut, . . . de sauver son pays*"[12]). Michelet described Jeanne as the true founder of the motherland (*la patrie*) because her love for France was so pure and so sublime that she inspired the people to revolt against their occupiers:

> For the first time, one feels, France is loved like a person. And she becomes such from the day that she is loved.
> Until then she was just a group of provinces, a vast chaos of fiefdoms, a vague idea of a great country. But from this day henceforth, through the strength of the heart, she is a nation.
> Beautiful mystery! Touching! Sublime! How the immense and pure love of a young heart inflamed an entire world, gave it a second life, the true life that love alone gives.
> (*Pour la première fois, on le sent, la France est aimée comme une personne. Et elle devient telle du jour qu'elle est aimée.*
> *C'était jusque-là une réunion de provinces, un vaste chaos de fiefs, grand pays, d'idée vague. Mais, dès ce jour, par la force du cœur, elle est une patrie.*
> *Beau mystère! touchant! sublime! Comment l'amour immense et pur d'un jeune cœur embrasa tout un monde, lui donna cette seconde vie, la vraie vie que l'amour seul donne.*[13])

Michelet believed in the role to be played in history by heroic, forceful personalities. Jeanne became for him the source of the first stirrings of a national spirit in France. This view of Jeanne was shared by other republican writers and thinkers, from moderates to socialists, who found her rebellion against Church authority and her bravery against long odds to incarnate the spirit of common people in postrevolutionary France. As the inspiration for the people, she represented republicanism in a time when France was trying to define itself as a democratic, secular nation.

Although intellectual republicans and socialists of the left like Lucien Herr, Charles Péguy, and Jean Jaurès praised Jeanne as a free-thinking unifier of the national identity, it was French nationalists of the right (conservative Catholics, monarchists, and strong-government proponents) who most vocally appropriated Jeanne as the pure, Aryan spirit of the French. Jeanne became for them the symbol of the French as a race as well as a nation. Between 1870 and 1914 Jeanne was for French nationalists the embodiment of all conservative virtues—rootedness to the soil, antimaterialism, popular origin—that served to bolster anti-Semitic views, which interpreted Jews to be foreign to France, materialistic and internationalist. For example, Jeanne's name was often evoked by those who stood against Captain Alfred Dreyfus, the Jewish army officer falsely accused of treason.[14] If the left had secularized public education by separating church from state, and if it was seen to be incapable of preparing France for the next battle with the Germans, the right adopted Jeanne as a symbol of a unified church and state and a strong army capable of regaining the provinces of Alsace and Lorraine, lost to the Prussians in the Franco-Prussian war of 1870.

This linking of Jeanne to right-wing partisan causes led to a period between the two world wars when French fascists regularly called upon Jeanne as their patron saint whose spirit would help to purify and revivify a decadent and corrupt France. On the other hand, during the German occupation of France between 1940 and 1944, and particularly at the liberation, Charles de Gaulle, leader of the Free French, was compared to Jeanne d'Arc.

More recently, Jeanne has been appropriated by the *Front National*, one of France's best-known right-wing political parties. Its leader is Jean-Marie Le Pen who, after service as an officer in the French paratroops during the Indochinese war and the Algerian conflict, was elected to the *Assemblée Nationale* in 1956. He founded the right-wing, nationalistic *Front National* in 1972. Since that time he has been elected by his constituents to a number of offices in French and European politics. He was a candidate for the presidency of France as late as 2002, having won almost 20 percent of the vote in the first round of elections.

The party stands for an autonomous France that can resist the current of globalization led by the United States and abetted, in Le Pen's opinion, by the centralizing forces of the European Union. The *Front National* is a classic nationalist party in its view that ethnic and political boundaries should coincide. It is particularly outspoken against immigration into France from North Africa. Le Pen has also been accused of making anti-Semitic remarks.

The *Front National* has adopted Jeanne d'Arc as its national heroine. Since 1979 it has chosen to celebrate her, first on the traditional holiday of May 8 and then on May 1, so that the party can express its

Paris, Wednesday, May 1, 2002. Supporters of extreme-right presidential candidate Jean-Marie Le Pen wave French flags and campaign posters during the National Front's traditional May Day march to honor Joan of Arc. (AP/World Wide Photos)

solidarity with workers on a holiday that is normally identified with the political left. Le Pen's usual speech on that occasion reveals his identification of Jeanne with the defense of national values and interests as he defines them:

> Globalism, communism, European unity, decadence, falling birthrates, unemployment, immigration, crime, corruption, political and cultural colonization, such are some of the threats that weigh upon us at the dawn of the twenty-first century . . . And it is there that we need Jeanne's example and her protection to intercede for us. Jeanne came to confound the treason of the Treaty of Troyes [through which the king of England became the inheritor of the crown of France and the dauphin, heir to the French throne, was disinherited in 1420], let us unite to undo the Maastricht Treaty [treaty that established the European Union, signed in 1992] and kick out the traitors. . . . Let us listen to Jeanne, always among us in the Motherland for which she gave her life almost six centuries ago.
> Let us listen to her; let us fight and God will give victory!

Long live life, long live truth, long live France, long live the
National Front, long live Jeanne!

*(Mondialisme, communisme, Européisme, décadence, dénatalité, chô-
mage, immigration, insécurité, corruption, colonisation politique et culturelle, telles sont quelques-unes des menaces qui pèsent sur nous à l'aube
du 21ème siècle . . . Et c'est là que l'exemple de Jeanne et sa protection
nous sont nécessaires pour intercéder. Jeanne est venue pour mettre en
échec la trahison du Traité de Troyes, unissons-nous pour jeter bas le
Traité de Maastricht et bouter les traîtres. . . . Écoutons Jeanne, toujours présente, dans la Patrie pour laquelle elle donna sa vie, il y a près
de 6 siècles.*

Écoutons-la, Bataillons et Dieu donnera la Victoire!

*Vive la Vie, vive la Vérité, vive la France, vive le Front National,
vive Jeanne!*[15])

For Le Pen, national independence, globalization, immigration,
family values, low birthrates (of Caucasian French children), decadent practices (drugs, homosexual unions, abortion), and cultural
dominance (primarily by the United States) are issues faced by
France that can be treated by a return to "pure" French values—
family, religion, traditions—of which the Front National is the latest
standard-bearer. For this political party, Jeanne d'Arc is the symbol
of resistance against all that is not "French." Jeanne has again been
resurrected in the service of the nation, albeit from the perspective of
ideologically charged partisan politics.

Thus, the national heroine is at issue in France because she can be
made to serve the collective French memory as a political and cultural agent for various ideologies. For some, she is the heroine who
resists political compromise and military timidity. For others, she
represents the will to battle doctrinaire hierarchy at the root of politically divisive partisanship. For yet others, she symbolizes an ideal of
French virtue, honor, and purity that resists corrupting foreign influences. As such, Jeanne has been at the forefront of discordant issues
in France for over two hundred years.

Discussion

Because culture "texts" like Jeanne d'Arc are inherited from the
past, we tend to regard them as somehow natural, made of whole
cloth, and truthful. But as we have seen, a culture writes its texts
according to its needs at a particular moment. It often does so within

a society at the prompting of those who would seize or hold power or change its distribution. Culture texts are therefore products that are the end point of a process within a particular context. They are vessels to be filled by the ideologies, visions, and aspirations of a group. If this is the case, how are we to interpret the culture texts represented by our heroes, and what is their significance? Can we view them as eternal truths valid for all moments, or are our heroes manufactured like any other form of cultural production?

It is important for a society to establish its cultural heroes as images of the way in which we best imagine ourselves to be, to account for our most noble premises and represent our highest aspirations.

Agree

The French have been correct in identifying Jeanne d'Arc as the national heroine because without her intervention France might well have become a branch of the English crown. Today it could be a former colony like Australia, Canada, India, or Kenya. Jeanne changed the course of French history and as such best represents the continuity of France as a distinct entity. Among nations, France is one that most highly prizes its patrimony and independence. There are few people in French history who have contributed more to that heritage than Jeanne. There is no doubt that she represents France's aspirations to be free and independent to the highest degree, which is why the French continue to celebrate her in modern times. André Malraux, famous novelist and a former French minister of culture, put it this way in 1964: "She remade the army, the king, France . . . It was easier to burn her than to rip the soul of France from her. . . . O Jeanne, who lies without a burial place, you who knew that the tomb of heroes is the heart of the living" (". . . *elle refit l'armée, le roi, la France. . . . Il était plus facile de la brûler que de l'arracher de l'âme de la France. . . . Ô Jeanne sans sépulcre, toi qui savais que le tombeau des héros est le coeur des vivants*"[16]).

Heroes and heroines of the past are designated as such precisely because they go beyond the boundaries of the ordinary. Their actions are so important and so exemplary that there is room for us constantly to reinterpret them in the light of current events. We can establish our culture heroes as images of the way we best imagine ourselves to be, to account for our most noble premises and to represent our highest achievements. Of course the culture hero is open to interpretation! It is because the hero goes beyond established norms, has the genius or the daring to try something different or to

14

recognize the high moral ground, that one can never limit heroic behavior to the literal events. When we recognize them as heroes, these persons outlive their destiny precisely because they are transcendent. They have saved or maintained important ideals, and we have the right to reinterpret them for our own time. The culture hero is the bridge between our past and our present.

Disagree

Jeanne d'Arc is an illusion. Although the historical Jeanne d'Arc played an important role in French history during the Hundred Years War, her real significance lies in the fact that, since then, she has been appropriated by every partisan cause and ideological position known in France during the past two centuries. Particularly in the modern period, Jeanne has become the puppet of opposing forces, a manufactured image serving the needs of the moment. Just what aspirations and motives are we talking about when we celebrate Jeanne? We can admire her as a historical figure, but she is not the representative of modern France that various causes have made her out to be. Study reveals her to be a creation corresponding to the agendas of the left or the right, the secularists or the religious, the misogynists or the feminists. What we imagine ourselves to be is usually of the moment. We have to ask, therefore, of which France is Jeanne the heroine?

We should not make of our culture heroes whatever we want. This opens them to erroneous interpretations and to mystification. We risk falsifying history or at least spinning it to serve our own aims. Jeanne's actions took place in a particular time and for a particular motive. It is not proper to make her represent ideals or aspirations that came after the fact. Jeanne is just a precursor to a practice that has become so pervasive in politics, finance, and even advertising that we can no longer take any pronouncement at face value. The creation of symbolic figures or traditions should be a natural practice of a people. They should emanate from the people over time, rather than be imposed from the top by those who stand to gain from a narrow interpretation. Our society has made this habit so routine as to have created professional spinmeisters.

Jeanne's claim of divine inspiration should be respected.

Agree

There are, on occasion, those beings who are able to translate a message of a higher order that can save a troubled people. In modern times, Mahatma Gandhi and Dr. Martin Luther King, Jr., have been called that kind of leader. People can clearly see the working of some transcendent force through them, be it divine will, historical unfolding, or striving for a higher moral plane. Jeanne d'Arc was no less a figure. When we scoff at those who claim divine inspiration, we do so because we fear being taken in or because we recognize that their goals do not correspond to the moral teachings of our religious practice. Jeanne expressed her confidence in the rule of rightful authority and her faith in deliverance in the terms of her day. She lived her life in witness to her ideals. If she were alive today, she might use different language or the scenarios of her visions might play differently, but she would be no less a messenger of fundamental truths.

Disagree

In every place, there are those who claim to have received a message from God. History is full of charlatans who have proclaimed themselves to be divine messengers but who have turned out to have feet of clay. What prevents them from being locked up as lunatics is that they are skillful at translating that message into action and having others go along with it. Those who came into contact with Jeanne d'Arc were right to distrust her. Her divine mission was really a political one, something the English recognized right away. Her enemies were correct in having her charged with heresy, thus eliminating her as a threat to their ambitions. They allowed their collaborators to attack her visions in order to reveal a much more worldly agenda. Jeanne promoted a redistribution of power disguised as the expression of God's will. She expressed her politics as the voice of divinity.

Questions and Activities

1. The Hundred Years War is the context that must be understood to fully appreciate the story of Jeanne d'Arc. Read a short history of the Hundred Years War, paying careful attention to the cast of characters and the sequence of events. (A readable version is Desmond Seward, *The Hundred Years War*, New York: Penguin Books, 1999.) Make a preliminary diagram of the events so that their unfolding is clear across a time line. Compare notes with a

partner or a small work group. Collectively make a series of illustrative posters from which you can give a background talk.

2. Find several portraits, sculptures, or other representations of Jeanne that portray her in different ways. How do the artists conceive of Jeanne according to their representation of her? Compare and contrast. Is she portrayed as a saint? A warrior? What motive might lie behind these representations? See, for example, Ingres's 1854 painting, *Joan of Arc at the Coronation of Charles VII* (*Jeanne d'Arc au sacre du roi Charles VII, dans la cathédrale de Reims*), at <http://www.hol.gr/cgfa/ingres/p-ingres25.htm>; the statue by François Rude (1852); Paul Gauguin's 1889 painting, *Jeanne d'Arc;* or Anna Vaughn Hayatt's statue (first equestrian sculpture of a woman by a woman, 1910). Other images are found on the Musée Jeanne d'Arc site, listed below, and on various sites referred to in the Resource Guide.

3. At the time of Jeanne's death, France could not be called a nation in the modern sense. It was the nineteenth century that celebrated Jeanne d'Arc as a founder during a time of nation-building in modern France. In 1882 French philosopher and historian Ernest Renan gave a lecture at the Sorbonne that was the basis for his famous essay, *What Is a Nation?* (*Qu'est-ce qu'une nation?*). He said, "The cult of ancestors is the most legitimate of all cults; ancestors have made us what we are. A heroic past, great men [sic], glory (I mean true glory), that's the social capital upon which to base the idea of a nation" ("*Le culte des ancêtres est de tous le plus légitime; les ancêtres nous ont faits ce que nous sommes. Un passé héroïque, des grands hommes, de la gloire (j'entends de la véritable), voilà le capital social sur lequel on assied une idée nationale*"). See the Resource Guide for the source of the full text. Argue for or against Renan's assertion in a persuasive essay. You may use either French or American examples.

4. Read Jean Anouilh's 1953 play about Jeanne d'Arc, *L'Alouette* (*The Lark*), as a class project. Jeanne is typical of Anouilh's heroines. The playwright defines the heroine as the person who can refuse when, in the face of all contrary logic or absurdity, she should assent. What does Anouilh intend by the heroine's refusal? Do you agree with this definition of heroism? Given the fact that the play was written shortly after World War II, read the characters' roles against the backdrop of events in France during the German occupation from 1940 to 1944. (Suggestion: read Bishop Cauchon as a Vichy collaborator, Jeanne as a member of the Resistance, and Warwick as a cynical German occupier.) Does Jeanne's

stance make sense to you today? Does the world have room for a Jeanne today in the light of any contemporary events?

5. Many films have been made about Jeanne d'Arc, going back to the earliest days of cinema. Your local video store or library may have Luc Besson's 1999 film, *The Messenger*, or Jacques Rivette's 1994 *Jeanne La Pucelle*. The classic film section may contain Otto Preminger's 1957 *Saint Joan*, with Jean Seberg, or Roberto Rosselini's 1954 *Joan of Arc* (*Giovanna d'Arco al Rogo*), starring Ingrid Bergman. Carl Dreyer's *The Passion of Joan of Arc*, 1928, has been re-released (DVD, Criterion Collection/Home Vision Entertainment, 1999). For a spoof on the legend, see scenes dedicated to the Maid of Lorraine in the 1988 film, *Bill and Ted's Excellent Adventure*. Write an analysis in which you explain how the director of the film has chosen to portray Jeanne. What aspects of her career are emphasized? Why do you think this is the case? Or, compare two films about Jeanne. Where do they differ? With what results for the viewer? (For an overview, see the article by Kevin J. Harty, "Jeanne au cinéma," in Wheeler and Wood, eds., *Fresh Verdicts*, cited in the Resource Guide.)

6. For the past decade, Jeanne d'Arc has been largely the property of the *Front National* (FN). Consult the Web site of this political party at <http://www.front-national.com/>. What is its agenda? How does the FN vision of Jeanne play to its program for France? Why does this political party consider her to be the embodiment of the true France? (See also the article by Nadia Margolis, "The 'Joan Phenomenon' and the French Right," in Wheeler and Wood, eds., *Fresh Verdicts*, referenced in the Resource Guide.)

7. How have we treated American heroes as cultural texts? Choose an American figure who has been controversial, and trace the fortunes of that person as he/she has been variously interpreted over time. Some examples might be Thomas Jefferson, Molly Pitcher, General Douglas MacArthur, President John F. Kennedy, the Reverend Martin Luther King, Jr. Why do we celebrate them? Are there details about their lives that we should weigh further in our consideration of them as American heroes? Should these facts change our opinion of them?

8. A recent example of an American heroine is Private Jessica Lynch, who was dramatically rescued from an Iraqi hospital during the Iraq war in 2003. As the story unfolded, different versions began to emerge. Form a group to trace the story of Private Lynch from various media accounts, and report to the class what happened to her. In what ways does the treatment of her story resemble that of Jeanne d'Arc? In what ways does it diverge from it? In what man-

ner might the real stories of both of these young women, Jeanne and Jessica, not be about them directly? Justify your answer. (See, for example, Mark Bowden, "Sometimes Heroism Is a Moving Target," *New York Times*, June 8, 2003, sec. 4; Ron Haggart, "What the Spin Doctors Ordered," *Globe and Mail* [Toronto], August 8, 2003; David D. Kirkpatrick, "Jessica Lynch Criticizes U.S. Accounts of Her Ordeal," *New York Times*, November 7, 2003. You may have seen the unauthorized television version of the story, *Saving Jessica Lynch*, first broadcast on NBC on November 9, 2003. Compare this version to the authorized biography of Jessica Lynch by Rick Bragg, *I Am a Soldier Too*, New York: Alfred A. Knopf, 2003.)

9. Do you think that Jeanne should be cited as a heroine of feminism? Argue in an essay that her demise was caused as much by her crossing of gender boundaries as it was by having confronted religious authority or having been used as a political pawn. You may want to reference the essays by Susan Schibanoff and Christine McWebb in Wheeler and Wood, eds., *Fresh Verdicts*, cited in the Resource Guide.

Vocabulary/Vocabulaire

Nouns/Substantifs

achievement	un accomplissement
ancestors	les ancêtres (m. & f.)
armor	l'armure (f.)
freethinker	un libre penseur
heresy	l'hérésie (f.)
hero	le héros; l'héroïne
Hundred Years War	la Guerre de Cent Ans
ideology	l'idéologie (f.)
meaning	la signification
political left	la gauche
political party	un parti politique
political right	la droite
Pope	le Pape
resister	un(e) résistant(e)
saint	un saint, une sainte

significance	signification, importance, conséquence (f.)
star (of film)	une vedette
warrior	un guerrier, une guerrière

Verbs/Verbes

canonize	canoniser (qqn.)
distrust	se méfier de
embody	incarner
mean, signify	signifier

Adjectives/Adjectifs

anticlerical	anticlérical –aux
partisan	partisan(e)
significant	significatif -ive
skeptical	sceptique

Expressions/Expressions

to be burned alive	être brûlé vif
dress like a man	s'habiller en homme
hear voices	entendre des voix
heroic past	un passé héroïque
main character	le personnage principal

Notes

1. Régine Pernoud, *Petite vie de Jeanne d'Arc* (Paris: Desclée de Brouwer, 1995), 34.

2. See Karen Sullivan, in "The Sign for the King," *The Interrogation of Joan of Arc* (Minneapolis: Minnesota University Press, 1999).

3. Pernoud, *Petite vie*, 98.

4. Ibid., 99–100.

5. Ibid., 107.

6. Voltaire, *Les Honnêtetés littéraires XXII*, in *Mélanges*, ed. Jacques Van Den Heuvel (Paris: Gallimard, 1961), 999.

7. Voltaire, *La Pucelle* [1755]. vol. 9 of *Oeuvres Complètes de Voltaire* trans. W. F. Fleming. Quoted in Philip Stewart, "Kisses, en Taille Douce."

A New History of French Literature. Edited by Denis Hollier (Cambridge: Harvard University Press, 1989), 512. (Paris: Garnier Frères, 1877), Chant XI, 177.

    8. Anatole France, *Vie de Jeanne d'Arc,* vol. 15 of *Œuvres complètes illustrées de Anatole France* (Paris: Calmann-Lévy, 1925–35), 29.

    9. France, vol. 16, *Lettre du Docteur Dumas,* 446.

    10. France, vol. 15, 68.

    11. Quoted in Michel Winock, "Jeanne d'Arc," in *Les Lieux de Mémoire,* vol. 3, ed. Pierre Nora (Paris: Gallimard, 1992), 694, 696. An English version may be found in *Realms of Memory,* vol. 3, trans. Arthur Goldhammer, ed. Lawrence D. Kritzman (New York: Columbia University Press, 1998).

    12. Jules Michelet, *Jeanne d'Arc* [1853] (Paris: Hachette, 1879), viii.

    13. Ibid., xv.

    14. Winock, "Jeanne d'Arc," 722.

    15. Jean-Marie Le Pen, "Fête de Jeanne d'Arc du 1er mai 2000," *Front National,* May 1, 2000, <http://www.frontnational.com/lesdiscours.php?id_inter=9> (accessed November 13, 2003).

    16. André Malraux, *Oraisons funèbres* (Paris: Gallimard, 1971), 90, 93, 101.

Bibliography

France, Anatole. *Vie de Jeanne d'Arc.* Vols. XV, XVI. *Œuvres complètes illustrées de Anatole France.* 25 vols. Paris: Calmann-Lévy, 1925–35.

Le Pen, Jean-Marie. "Discours de la Fête de Jeanne d'Arc du 1er mai 2000." <http://www.frontnational.com/lesdiscours.php?id_inter=9>.

Malraux, André. *Oraisons funèbres.* Paris: Gallimard, 1971.

Michelet, Jules. *Jeanne d'Arc* [1853]. Paris: Hachette, 1879. Translated by Albert Guérard as *Joan of Arc.* Ann Arbor: Michigan University Press, 1957. Translation does not include the introduction found in this chapter.

Pernoud, Régine. *Petite vie de Jeanne d'Arc.* Paris: Desclée de Brouwer, 1990.

Voltaire. *Les Honnêtetés littéraires* in *Mélanges.* Edited by Jacques Van Den Heuvel. Paris: Gallimard, 1961.

———. *La Pucelle* [1755]. *Oeuvres Complètes de Voltaire.* Vol. 9. Paris: Garnier Frères, 1877.

———. *The Maid of Orleans.* Translated by W. F. Fleming, Vols. 40 and 41. *The Works of Voltaire.* Akron: Werner, 1905. Quoted in Philip Stewart. "Kisses, en Taille Douce." *A New History of French Literature.* Edited by Denis Hollier. Cambridge: Harvard University Press, 1989.

Winock, Michel. "Jeanne d'Arc." *Les Lieux de Mémoire.* Vol. III, 3. Edited by Pierre Nora. Paris: Gallimard, 1992. An English version may be found in *Realms of Memory.* Vol. III. Translated by Arthur Goldhammer. Edited by Lawrence D. Kritzman. New York: Columbia University Press, 1998.

Resource Guide

Further Reading

Balladur, Edouard. *Jeanne d'Arc et la France: le mythe du sauveur*. Paris: Fayard, 2003.

Crane, Susan. "Clothing and Gender Definition: Joan of Arc." *Journal of Medieval and Early Modern Studies* 28 (1996): 297–320.

Duby, Andrée, and Georges Duby. *Les Procès de Jeanne d'Arc*. Folio Histoire 69. Paris: Gallimard, 1995.

Krumeich, Gerd. *Jeanne d'Arc à travers l'histoire*. Paris: Albin Michel, 1993.

———. "Joan of Arc between Right and Left." In *Nationhood and Nationalism in France: From Boulangism to the Great War, 1889–1919*, 63–73. London: Routledge, 1992.

Margolis, Nadia. *Joan of Arc in History, Literature and Film*. New York and London: Garland Publishing, Inc., 1990.

Pernoud, Régine. *Jeanne d'Arc: la reconquête de la France*. Paris: Gallimard, 1997.

———. *Jeanne d'Arc par elle-même et ses témoins*. Paris: Editions du Seuil, 1962. English translation *Joan of Arc: By Herself and Her Witnesses*. Translated by Edward Hyams. New York: Scarborough House, 1994.

———. and Marie-Véronique Clin. *Joan of Arc: Her Story*. Translated by Jeremy Duquesnay Adams. New York: St. Martin's Press, 1999.

Renan, Ernest, "What is a Nation." In *Becoming National: A Reader*. Edited by Geoffrey Eley and Ronald Suny. New York: Oxford University Press, 1996. <http://ourworld.compuserve.com/homepages/bib_lisieux/nation01.htm>

Searle, William. *The Saint and the Skeptics: Joan of Arc in the Work of Mark Twain, Anatole France and Bernard Shaw*. Detroit: Wayne State University Press, 1976.

Sullivan, Karen. *The Interrogation of Joan of Arc*. Minneapolis: Minnesota University Press, 1999.

Wheeler, Bonnie, and Charles T. Wood, eds. *Fresh Verdicts on Joan of Arc*. Garland Reference Library of the Humanities. Vol. 1976. New York: Garland, 1996.

Woodward, Kenneth L. *Making Saints: How the Catholic Church Determines Who becomes a Saint, Who Doesn't, and Why*. New York: Simon & Schuster, 1990.

Films

For an evocation of the battle of Azincourt (Agincourt, in French) see Shakespeare's *Henry V* (1989). Dir. Kenneth Branagh. Perf. Kenneth Branagh. MGM Home Entertainment, 2000. Many feature films about

Jeanne have been made over the years, some of the better known of which are listed here. For information on films and availability, see the Internet movie Database: <http://www.imdb.com/>.

Jeanne d'Arc. Dir. Georges Méliès. Perf. Jeanne d'Alcy. Star Films. 1899–1900.

Jeanne la Pucelle. Dir. Jacques Rivette. Perf. Sandrine Bonnaire. 1993. Videocassette. 2 Vols. Facets Multimedia, 2001.

Joan of Arc. Dir. Victor Fleming. Perf. Ingrid Bergman. RKO, 1948. Videocassette. Vid-America, 1991.

Joan the Woman. Dir. Cecil B. Demille. Perf. Geraldine Farrar. Paramount. 1917. Videocassette. Kino Video, 1997. DVD. Image Entertainment, 2001.

La Passion de Jeanne d'Arc. Dir. Carl-Theodore Dreyer. Perf. Maria Falconetti. Société Générale de Films, 1927–28. Videocassette. *The Passion of Joan of Arc*. Home Video Entertainment, 1999.

Le Procès de Jeanne d'Arc. Dir. Robert Bresson. Perf. Florenz Carrez. 1962. Not yet released in the United States on videocassette or DVD.

Saint Joan. Dir. Otto Preminger. Perf. Jean Seberg. United Artists, 1957. Videocassette. Warner Studios, 1996.

The Messenger: The Story of Joan of Arc. Dir. Luc Besson. Perf. Mila Jovovich. 1999. Videocassette. Columbia Tri-Star, 2000.

Web Sites

International Joan of Arc Society
    <http://www.smu.edu/ijas/>
The Catholic Encyclopedia entry on Joan of Arc. Contains many cross-links and references
    <http://www.newadvent.org/cathen/08409c.htm>
Jeanne d'Arc Museum in Rouen
    <http://www.jeanne-darc.com/>
Front National
    <http://www.front-national.com/>
Representations in painting
    <http://www.artchive.com/>
    <http://cgfa.sunsite.dk/>
Nationalism
    <http://www.nationalismproject.org/>

CHAPTER 2

The Trial of Maurice Papon:
Holding France Accountable

Between 1940 and 1944, during Germany's occupation of France, the Vichy state replaced the French Republic. Of interest in the reopening of French memory of this period is the recent trial for complicity in crimes against humanity of a former high-ranking official under the Vichy government. When people publicly reevaluate their history, one can catch a rare and honest glimpse of the national character. How would France react to this trial, occurring almost fifty years after the fact? Would the resurrection of hard memories prove to be beneficial to the country as a whole, or would it merely aggravate old prejudices? Does the opening of old wounds serve to enhance morale in the long run, or does it promote defensive attitudes in a people?

Background

The French were prepared for war. They sat behind their Maginot line of communicating trenches and pillboxes, confident that they could turn back the attack. When it came on May 10, 1940, the German lightning assault on the west did not unfold according to French plans. The Luftwaffe pulverized Rotterdam from the air.

Paratroopers dropped onto Dutch soil. Holland fell in five days. At the same time, attacking through the Ardennes forest in Belgium, the Germans broke through the French lines, reaching the river Oise on May 18. Turning toward the west, they cut off the French and British forces that had advanced to meet the threat. Colonel Charles de Gaulle slowed the Germans momentarily at Moncornet, but the units that the French committed piecemeal were no match for the concentrated German armored and air assaults. Belgium fell on May 28. Although the British heroically evacuated the beach at Dunkirk, saving over three hundred thousand British and French soldiers, the French had lost thirty divisions. With France in a state of panic, despair, and often denial, the Germans marched into Paris on June 14, 1940. The largest army in the west had fallen in a matter of six weeks; a new era was to begin in France.

Vichy

Shortly after the fall of Paris, Marshal Philippe Pétain, respected hero of the battle of Verdun during World War I, signed an armistice with Germany. For him and his supporters, armistice meant saving what one could, even though it also dictated collaboration with the Germans. For others, armistice was a shameful sellout. In this vein, General de Gaulle made his famous broadcast from London on June 18, 1940, urging the French to fight on and to resist occupation. Under the terms of the armistice, France was split into two main parts: the north and the Atlantic coast under the direct control of the Germans, and the south governed by a new French state located at Vichy. In July 1940 the National Assembly voted to give Marshal Pétain—then eighty-four years of age—full executive and legislative powers. Symptomatic of the constitutional changes that had taken place, the motto of the republic, "*Liberté, Égalité, Fraternité,*" was changed to "*Travail, Famille, Patrie*" (Work, Family, Country), reflecting the ideology of the Vichy state.

If France had fallen so rapidly, Vichy was eager to assign a good part of the blame to the "enemy within," to those whose values and allegiances were not "French." In October 1940, the same month in which Hitler and Pétain decided upon political collaboration, the roundup of communists began and the first of the anti-Jewish laws were passed, made more stringent by a second series in June 1941. The Vichy government promulgated these racial laws with no special urging from the Germans. Jewish French citizens were excluded from elective office and from government service, from the courts and from the army, from the performing arts and the media. Access to universities and professions was severely limited. Jewish-owned businesses were forcibly liquidated. French police began to round up foreign-born Jews, who were subsequently deported by the Germans to death camps. Seventy-five thousand Jews from France later met the same fate, and few returned alive.

At the Prefecture of the Gironde in Bordeaux, the regional administrative center for three departments in southwest France, a young administrator, Maurice Papon, who was making rapid progress up the ranks of Vichy's administration, was named general secretary. As one of his functions, he was in charge of the special section that kept tabs on Jews within the area. He signed orders to round up Jews and to have them transported to Drancy, a French-run transit camp outside Paris, from which the Germans then shipped detainees to the death camp at Auschwitz in Poland. After the war, Papon continued his government career, serving as a prefect in North Africa, as the prefect of police of Paris, and as a minister of the budget. He was able to rise so high, in part, because General de Gaulle, first as head of the Free French and later as president of France (1958–1969), never recognized the legitimacy of the Vichy government, nor did he wish to have collaboration seen as anything more than a momentary aberration. Although former Nazis like Klaus Barbie and vicious collaborators like Paul Touvier were later tried and convicted in French courts in 1987 and 1994, no one of Papon's stature had been brought to trial since the end of the war. Papon's activities came to public attention only in 1981, when his wartime role was reported in the press.

The Indictment

In 1983 Papon was indicted for crimes against humanity. In 1996 the courts changed the charge to complicity in crimes against humanity, with reference to eight convoys, numbering 1,410 Jews representing sixteen different nationalities. Of these, 778 were French and 207 were children. Between 1942 and 1944 they were transported by the French to the camp at Drancy and from there by the Germans to Auschwitz.[1] The precedent for the indictment is found in the *Nuremberg War Crimes Trial Proceedings* of 1945, Article 6(c), which defines crimes against humanity as "namely, murder, extermination, enslavement, deportation, and other inhumane acts committed against any civilian population, before or during the war; or persecutions on political, racial or religious grounds in execution of or in connection with any crime within the jurisdiction of the Tribunal, whether or not in violation of the domestic law of the country where perpetrated." Further, the Nuremberg Proceedings stated that "Leaders, organizers, instigators and accomplices participating in the formulation or execution of a common plan or conspiracy to commit any of the foregoing crimes are responsible for all acts performed by any persons in execution of such plan."[2]

The Trial

What was to be France's longest criminal trial on record, as well as one of the most expensive, opened in Bordeaux on October 8, 1997. From the outset, the lynchpin of Papon's defense was the argument that he could not have conspired against the human rights of the victims because he did not know that the fate of the deportees would be death in the Nazi gas chambers, and that although the policy of the Vichy government toward Jews was racially motivated and prejudicial, it was not genocidal. In other words, because Vichy did not conspire in Hitler's Final Solution for the elimination of European Jewry, and because it was never declared a criminal state, the actions of its representative, Papon, could not be construed as criminal under the Nuremberg statutes.

Philippe Burrin, a Swiss historian and witness, addressed these issues by asking rhetorically if high officials of the Vichy government could have ignored the fate that awaited the deported Jews, and if these officials could have refused to participate in their deportation. His response was that an order by the Germans could not be refused, but that certain officials, particularly after 1943, asked for transfers or created incidents that would get them transferred.[3] His response to the question concerning foreknowledge of the fate of the victims was that the events were so extraordinary, and Hitler was so fanatically anti-Semitic, that highly placed officials of the Vichy regime could have known or should have imagined what fate awaited the Jews.[4]

Papon claimed that he saved at least 130 Jews from deportation by crossing their names off the lists of those to be rounded up for transportation to Drancy.[5] Moreover, in 1958, fourteen years after the fact, Papon obtained documents showing him to have been a member of the French Resistance. The defense portrayed Papon as a clandestine resister against the Germans, a patriot who rescued Jews and who sheltered de Gaulle's agents.

The defense maintained that Papon should not have been singled out as a sacrificial lamb to assuage the collective guilt of the French for having permitted the Vichy regime and its cruelty. To judge Papon fifty years after the facts would be to try history and France's role in it. Moreover, to go back now would mean that all government foreign policy roles would have to be revisited to determine whether France and its representatives bore any guilt at any time. Such a policy would effectively end French government.

During his long summation, Papon's lead lawyer conceded that his client could be considered "responsible without being guilty." At other moments he characterized Papon as having been present during the events of 1942–1944, but not directly responsible for them. He was trying to draw a fine line between participation and guilt. Because Vichy was not Hitler's Third Reich, nor was it ever declared a criminal state or an accomplice of the Nazis, he argued, one could not declare Papon to have been an accomplice of Nazi Germany, the avowed aim of which was the criminal, genocidal elimination of a people.[6]

For its part, the state prosecutors and the attorneys for the civil litigants contested these interpretations. Historians testified that high-ranking officials should well have known that the final outcome for the deportees was death. One of the Nazi's cover stories for transports to concentration camps took the form of involuntary deportations to supply labor for German war industries. If only able-bodied men had gone, that argument might have been plausible. But when men, women, young children, the old, the infirm, and the mentally ill were taken, suspicions had to have been aroused. Moreover, the word began to spread in the French detention camps. Samuel Schinazi, who had been arrested for resistance activities, testified, "But when I got to the Mérignac[7] camp I learned little by little through conversations of the existence of gas chambers and the systematic extermination of deported Jews. . . . We lived in a permanent state of anguish" ("*Mais quand je suis arrivé au camp de Mérignac, petit à petit, j'ai appris au cours de conversations l'existence de chambres à gaz et de l'extermination systématique des juifs déportés. . . . Nous vivions dans une angoisse permanente*"[8]).

The defense called many members of the Resistance who claimed not to have known about the Nazi death camps, but the prosecution countered with resisters who had been reading the underground press and who had listened to broadcasts by the BBC in which the death camps were spoken of. On December 12, 1942, in a joint communiqué, the American, English, Russian, and Free French allies denounced the Nazis for practicing cold-blooded extermination. In occupied France, certain officials who held the same administrative level as Papon took measures to protect Jewish children and to find Christian families to shelter them.[9]

In fact, if Papon claimed to have saved Jews, the logic of his argument flew in the face of the defense's position that he did not know what fate awaited them. If he was saving them, from what fate was he saving them? If the outcome was merely unpleasant but not mortal, why would he put himself in jeopardy by saving people? One of the dramatic moments of the trial came with the journalistic revelation that Papon had not saved 130 Jews. He claimed to have taken those names off the deportation lists, but in reality he had signed release documents for people who were found not to be Jewish under Vichy's racial laws.[10]

In the areas for which Papon was responsible, actions sometimes went beyond what the Germans were demanding. René Bousquet, secretary general of the police under Vichy, and SS general Karl Oberg, head of security services for the Third Reich in France, had signed accords in 1942 under which only foreign Jews and only those over sixteen were to be deported. Papon signed deportation orders for French Jews and for those under sixteen on several occasions. He testified that Drancy was known to be a transit camp for deportation to the east; once at Drancy the Jews' fate was sealed, but he claimed that this knowledge was only possible in light of what is known today. In fact, shortly thereafter, in the fall of 1942, orders came down from the Germans to include Jews of all nationalities and all ages. Jewish children who had been separated from their parents were then living with host families in the Bordeaux region. The Prefecture knew where they were housed. As the orders were received, it would have been possible to warn their hosts, although Papon claimed that the Germans knew exactly where each child was located anyway. Nonetheless, the offices for which he was responsible held the lists.[11] Consequently, the circumstantial evidence pointed to the Prefecture's responsibility in alerting the Germans to the whereabouts of the children. Papon countered that the Prefecture never issued an order for their roundup, but merely let it be known to the

French police that such an order existed. He maintained that he increasingly stalled for time, and that he ordered his staff to go as slowly as possible.[12]

The Verdict

After almost six months of testimony, more than six thousand documents, nearly one hundred witnesses, and briefs amounting to fifty thousand pages, the trial came to a close. The civil complainants alleged the active participation of the Vichy government in Germany's policy of deportation, Papon's participation in that policy, and his knowledge of Hitler's Final Solution for the extermination of the Jews. In affirming these allegations, they maintained that the court would reiterate what President Jacques Chirac had recognized three years earlier, that "The criminal insanity of the occupying forces was backed up by French people and by the French State" ("*La folie criminelle de l'occupant a été secondée par des Français, par l'État français*"[13]). The public prosecutor, however, while affirming Papon's responsibility for the eight convoys in question, asked for twenty years imprisonment (rather than life, the maximum penalty) because of doubts about his foreknowledge of the Holocaust. For his part, Papon claimed in his final statement that he was being made a scapegoat for Vichy and that, if he were to be found guilty, all state affairs would be paralyzed for fear of prosecution at a later date.[14]

On April 2, 1998, after nineteen hours of deliberation, the 768 counts of the indictment for unlawful arrests, imprisonment, and deportations were read. Papon was found guilty in the matter of four of the eight deportation convoys. For having ordered those arrests, imprisonments, and deportations, Papon was found guilty of inhuman acts, as defined by the Nuremberg Tribunal, and of complicity in crimes against humanity. The jury did not find him responsible for the murder of the victims, which suggested that he had no knowledge of the Final Solution. The court sentenced him to ten years' imprisonment. Maurice Papon was eighty-seven years old.

The Aftermath

Immediately upon the reading of the verdict, Papon was freed pending appeal. In fall 1999, after the failure of his appeal, the news broke that Papon had fled. French authorities initiated an international manhunt. He was quickly located in Gstaad, Switzerland, repatriated

Convicted war criminal Maurice Papon, center, arrives at the Paris Court House with his lawyer Jean-Marc Varaut, second left, February 5, 1999, for a hearing in his lawsuit against author and historian Jean-Luc Einaudi for statements he made about Papon's role in the deaths of Algerian demonstrators when Papon was Paris police chief in 1961. (AP/World Wide Photos)

upon the request of the French police, and jailed. In spring 2001 the European Court of Human Rights (*la Cour européenne des Droits de l'Homme*) rejected Papon's appeal for release on the grounds that imprisonment at his advanced age of ninety years and his infirmities constituted "inhuman and degrading treatment," which is prohibited by the European Convention on the Rights of Man. The court stated that Papon's health was "good" for a man of his age and that France's penal system was providing adequate medical care. At this point, the only other avenue for Papon was an appeal to the president of France for a pardon.

In summer 2001 twenty public figures, including two former French prime ministers and former members of the Resistance, made the appeal. Humanitarian concerns having to do with Papon's advanced age accounted for some of their motivation. They also objected to Papon alone being held accountable for acts committed sixty years earlier, when others were equally or even more to blame. Thus, the debate concerning the collective memory of France's past and the ultimate responsibility for it resurfaced. President Jacques Chirac refused the appeal in October 2001. Nevertheless, the case continued.

In July 2002 the Administrative Tribunal of Paris awarded one symbolic euro to a civil litigant, announcing in its decision that Vichy was not a mere parenthesis in French history, but that, on the contrary, the state was to be held responsible for crimes carried out by Papon. In September 2002 Papon, age ninety-two, was freed from prison under a French law that had been voted in March 2002, under which a prisoner may petition to have a sentence set aside if the detainee's health is shown to be mortally endangered by the conditions of imprisonment. In July 2003 the Council of State (*le Conseil d'État*), France's highest administrative authority, ordered the reinstatement of Papon's pension, declaring that no penalties could be assessed that deny a defendant's civil rights.

Swearing to carry on the fight to clear his name, Papon has kept his lawyers busy with appeals. In February 2004 the case was referred to France's highest appellate court, based upon a decision by the European Court of Human Rights. That appeal will be heard in May 2004. In a rare interview, Papon declared in February 2004, "I never found myself in the position of causing an event that produces remorse, [so] I don't see why I would express any. To express remorse you have to have a guilty conscience." (*"Je ne me suis jamais trouvé dans la position d'engendrer un événement qui porte au remords, je ne vois pas pourquoi j'en exprimerais. Pour exprimer des remords, il faut que la conscience soit coupable."*[15])

Discussion

The wave of revelations about Vichy opened the floodgates of books, articles, films, television programs, and debates on the responsibility of France to face up to its past during the occupation from 1940 to 1944. The collective memory, and consequently the national character, is being brought into consideration.

Should the wave of reexamination of the past continue?

Agree

The wave of reexamination of the past should continue. France failed to mourn or to atone properly for the Vichy regime. The result was a broad acceptance of the myth of a general resistance to the Germans under a regime that was supposedly championed by only a few atypical Frenchmen. This history denied the reality of Vichy's crimes. It is a worse blot on the national honor not to speak of these years than to open old wounds. Since 1789 France has considered itself to be a country of universal values, of freedom and enlightenment in which the Rights of Man are respected. France would be less than honest if it did not admit that it did not always live up to its ideals. Further, until the young can come to grips with what their elders did during the war—not only their heroism but their cowardice and blind spots as well—it will not be possible for France to move forward while carrying the burden of a fractured past.

Disagree

Community solidarity, the necessity to forget traumatic events, the need for closure, and the duty to get on with the present all require that the Vichy period be put to rest. The continuation of debates and recriminations are destructive and lead to intergenerational bickering and distrust. While some resisted and some collaborated, most were the victims of a situation beyond their control. In any war, underlying jealousies and hatreds are bound to surface. World War II was no exception. At the dawn of the twenty-first century, with most of the principal actors dead, it makes no sense to reopen history. As for the current generation, denunciations of their elders by younger men and women are too easy and serve no useful purpose. They have no idea what living through the war meant, of having to put up with an onerous occupation, its dangers and its arbitrariness. The young need to turn their energies toward solving today's problems.

Was the sentence in the Papon case appropriate?

Agree

The sentence was appropriate, and therefore justice was served. Maurice Papon was found guilty of complicity in crimes against humanity by virtue of the racial motivation for the arrest, confinement, and deportation of his victims as defined by the Nuremberg

Tribunal. One can argue, in fact, that the sentence was severe because, at his advanced age, a ten-year sentence was tantamount to life. Nonetheless, he was sentenced to ten years rather than a longer term because it appears that the jury was not convinced that he had firsthand knowledge that the people he deported would be murdered. They could not say that he had carried out his inhuman acts on behalf of Nazi Germany and its racial policy of extermination of the Jews. A less severe sentence or an acquittal would have signaled a return to the myth that France was only the hapless victim of the German occupation, that she resisted to the best of her ability, and that the Vichy government was a historical aberration whose authority was not widely accepted.

Disagree

The term of imprisonment in the Papon case was a politically correct judgment rather than justice fully served. A life sentence would have been appropriate. The fear that Papon might have been seen as a scapegoat for Vichy would not have been justified, nor would it have been possible to say that France still had not truly come to grips with its past. In fact, it would have been interpreted in the opposite sense, that France finally had the courage to make an example of a man who not only collaborated in murderous policy by coldly signing documents, but who then went on to become powerful and influential after the war. France never had the will to confront such men until this moment. Consequently, a decision to punish Papon severely would have given notice that France was admitting past crimes and that it had knowingly left stones unturned.

Questions and Activities

1. The French army was protected by the powerful defenses of the Maginot line at the outbreak of hostilities in France during World War II. This strategy failed. What was the problem with French tactical thinking? (See, for example, J. E. Kauffmann and H. W. Kauffmann, *The Maginot Line: None Shall Pass*, Westport, CT: Praeger, 1997.) Report to the class in a poster session.

2. Who was Marshal Philippe Pétain? Why was he so respected at the beginning of World War II? What were his ideas during the occupation of France? (Many of the books and Web sites in the Resource Guide contain information.)

3. Who was General Charles de Gaulle? What role did he play in World War II? In its aftermath? Create an interview show in which the guests are Pétain and de Gaulle. Have them discuss their views before a panel of journalists.

4. In 1987 Klaus Barbie, a former Nazi who had been living in Bolivia, was put on trial in France and sentenced to life imprisonment. Who was this man, and why was he put on trial in a French court? Report to the class. (See, for example, Alan Finkielkraut, *Remembering in Vain: The Klaus Barbie Trial and Crimes against Humanity,* New York: Columbia University Press, 1992, or Lawrence Douglas, *The Memory of Judgment,* New Haven: Yale University Press, 2001, esp. 187–96.)

5. In 1994 Paul Touvier, a French citizen, was tried in a court at Versailles and was sentenced to life imprisonment. What were the strange circumstances surrounding this case? Report to the class. (See, for example, Richard J. Golsan, ed., *Memory, the Holocaust, and French Justice: The Bousquet and Touvier Affairs,* Hanover, NH: University Press of New England, 1996. For a fictional treatment written like a thriller, see Brian Moore, *The Statement,* New York: Knopf, 1995.)

6. Appoint a respondent in the class who, after having heard the reports on Barbie and Touvier, will address the contention that neither the Barbie nor the Touvier case had settled the issue of Vichy in the courts. Why did many think that this might be so?

7. Assume the role of a television producer who wants to make a documentary of the Papon trial. Present your storyboard to the class in the form of a poster presentation or a computer slide show.

8. Make a video of the Papon trial in which one student plays the role of prosecutor, one plays the role of defense attorney, and one plays the role of Maurice Papon. Other witnesses may be called, of course.

9. One of the works credited with reopening the closed collective memory of the occupation is Marcel Ophuls's long 1971 documentary film, *The Sorrow and the Pity* (*Le Chagrin et la pitié*). (DVD, Image Entertainment, 2001, also available on videocassette.) Form a viewing group of four to five persons. Note the different ideas, perspectives, and ideologies presented. Along with several other students in your group, present the different voices and perspectives represented.

10. Robert O. Paxton, an American historian, created a sensation with the publication of his book, *Vichy France: Old Guard and New Order, 1940–1944* (Columbia University Press, 1972). He is credited with having introduced the French to the Vichy regime

and of having exposed the extent to which Vichy willingly collaborated with the Germans. List and critique the arguments that he uses that so ignited debate in France.

11. In December 1964 the ashes of the French resistance fighter Jean Moulin were transferred to the Panthéon, thus making him the nation's choice for remembrance of the Resistance. Who was this man? (See, for example, <http://www.crrl.com.fr/archives/JMoulin/sommaire.htm> or <http:// www.spartacus .schoolnet.co.uk/2WWmoulin.htm.>) What controversy surrounds him? (You may also want to read André Malraux's funeral oration for him, "Transfert des cendres de Jean Moulin au Panthéon," in *Oraisons funèbres*, Paris: Gallimard, 1971.)

12. Until the 1980s in France, most textbooks spent little time on World War II and fewer words on Vichy's collaboration with the Germans. What do your textbooks say about America's involvement in Vietnam? How is that conflict treated? Ask your teachers about changing perceptions of history and America's role as reflected in the history texts used in your school. Report your findings to the class.

13. During his trial Maurice Papon argued that the long French tradition of public administrators (*hauts fonctionnaires*) required him to stay at his post to keep the wheels of government running. If all administrators had left their desks, the argument goes, chaos would have been the result. Do you agree with this argument? Debate the question with classmates.

14. A second controversy surrounding Maurice Papon concerns the events of October 17, 1961, in Paris. What happened then? What were the repercussions in 1999? Research these events and report to the class. (As a start, see part III of Golsan, ed., *The Papon Affair* listed in the Resource Guide.)

15. Former U.S. Secretary of State Henry Kissinger has been accused of war crimes during the 1970s in the Vietnam conflict and in the overthrow of the Allende government in Chile. He has been summoned by foreign courts, before which he has refused to appear. Familiarize yourself with this situation. Kissinger claims that "people should ask whether it is actually feasible to conduct international policy if high officials, 30 years after the event, are hounded on tactical matters" (http://www.telegraph.co.uk/news/main.jhtml?xml=/news/2002/04/28/nkiss28.xml). In what way might this position be similar to Maurice Papon's argument during the trial? Do you think that Kissinger should answer for his policies before foreign courts? Why or why not?

16. In France criminal trials take place in the *Cour d'assises*, which is presided over by three judges. The jury is composed of nine jurors, citizens in good standing, chosen at random from a list. Jurors may ask questions of the accused, as may the judges. Judges are part of the independent magistrature; they are career jurists, not political appointees. At the conclusion of the trial, both the jury (*les jurés*) and the judges (*magistrats*) deliberate together on the question of innocence or guilt and on a penalty if the accused is found guilty. Compare this to the American system in which the jury deliberates on its own. Which system would you prefer? Why?

17. Most of the surviving civil litigants in the Papon trial asked for symbolic damages of one franc; fewer asked for a larger amount of money to compensate for their suffering. Which is the more appropriate settlement in your opinion?

18. If the Papon case cleared the air by coming to grips with the past, it might be argued that the United States should pay reparations for slavery in order to apologize for that terrible institution in this country. Some people have argued that reparations would only increase interracial tensions, that slavery was not illegal at the time, and that reparations are another form of affirmative action. (See reference to the debate at <http://www.arm.arc.co.uk/> and <http://www.africana.com/> using the search functions to find "reparations.") What is your opinion?

19. The International Criminal Court treaty received the sixty ratifications needed to commence operation on July 1, 2002. The Bush administration has announced that it does not consider itself bound by President Bill Clinton's signature on the treaty for the creation of a permanent war crimes tribunal. Should such a tribunal exist? Should the United States be a signatory to the treaty and be bound by it? Research the question and express your views in a paper. The Web site of the International Criminal Court is found at <http://www.un.org/law/icc>. Lexis-Nexis indexes a number of current articles on this topic.

Vocabulary/Vocabulaire

Nouns/Substantifs

accused person	l'accusé(e)
acquittal	l'acquittement (m.)
appeal	un pourvoi en cassation

arrest	l'arrestation (f.)
civil plaintif	une partie civile
civil rights	les droits civiques (m. pl.)
court	la cour
defendant	un(e) inculpé(e)
deportee	un(e) déporté(e)
gas chamber	une chambre à gaz
guilt	la culpabilité
issue	une question
Jew	un Juif, une Juive; Israélite
lawyer	un avocat
prosecution	l'accusation (f.)
prosecutor	le procureur
representative	un représentant, un délégué
roundup	une rafle
scapegoat	un bouc émissaire
sentence	la peine
state	un état
suffering	la souffrance
survivor	un survivant
testimony	le témoignage
trial	un procès
witness	un témoin (un témoin à charge—witness for the prosecution; témoin favorable à la défence—defense witness)

Verbs /Verbes

appeal	se pourvoir en cassation
arrest	arrêter
conspire	conspirer contre; agir de concert avec (qqun)
indict	inculper (qqun)
round up	rafler

sentence	condamner (e.g., condamner qqun à dix ans de réclusion criminelle)
serve a sentence	purger une peine
suspect	se douter (de qqch)
witness, testify	témoigner

Adjectives/Adjectifs

guilty	coupable
Jewish	juif, juive

Expressions/Expressions

anti-Jewish laws	le statut des juifs
court session	une audience
crime against humanity	un crime contre l'humanité
fact of law	une question de droit
find someone guilty/innocent	prononcer qqun coupable/innocent(e)
have a guilty conscience	avoir mauvaise conscience
important civil servant	un haut fonctionnaire
Nuremberg Tribunal principle	l'arrêt du tribunal de Nuremberg
to be freed	être remis(e) en liberté
to be judged	être jugé(e)

Notes

1. *Le Procès de Maurice Papon,* vol. 1 (Paris: Albin Michel, 1998), 12. For a concise version of the trial events see Jean-Jacques Gandini, *Le procès Papon* (Paris: Librio, 1999), 14–15, 46.

2. The online Avalon Project at Yale University is a valuable source for many diplomatic and legal documents. For the Nuremberg Proceedings, see <http://www.yale.edu/lawweb/avalon/imt/proc/imtconst.htm#art6>.

3. *Procès* 1, 400.

4. Ibid., 403.

5. Ibid., 502, 506–507, and <http://www.liberation.com> December 12, 1997.

6. "Varaut: Vichy n'était pas complice du reich," <http://www
.liberation.com> March 25 and 31, 1998; *Procès* 2: 869–88; 890–945.
Varaut's summation was also published separately as *Plaidoirie de Jean-
Marc Varaut devant la Cour d'assises de la Gironde au procès Maurice Papon*
(Paris: Plon, 1998).

7. Mérignac-Beaudésert was a French internment camp located outside
of Bordeaux, from which Jewish internees were shipped to Drancy for trans-
port to the German death camps.

8. *Procès* 1, 157.

9. Gandini, *Le procès Papon,* 82–90.

10. Annette Lévy-Willard, "Papon n'a jamais sauvé 130 Juifs," <http//
www.liberation.com>, December 3, 1997.

11. Pascalle Nivelle, "Au revoir les enfants," <http://www
.liberation.com> December 23, 1997.

12. *Procès* 1, 502, 505, 764.

13. July 16, 1995, speech at the commemoration of the Vel' d'Hiv'
roundup of Jews on July 16, 1942. The original of this speech is available at
<http://www.elysee.fr/rech/rech_.htm>.

14. *Procès* 2, 949–950.

15. Denis Demonpion, "Le dernier plaidoyer de Papon," *Le Point* 1640,
February 19, 2004, 22.

Bibliography

Gandini, Jean-Jacques. *Le procès Papon.* Paris: Librio, 1999.
Le Procès de Maurice Papon. 2 vols. Paris: Albin Michel, 1998.
    (The trial transcript.)
<http://www.lemonde.com>
<http://www.libération.com>

Resource Guide

Further Reading

"A Time to Remember." Special issue, *Contemporary French Civilization*
    19, no. 2 (1995).
Azéma, Jean-Pierre. *Vichy, 1940–44.* Paris: Perrin, 1997.
Burrin, Philippe. *La France à l'heure allemande.* Paris: Seuil, 1995.
    English version: *France under the Germans: Collaboration and
    Compromise.* Translated by Janet Lloyd. New York: The New
    Press, 1997.
———. "Vichy." In *Les Lieux de mémoire,* t. III: *Les France,* vol. I: *Conflits
    et partages.* Edited by Pierre Nora, 320–45. Paris: Gallimard, 1992.

Cointet, Jean-Paul. *Histoire de Vichy*. Paris: Plon, 1995.

Conan, Éric, and Henry Rousso. *Vichy: un passé qui ne passe pas*. Paris: Fayard, 1994. In English: *Vichy, an Ever-Present Past*. Translated by Nathan Bracher. Hanover, NH: University Press of New England, 1998. A sequel to Rousso, below.

Golsan, Richard J., ed. *The Papon Affair: Memory and Justice on Trial*. New York and London: Routledge, 2000.

Kedward, H. R. *Occupied France: Collaboration and Resistance*. Oxford: Basil Blackwell, 1985.

Kritzman, Lawrence, ed. *Auschwitz and After. Race, Culture and the "Jewish Question" in France*. New York: Routledge, 1995.

Malraux, André. *Oraisons funèbres*. Paris: Gallimard, 1971.

Marrus, Michael R., and Robert O. Paxton. *Vichy France and the Jews*. New York: Basic Books, 1981.

Paxton, Robert O. *Vichy France, Old Guard and New Order 1940–1944*. New York: Columbia University Press, 1972.

Rousso, Henry. *Le syndrome de Vichy de 1944 à nos jours*. Paris: Seuil, 1987. In English: *The Vichy Syndrome: History and Memory in France since 1944*. Translated by Arthur Goldhammer. Cambridge: Harvard University Press, 1991.

Sweets, John. *Choices in Vichy France: The French under Nazi Occupation*. Oxford: Oxford University Press, 1986.

"The Vichy Syndrome." Dossier. *French Cultural Studies* 19, no. 2 (1995).

Violet, Bernard. *Le dossier Papon*. Paris: Flammarion, 1997.

Zuccotti, Susan. *The Holocaust, the French, and the Jews*. New York: Basic Books, 1993.

Films

There is a rich vein of films to be mined on the subject of the 1940–1944 occupation of France. If you see only one, you should view this groundbreaking documentary:

The Sorrow and the Pity. (*Le chagrin et la pitié*, 1971). Dir. Marcel Ophuls. Videocassette. Milestone Film & Video, 2000. DVD. Image Entertainment, 2001. (English subtitles.)

Ophuls, Marcel. *Le Chagrin et la pitié*. Paris: Éditions Alain Moreau, 1980. This is the scenario of the film. In English: *The Sorrow and the Pity: A Film by Marcel Ophuls*. Translated by Mireille Johnston. New York: Outerbridge and Lazard/Dutton, 1972.

For other viewing, see the film and visual culture bibliography at <http://ghc.ctc.edu/Socsci/MSCHOLZ/vichy.htm>.

Newspaper and Periodical Resources

Lexis-Nexis is an excellent source for newspapers articles on issues in France. Note that both English-language and foreign-language news articles are indexed. Ask your librarian about OCLC First Search as another fruitful database for searching articles.

Web Sites

Newspapers: Among widely read daily French newspapers, recent articles are free; others, in the archive section, are fee-based or by subscription.

Elite newspaper, *Le Monde:* <http://www.lemonde.fr>
Popular daily, moderate left, *Libération:* <http://www.liberation.fr/>
Venerable, moderate right, *Le Figaro:* <http://www.lefigaro.fr/>
Online dossier on the Papon trial by *Sud-Ouest,* a large regional newspaper: <http://www.sudouest.com/papon/direct/index.html>. Dossier of the trial is still free.
World War II sites containing history, maps, main actors:
<http://www.bbc.co.uk/history/war/wwtwo/>
<http://www.spartacus.schoolnet.co.uk/2WW.htm>
<http://www.fordham.edu/halsall/mod/modsbook45.html>
<http://www.mtholyoke.edu/acad/intrel/ww2.htm>
<http://ghc.ctc.edu/Socsci/MSCHOLZ/vichy.htm>

CHAPTER 3

The Aussaresses Revelations: A Tortured Memory

To read the account of Louisette Ighilahriz's three-month imprisonment at the hands of French officers requires a strong stomach. During the so-called Battle of Algiers in 1957 this Algerian woman, then a fighter in the war for Algerian independence, was wounded in a French ambush and captured. Tortured for information about her associates and their plans, she was kept tied down and naked, covered in her own blood and excretions. Her story is shocking, but its kind was not unknown in France.[1] It made the headlines because Louisette Ighilahriz later sought to thank the person who saved her life, a military doctor by the name of Richaud who, appalled by her condition, put her into the hospital.

In fall 2001 a historic ruling by a French court awarded Mohammed Garne a small pension because he had become the first person in France to be recognized as a war victim due to criminal acts occurring before his birth. In 1959 his mother Kheira, then sixteen, was sequestered by French soldiers and repeatedly raped. Garne was awarded damages for his physical problems because of the injury he sustained as a fetus when his mother was beaten and tortured in an attempt to get her to miscarry. The verdict capped his thirteen-year effort to get justice.[2]

This decision was made public some days before the beginning of the trial of Paul Aussaresses, a former French army general, who had published his memoirs of the Algerian war in 2001. He revealed that he had ordered Algerian terrorist suspects to be tortured or summarily executed. Beatings, electrodes attached to earlobes and genitals or shoved down the throat, and forced ingestion of water were some of the methods used to gather intelligence. Two elements in Aussaresses's commentary were particularly shocking. The first was his tone of absolute conviction and his utter lack of regret about what he had done. In fact, his rationale was very clear: It was necessary to perform extraordinary acts in extraordinary times when the enemy was not clearly defined in terms of traditional military operations. The second shocking allegation was that the French government knew about torture in Algeria, tolerated it, and even recommended it. Aussaresses stated that François Mitterrand, then minister of justice and later president of France (1981–1995), had sent an emissary to Algeria to keep him informed and to provide cover for the torturers.[3]

Although many publications had already alleged torture in Algeria and often detailed it with gruesome eyewitness accounts, the revelations of the new millennium seemed to seize the French conscience with a poignancy that had not been demonstrated before. In order to understand the context in which French memory opened one of its suppressed chapters, we need to review the history of French involvement in Algeria.

Background

The French Adventure in Algeria

History gives many lessons from which one learns that rash behavior leads to unfortunate consequences. Such is the incident in which the Dey of Algiers, the ruling official of the Ottoman Empire, struck the French consul with a fly-whisk, thus precipitating the 1830 French expedition against Algeria. Actually, he whisked him because the French government refused to honor an unpaid debt dating from the French Directory of 1795–1799. Apologies were demanded and refused. A French ship arriving for talks was bombarded; an ineffective French blockade of Algerian ports was answered by the seizure of French interests. Because Charles X, the last of the Bourbon monarchs, wanted to give prestige to his restored dynasty, political motivation was at the heart of the French expedition against Algeria, as it also was for his successor, the constitutional monarch Louis-Philippe.

In June 1830 an expeditionary corps of thirty-seven thousand French soldiers arrived off the Algerian coast. It faced fifty thousand Arabs whose fighting qualities were uneven and who lacked the French advantage in artillery. Algiers fell on July 5, 1830, but conquest was not a given because the Muslims did not yield quietly. By 1837 Abd el-Kader, an Islamic purist of considerable military and diplomatic skills, was recognized by France as ruler of two-thirds of Algeria. Because he was convinced that over time the French would dominate, he broke the peace in 1840. The French were faced with the choice between a complete evacuation of Algeria or total conquest. They chose the latter course of action.

General Thomas-Robert Bugeaud, commander of the French forces, used the tactic of the *razzia*, the systematic destruction of cattle, crops, grain stores, and warehouses, to force local Muslims into submission. Captives were treated harshly. The countryside he left behind was devastated. After seven years of fighting, Abd el-Kader surrendered on December 3, 1847.

The French government expropriated land and began to turn it over to colonizers recruited for resettlement. The French Second Republic (1848–1852) declared Algeria an integral part of France and carved part of it into French departments. The French philosophy of assimilation—the obligation to uplift indigenous populations by sharing the benefits of French civilization and technology—began at this point. Under the Second Empire (1852–1870) Emperor Napoleon III declared Algeria to be an Arab kingdom that France was required to protect and "civilize." Arabs would be given land to cultivate, while Europeans would concern themselves mainly with commerce and industry. By the end of the Second Empire in 1870, this policy had again changed. The Third Republic (1875–1940), having lost Alsace and Lorraine to the Prussians during the Franco-Prussian war of 1870, concentrated on the development of French overseas conquests. From 1871 and until World War I, France encouraged immigration to Algeria. Between 1872 and 1914 the European population grew from roughly 250,000 to 750,000.[4]

Huge areas of land were given to the colonists for free or were sold very cheaply. Dispossessed of their lands, local Arab populations were increasingly impoverished. At the outbreak of the Algerian war in 1954 the settlers (*colons*) were in control of the best Algerian land.

The philosophy of assimilation—known as integration in the post-1954 years—theoretically aligned the rights and duties of local populations with those of Europeans, but the reality of assimilationist policies meant that French laws replaced local institutions, while Arabs did not have the same guarantees as the French in the areas of education, taxation, and salary. Although a small Arab elite was allowed to form by virtue of some space allotted to them in the French educational system, the net result of assimilation was to unhinge local society.[5]

By the 1930s the colonial order was showing strain. Most Algerian peasants (*fellahs*) were paupers. Nonetheless, the hundredth anniversary of the conquest in 1930 was led by a press campaign in France that portrayed colonization in flattering terms. Efforts of the socialist *Front Populaire* (1936–1938) to increase Algerian representation in the parliament, to give elector rights to some Algerians, and to allow some to become French citizens were met by furious protests among Europeans in Algeria. Among the Muslim population disillusionment and embitterment were growing, not only among more radical nationalist groups, but among many moderates as well. Ferhat Abbas, a moderate politician, originated a manifesto in which he rejected assimilation, proposing an autonomous Algerian state federated with France, an idea that had already been in the air.[6] Now Algerian leaders turned down French proposals for increased assimilation and representation.

The War for Algerian Independence

Trouble broke out in Algeria in 1945 after World War II. A demonstration at Sétif on May 8, 1945, degenerated into riots in which about one hundred French were killed. Savage repression by French armed forces, which included indiscriminate bombardments, followed. While official estimates of 1,500 dead were made public, the real figure more likely was between 6,000 and 8,000.[7] In the aftermath, local hostility toward the French and increasing nationalism were evident.

The administration and economy of Algeria clearly functioned to the benefit of its French population, which now numbered almost one million. Eighty percent were born in Algeria (*les pieds noirs*). By this time they considered themselves to be the legitimate owners of the country. They were largely an urban population engaged in business and administration, and while there were many small farmers among their number, most French had achieved a respectable standard of living, often higher than that of their counterparts in metropolitan France. These very conservative descendants of colonists were generally set against all reform. About two million of the nine million Algerians had reached some European standards, but three-quarters of the population was still not assured of a decent living. The Muslim population suffered through continuous stagnation. Only 13 percent of Arab children had access to public schooling.[8] No political reforms were in sight, nor were any major plans to improve the material conditions of life undertaken on behalf of the Algerians. The metropolitan French remained mainly indifferent to affairs in Algeria.

The post-World War II generation of Algerians had grown tired of the racism and inertia of the French colonial government. Many young Algerians, having served with the Free French forces, were ready to turn their military experience against the French. Significant, too, was their knowledge of the French defeat at the hands of the Germans and against the Viet Minh in Indochina, which removed the aura of invincibility from the French army. It was a generation that would not shy away from violence to gain its ends. New leaders like Ahmed Ben Bella (later the first president of an independent Algeria) emerged. They formed several revolutionary committees that finally surfaced as the National Liberation Front (*Front de Libération Nationale*, the FLN). In July 1954 the Algerian revolutionaries made the decision to train and arm for a protracted struggle for their independence. Early on the morning of November 1, 1954, the insurrection broke out. Some limited attacks on French installations took place, but what was to follow would be long and terrible.

The French government treated the uprising as acts of sedition rather than the beginning of a war of national liberation. Since Algeria was a part of France, it could not be given up like other colonies in North Africa (Tunisia and Morocco were granted independence in 1956) or in sub-Saharan western Africa. On November 7, 1954, François Mitterrand, then minister of justice, said, "Algeria is France and France will not recognize any authority there but its own" (*"L'Algérie c'est la France et la France ne reconnaîtra pas chez elle d'autre autorité que la sienne"*[9]). Several days later, on November 12, Pierre Mendès-France, president of the Counsel of Ministers, echoed this when he said that there would be no compromise with sedition and that "The Algerian departments constitute a part of the French

Republic. They have been French for a long time and irrevocably so" (*"Les départments d'Algérie constituent une partie de la République française. Ils sont français depuis longtemps et d'une manière irrevocable"*[10]). A state of emergency was declared in April 1955, providing the legal status for extraordinary action. The National Assembly declared special powers in Algeria, which coincided with a call-up of reservists and an extension of military service.

Riots on August 20 and 21 were serious. Thousands of French as well as Algerians suspected of being sympathetic to the French were murdered, including women and children. Increasingly fearful, the French population demanded extreme measures. It became more and more obvious that the official line of a police action could not be taken seriously. By the end of 1955 terrorist acts now numbered one thousand per month.[11] The army reacted to ambushes and raids by the FLN in the countryside; but, frequently lacking good intelligence, French soldiers sometimes shot up and terrorized innocent villages. FLN fighters sometimes mutilated their victims, both French soldiers and settlers as well as unsympathetic Arabs, providing the French with a rationale for reprisals. French soldiers sometimes subjected Moslem suspects to electric torture (*la gégène*) by hooking them up to the magnetos of field telephones. Summary execution (*la corvée de bois*) often followed.

The FLN wanted to demonstrate its hold on urban populations as well as upon the countryside. On December 30, 1956, bombs exploded in the Milk Bar and the Caféteria, two cafés popular with European young people, leaving four dead and fifty-two wounded, including several children. On January 7, 1957, General Massu, commanding the Tenth Parachute Division, was given complete police powers in Algiers because the regular police forces could not prevent attacks or find their perpetrators. Troop strength was increased to four hundred thousand by the end of 1957.[12]

The French won the so-called battle of Algiers of 1957 largely through the torture of suspects.[13] By the same measure, the revelation of torture had both domestic and international repercussions, opening new questions in France concerning the legitimacy of the war. Pressure from the international community for a negotiated settlement increased, while continued military action, searches of villages (*ratonnades*), detentions, brutal treatment, summary executions, removal of populations to resettlement camps, and pressure by the FLN (which executed Algerians deemed disloyal to its cause) kept the local population on the side of the FLN.

Charles de Gaulle and the End of the Algerian War

By spring 1958 the war in Algeria had been going on long enough to be seen as inconclusive in metropolitan France. The French government of the Fourth Republic (1946–1958) was incapable of resisting pressure from the French citizens of Algeria and was rapidly undergoing crisis. Waiting in the wings was Charles de Gaulle, the World War II hero of France, who had left the presidency twelve years earlier in 1946, disgusted by party politics. He had retired to his home at Colombey-les-Deux-Eglises to write his memoirs and await the call to return to public service. When the colons and the army combined efforts to bring down the colonial government in Algeria and called for the return of de Gaulle to power, he let it be known in May 1958 that he was "ready to assume the powers of the republic."[14] His historical stature was enhanced for the colonizers because he had kept the French Empire together during the war, and for the colonized he was remembered for his 1944 Brazzaville declaration in which he referred to self-administration and self-governance for the colonies.

De Gaulle set a high price for his return, nothing less than the elimination of the Fourth Republic and the formulation of a Fifth Republic under a new constitution and government. Meanwhile, General Salan, commander-in-chief in Algeria, was making plans for paratroops from Algeria to drop on Paris and to create a coup d'état in favor of de Gaulle. The regime could not resist the pressure for some resolution of the crisis in Algeria and the threats of an invasion by its own army. President René Coty invited de Gaulle to form a government. On June 1, 1958, the National Assembly accepted him. De Gaulle's takeover put him in the position of the man of destiny who would again shoulder the nation's burden in its hour of need. He was sixty-seven years of age.

De Gaulle made his first speech in Algeria on June 4, 1958. His ambiguous first sentence to the crowd of *pieds noirs* and Muslims was "*Je vous ai compris*" ("I have understood you").[15] He kept his cards close to his chest, but while he would have liked to retain Algeria for France in some kind of federated relationship, war-weariness, world opinion, de Gaulle's own lack of sympathy for the colonizers of Algeria, an unsuccessful putsch organized by dissident army generals, and bombings in Algeria and France by the OAS (the right-wing *Organisation de l'armée secrète* headed by General Salan) led to the beginning of the end. De Gaulle held a referendum in July 1962 in which Algerians could vote for a freer and more enlightened relationship with France or complete independence. Algerians voted massively and overwhelmingly for independence. After seven and a half years of war, the French government and the FLN signed the Evian accords in March 1962, agreeing to a cease-fire and to Algeria's self-determination.

The Aussaresses Outcome

In 2001 General Aussaresses and his publishers were indicted in France over the publication of his book, *Services spéciaux*. The charge was an unusual one, "complicity in apologetics for war crimes." Because of several amnesties granted in the decade after the war, Aussaresses and others could not be charged with war crimes directly. The defense presented the old general as a World War II Resistance hero who fought in Algeria in a terrible war against an enemy who used terrorism to attack not only French soldiers but also civilians on both sides. For the civil litigants, the conduct of the Algerian war was on trial. What outraged many people was not Aussaresses's wanting to speak about torture, but his legitimizing of it. Lawyers pointed out that this legitimization was manifested in the detached tone of the book. The defense disparagingly countered that it would be necessary to put handcuffs on the tone.[16] The prosecutor asked for a fine of 100,000 francs against the publishers of the book for having exploited the cold-blooded recounting of torture in the interest of their sales receipts. The trial ended on November 28, 2001. Paul Aussaresses was found guilty of complicity in defending war crimes. He was fined 7,500 euros, taken off the generals' list, and suspended from the Legion of Honor. He was spared the maximum penalty of five years in prison and a fine of 45,000 euros. The court was more interested in the clinical, factual presentation of what Aussaresses did than in his absence of regret. The judges condemned presenting acts of torture as inevitable and legitimate because the net effect is to remove the inherent moral reprobation of these acts in the eyes of the reader. Aussaresses's lawyer protested the verdict as an act of censorship and stated that he would appeal on the grounds that armchair spectators cannot make themselves retroactive field commanders in a war that they did not live through.[17] The book's editors were fined 15,000 euros because the court found that the publishers had sought out the retired general to encourage him to publish, not so much for history's sake, as their lawyers maintained, but for the sake of publicity and sales. An appeal of the fines was denied in April

Former French Gen. Paul Aussaresses holds his book *Special Services: Algeria 1955–57* during an interview in Paris, May 7, 2001. (AP/World Wide Photos)

2003. In June 2003 the French Court of Appeals (*la Cour de cassation*) reaffirmed earlier court decisions not to allow Paul Aussaresses to be indicted for crimes against humanity, citing the 1968 amnesty, which precluded any further action.

Discussion

The foregoing sets the stage for a discussion of a problem that did not end with the Nazi concentration camps or with Algeria. One only need think of Vietnam, Argentina, Chile, Guatemala, El Salvador, Bosnia, Rwanda, and many other places.

Amnesty was the appropriate action in the Aussaresses case.

Agree

Amnesties are granted for good reasons. Legally, an amnesty is not a pardon. It is meant to promote reconciliation; in declaring that certain acts can be forgotten, it permits acrimonious public debate to die down and it gives society time to heal itself. Unlike a pardon, amnesty does not concern individuals, only a general class of actions. Amnesty therefore takes a neutral stance on those actions, but not on the individuals who committed them. This is why General Aussaresses could be indicted for actions not covered by the amnesty laws, such as making excuses for torture. If the French government admitted to collective responsibility for torture in Algeria, the perpetrators would have to be punished; the government would have to rescind its amnesty, thereby losing credibility; huge reparations would have to be paid; and the thousands of soldiers who did not torture would be tarred with the same brush.

Disagree

Clearing the national conscience is the duty of any civilized country when it has violated its own principles and best instincts. If the weight of the past is left hanging, it is for the present to deal with it lest it become a weight on the national soul. France could not even pass a commemoration law on the fortieth anniversary of the cessation of the war. It was only in 1999 that the designation of "war" rather than "events" or "maintaining order" in Algeria was made official. It is clear that the country is still traumatized and that successive governments since 1962 have been unwilling to recognize responsibility for inhuman acts carried out by the French in Algeria. The passage of amnesty laws can be explained by political ideology or by a genuine desire to reconcile with the past, but the effect has been merely to bury it. For France to cure itself, it must find a way to make things right by granting reparations to those who suffered and by finding the proper symbolic gestures of apology. A good model might be that of South Africa, which in declaring amnesty for crimes committed under apartheid, insisted upon a truth-telling commission and the assumption of accountability and responsibility on the part of those who committed heinous acts.

Terror tactics are sometimes necessary to accomplish legitimate goals.

Agree

As distasteful as terrorist violence is, over time many have opted for it as the only way to fight for their cause. Some have argued that "terrorist" has become a politicized word that does not take into account the legitimate struggle for rights. Terrorism is the armament of the weak. In order to overcome impossible odds in the struggle for one's goals, no limits can be recognized. One person's terrorist is another person's patriot. When the conditions of life become unbearable and those who oppress will not listen to the supplications of the oppressed, any act is permitted to gain relief. Terrorism is effective because it is inexpensive, it creates publicity, it can accomplish political goals (which can be as important as military victories), it polarizes opinion among the opposition, and it provokes psychological stress and anxiety among one's enemies.[18] The terrorist must be willing to sacrifice his or her own life or to face horrible consequences if caught. The label "terrorist" is a political designation applied by the strong to the weak.

Disagree

The terrorist may not always be synonymous with the freedom fighter. Terrorists are often young and malleable. They are subject to the reigning ideologies of the day and can be manipulated by others for political ends. Ideology is the rationale for many terrorist actions, but the underlying cause is often economic and social despair that can be cured by other means. The terrorist is willing to sacrifice all principle in the name of his or her goals, using any means to justify them. The terrorist accepts the death of the innocent. The terrorist simply chooses among various instruments of violence rather than between violence and nonviolence. The examples of Mahatma Gandhi and the Reverend Martin Luther King, Jr., in their choice of nonviolent protest speak loudly in this case.

Torture by governments is sometimes justified.

Agree

The use of torture may be justified when faced with terrorists who target innocent civilians. General Aussaresses was clear in his book. He wrote, "For as surprising as it was, the use of this kind of violence, unacceptable in ordinary times, could become unavoidable in a situation that superseded normal limits. . . . A piece of information obtained in time could save dozens of human lives" ("*Car pour surprenant qu'elle fût, l'utilisation de cette forme de violence, inacceptable en des temps ordinaires, pouvait devenir inévitable dans une situation qui dépassait les bornes. . . . Un renseignement obtenu à temps pouvait sauver des dizaines de vies humaines*"[19]). If a terrorist has planted a bomb on a school bus and will not reveal where it is located, the authorities must employ every means to save innocent lives. One only need think of the events of September 11, 2001, to appreciate this position. As the threat is magnified (let us suppose a terrorist who knows the whereabouts of a nuclear bomb that has been smuggled into an American city), one can afford even less to hesitate to force this person to talk. The ethical thing to do is to sacrifice one person in order to save many.

Disagree

The use of torture is a slippery slope. One may be tempted to use it occasionally and in extremis, but it is rare that recourse to duress, even among civilized peoples, has remained occasional. Once allowed, even with repugnance, torture becomes another arm in waging war and thus becomes routine. The outcome of the war is decided not on the battlefield, but in torture dungeons. Members of an army, usually proud of service in the defense of their country, become haunted by their acts, as did many French soldiers in the aftermath of the Algerian war. To employ "torture lite" techniques, with which some American agencies have been accused, or to turn prisoners over to allies whose methods are more brutal is an equivocation. Even in the face of an enemy who targets innocent bystanders, to choose not to torture is the moral path because it says that one does not accept that ends justify means.

Questions and Activities

1. Research the condition of Algeria since independence. Report to the class on the current state of affairs in Algeria, particularly with reference to the rise there of militant Islam.

2. In March 2003 Jacques Chirac made the first trip to Algeria by a French president since the former colony gained independence in 1962. What was the purpose of this trip? How did it play to the colonial past as well as to present realities in France? Report to the class on the intent and purposes of Chirac's Algeria trip. (See, for example, the analysis by Michael R. Shurkin for the Brookings Institution at <http://www.brookings.edu/fp/cusf/analysis/index.htm>.)

3. General Aussaresses's book was published in the United States under the title *The Battle of the Casbah: Terrorism and Counter-Terrorism in Algeria 1955-1957* (New York: Enigma Books, 2002). Given what you know about this book and the opinion of its author, imagine a meeting of your school board at which a

public argument breaks out over acquisition of the book for your school library. In teams of three or four, prepare arguments for and against acquiring the book. Another team will represent the school board and give its opinion after arguments for and against have been made.

4. The name *Harkis* was given to the two hundred thousand Algerian militiamen who fought alongside the French during the Algerian war. Research the fate of the *Harkis* in order to report to the class on this aspect of the unfinished business of the Algerian war. (*The Wall Street Journal* of October 17, 2001, and the *Financial Times* [London] of March 16, 2002, published articles including this topic. Note the speech of President Jacques Chirac on September 25, 2001, archived at <http://www.elysee.fr>. See also numerous newspaper articles, such as the one by Sylvia Zappi in *Le Monde*, September 25, 2001.)

5. It can be said that the Algerian war spilled over into the streets of Paris on October 17, 1961. What happened in Paris on that date? How were those events connected to the war in Algeria? Make a written report or give a presentation on the topic along with several other members of the class. (See, for example, <http://www.histoire .fr/vert/html/algerie_2.htm#debut>, and Brigette Jelen, "*17 octobre 1961–17 octobre 2001: une commémoration ambiguë*, "French Politics, Culture and Society" 20, no. 1 (2002):30–43.)

6. Lionel Jospin, French prime minister from 1997-2002 has stated that the torture and acts of violence in Algeria do not call for collective repentance, but rather for merely telling the truth about what happened. He reasoned that repentance would be an insult to the thousands of young soldiers who served France, who did not torture, and who refused to go along with the putsch of the generals. Others have said that only a public statement of repentance will heal the national bad conscience over Algeria because history is not simply facts but also the memory of those facts held by a collectivity. Debate the question: Resolved: France must solemnly repent and apologize for its actions in Algeria in order to bring the past to a close.

7. One high-ranking officer who did not condone the practice of torture was General Paris de Bollardière, who refused General Massu's directive to "accentuate police work," taken as a euphemism to get intelligence by any means. General de Bollardière wrote that moral values could not be sacrificed in the name of immediate efficaciousness. He was sentenced to sixty days in a military prison. Write a letter to the president of the French Republic in which you ask that de Bollardière be pardoned, stating your reasons.

(You may want to refer to Maran, *Torture and the Role of Ideology*, 106-23, cited in the Resource Guide.)

8. General de Bollardière wrote, "The reasons for ceding to the practice of violence and torture can only be explained by the impotence of the torturers" (*Bataille d'Alger, Bataille de l'Homme*, Paris: Desclée de Brouwer, 1972, 146). Do you agree with this evaluation of torturers? Explain why or why not.

9. French author and philosopher Albert Camus stated that "it is better to suffer certain injustices than to commit them, even to win wars, and that such deeds do us more harm than a hundred guerrilla forces on the enemy's side"[20] (*"Il vaut mieux souffrir certaines injustices que les commettre, et que de pareilles entreprises nous font plus de mal que cent maquis ennemis"*[21]). Do you agree with this statement? Create an informal debate between proponents and opponents in the class.

10. During the Algerian war, François Mauriac, the 1952 Nobel Laureate in Literature, wrote in *L'Express* on March 17, 1957, that "The most shared thing in the world is not good sense, it is cruelty" (*"La chose au monde la mieux partagée n'est pas le bon sens, c'est la cruauté"*). State your agreement or disagreement with Mauriac's opinion and give your reasons for it.

11. French Professor Pierre-Henri Simon, wrote in his book *Contre la torture* (Paris: Seuil, 1957, 23), "The feeling of collective guilt is a spontaneous form of the passion for honor" (*"Le sentiment de la culpabilité collective est une forme spontanée de la passion de l'honneur"*). Do you think he is correct? State your reasons for or against.

12. After the Algerian war, the French passed several amnesties that protected participants from prosecution. Since then, the International Criminal Court was established by the Rome Statute in 1998, subsequently ratified by over one hundred countries. Its role is to try individuals accused of crimes against humanity, genocide and serious war crimes. United States policy currently prescribes that, should an American soldier be alleged to have committed a war crime, that person would be tried under constituted processes of American military law, but not by an outside tribunal. The United States ratified the Rome Statute in 2000, but nullified its signature in 2002. Opponents of this policy counter that the United States is putting itself above international law and is antagonizing its allies. In the light of events since September 11, 2001, do you think that the United States should ratify the Rome Treaty of 1998 establishing the International Criminal Court? Research the question in order to write a paper justifying your opinion or form a debate with members of the class. (See, for example, <http://www.amicc.org>, <http://www.un.org/law/icc/

general/overview.htm>, <http://www.un.org/law/icc/index
.html>; "The International Criminal Court," *New York Times*, March
29, 2003, A24, or, July 2, 2003, A8.)

13. Faced with insurrection, the French voted a law on April 3, 1955,
declaring a state of emergency in which police powers were aug-
mented, limits were placed on movements of individuals and on the
press, and the army was given police powers. In the aftermath of the
attacks of September 11, 2001, the United States created new laws
and procedures to hold suspected terrorists, expand wiretaps and
electronic eavesdropping, and hold American citizens in military
rather than civilian incarceration. This culminated in the Patriot Act,
signed into law on October 26, 2001, by President George W. Bush.
Discuss the need to create special laws in special times. Is the price of
security worth the abrogation of certain civil rights? (See, for example, "Wider Military Role in U.S. Urged," in which Eric Schmitt
writes about the ongoing discussion concerning revisions to the
Posse Comitatus Act of 1878, in *New York Times*, July 21, 2002;
"After Sept. 11, a Legal Battle on the Limits of Civil Liberty," *New
York Times*, August 4, 2002; or "Expanded Powers of Justice
Department," *New York Times*, March 15, 2003.)

14. The French record in Algeria and other violations of human rights
by many parties elsewhere in the world have led to a decade
of openness on questions like torture. What is the official position
of the United States on torture? Find the answers to this question
by searching the Convention against Torture and Other Cruel,
Inhuman or Degrading Treatment or Punishment, signed by
the United States in 1992 and ratified in 1994; The Torture
Victims Protection Act of 1992; and Executive Order 13107,
signed by President Bill Clinton in December 1998
(<http://www.archives.gov/federal_register/executive_orders/
disposition_tables.html>). You may also want to consult Don Van
Natta, Jr., et al., "Questioning Terror Suspects in a Dark and Sur-
real World," *New York Times*, March 19, 2003, and the opinions
of Alan Dershowitz in *Why Terrorism Works* (New Haven: Yale
University Press, 2002).

Vocabulary/Vocabulaire

Nouns/Substantifs

censorship	la censure
colonist	le colon
duress	la contrainte
fighter	un(e) combattant(e)

fine	une amende
information	un renseignement
publishers	éditeurs (m. pl.)
remorse	le remords
repentance	le repentir
suffering	la souffrance
torturer	un tortionnaire
trial	un procès
witness	un témoin

Verbs/Verbes

admit	avouer
condone	pardonner
deny	nier
fine	condamner qqun à une amende
indict	inculper (qqun), poursuivre qqun en justice
repent	se repentir de qqch

Adjectives/Adjectifs

barbaric	barbare
Moslem	musulman(e)

Expressions/Expressions

counterterrorism	la contre-terreur
defending war crimes	apologie (f.) de crimes de guerre
dirty work	le sale travail
justify an act	justifier un acte
present something favorably	presenter qqch sous un jour favorable
show remorse	éprouver des remords
summary execution	une exécution sommaire
the end justifies the means	la fin justifie les moyens
to be aware of	être au courant de

to be indicted	être inculpé(e), poursuivi(e)
to be judged	être jugé(e)
to be on slippery ground	être sur un terrain glissant

Notes

1. See, for example, Florence Beauge, "Torturée par l'armée française en Algérie, Lila recherche l'homme qui l'a sauvée," *Le Monde,* June 20, 2000, 1. (Lexis-Nexis, accessed June 11, 2002.)

2. Johannès Franck, "Mohamed Garne, né d'un viol pendant la guerre d'Algérie, reconnu comme victime," *Le Monde,* November 24, 2001, Société, 10. (Lexis-Nexis, accessed July 9, 2002.)

3. Paul Aussaresses, *Services spéciaux: Algérie 1955-1957* (Paris: Perrin, 2001), 155.

4. Bernard Droz and Evelyne Lever, *Histoire de la guerre d'Algérie, 1954–1962* (Paris: Editions du Seuil, 1982), 18.

5. Ibid., 20–21.

6. Ibid., 31.

7. Martha Crenshaw Hutchinson, *Revolutionary Terrorism: The FLN in Algeria, 1954–1962* (Stanford, CA: Hoover Institution, 1978), 5.

8. Droz and Lever, *Histoire,* 43.

9. Quoted in ibid., 62.

10. Ibid., 55.

11. Droz and Lever, *Histoire,* 78.

12. Ibid., 128–29.

13. Ibid., 131.

14. Alistair Horne, *A Savage War of Peace: Algeria 1954–1962* [1977] (New York: Viking Penguin, 1987), 290.

15. See the texts of the General's speeches at <http://www.charles-de-gaulle.org.>

16. Johannès Franck, "100 000 francs d'amende requis contre le général Aussaresses et ses éditeurs," *Le Monde,* November 30, 2001. (Lexis-Nexis, accessed November 11, 2001.)

17. Brigitte Vital-Durand, "Aussaresses paie pour son Algérie," *Libération,* January 26, 2002, 14. (Lexis-Nexis, accessed June 6, 2002.)

18. Hutchinson, *Revolutionary Terrorism,* 18–39.

19. Aussaresses, *Services spéciaux,* 30–31.

20. Albert Camus, *Resistance, Rebellion and Death* [1961], trans. Justin O'Brien (New York: Vintage, 1994), 114.

21. Albert Camus, *Actuelles III. Chronique algériennes 1939–1958* (Paris: Gallimard, 1958), 15.

Bibliography

Aussaresses, Paul. *Services spéciaux: Algérie 1955-1957.* Paris: Perrin, 2001.

Droz, Bernard, and Evelyne Lever. *Histoire de la guerre d'Algérie, 1954–1962.* Paris: Seuil, 1982.

Horne, Alistair. *A Savage War of Peace: Algeria 1954–1962.* [1977.] New York: Viking Penguin, 1987.

Hutchinson, Martha Crenshaw. *Revolutionary Terrorism: The FLN in Algeria, 1954–1962.* Stanford, CA: Hoover Institution, 1978.

<http://www.lemonde.fr>

<http://www.libération.com>.

Resource Guide

Further Reading

Alleg, Henri. *La question.* Paris: Editions de Minuit, 1961.

Bacholle-Bošković, Michèle. "La Guerre d'Algérie expliquée à nos enfants." *The French Review* 76, no. 5 (2003): 968–82.

Camus, Albert. "L'Hôte." In *L'Exil et le royaume.* Paris: Gallimard, 1957.

Cohen, William B. "The Sudden Memory of Torture: The Algerian War in French Discourse, 2000–2001." *French Politics, Culture and Society* 19, no. 3 (2001): 82–94.

de Bollardière, Jacques Paris. *Bataille d'Alger, bataille d'homme.* Paris: Desclée de Brouwer, 1972.

Delacampagne, Christian. "Torturante Mémoire." *French Politics, Culture and Society* 19, no. 3 (2001): 95–107.

Evans, Martin. "From Colonialism to Post-colonialism." *French History since Napoleon.* Edited by Martin S. Alexander. London: Oxford University Press, 1999.

Maran, Rita. *Torture and the Role of Ideology: The French-Algerian War.* New York: Praeger, 1989.

Massu, Jacques. *La vraie bataille d'Alger.* Paris: Plon, 1971.

Rey-Goldzeiguer, Annie. *Aux origines de la guerre d'Algérie 1940–45.* Paris: La Découverte, 2002.

Rotman, Patrick, and Bernard Tavernier. *La Guerre sans nom: les appelés d'Algérie 1954–62.* Paris: Éditions du Seuil, 1992.

Roy, Jules. *J'accuse le general Massu.* Paris: Seuil, 1972.

Talbot, John E. *The War without a Name: France in Algeria, 1954–1962.* New York: Knopf, 1980.

Vidal-Naquet, Pierre. *Les crimes de l'armée française: Algérie 1954–1962.* Paris: Maspero, 1975.

———. *La torture dans la république: essai d'histoire et de politique contemporaines (1954–1962).* Paris: Editions de Minuit, 1998.

In English: *Torture: Cancer of Democracy*. Hammondsworth: Penguin, 1963.

Films

The Battle of Algiers (Battaglia di Algieri). Dir. Gillo Pontecorvo. Stella Productions, 1966. A tough but must-see film, available in VHS format: Rhino Video, 1993. This film has recently been shown at the Pentagon within the context of the war in Iraq. See Michael T. Kaufman. "What Does the Pentagon See in 'Battle of Algiers'?" *New York Times* September 7, 2003.

The Intimate Enemy: Violence in the Algerian War. Dir. Patrick Rotman. Broadcast on French TV in March 2002; watch for U.S. release. *L'ennemi intime*. DVD—Zone 2 France Television Distribution, 2002.

La Guerre sans nom. Canal + and GMT Productions. 1991. Dir. Bernard Tavernier and Patrick Rotman. DVD: Imperial Entertainment— Zone 2. In English: *The Undeclared War*. 1992. Little Bear Films. French draftees talking about their Algerian war experiences. Difficult to find.

L'Honneur d'un capitaine. Dir. Pierre Schoendoerffer. Perf. Nicole Garcia, Jacques Perrin. Videocassette. Beta/TF1 Films Production, 1982. DVD, 1999. Addresses the question of honor or truth. Contains footage of Algerian war combat. Difficult to find in United States.

Muriel. Dir. Alain Resnais, 1963. VHS: Hen's Tooth Video, 1998. Characters haunted by the past, including the Algerian War.

Commentary on Film

Dine, Philip. *Images of the Algerian War*. Oxford: Clarendon Press, 1994. See, in particular, chapter 8, "Cinema Images of the Algerian Conflict, 1954–1992."

Hill, Leslie. "Filming Ghosts: French Cinema and the Algerian War." *Modern Fiction Studies* 38, no. 3 (1992): 787–803.

Melville, Jean Pierre. "Le Chagrin et la pitié." *Sight and Sound* 40, no. 4 (1971): 181 ff.

Wilson, David. "Politics and Pontecorvo." *Sight and Sound* 40, no. 3 (1971): 160–61.

Newspaper and Journal Articles

Lexis-Nexis (<http://web.lexis-nexis.com/universe/>) is an excellent source for online searching of newspaper articles, both in English and in French. See whether it is available in your school library or in a nearby public or college library. OCLC First Search is a source to ask your librarian about for journal articles.

Web Sites

The *Institut National de l'Audiovisuel* (INA) site contains interesting historical footage of the events in France and Algeria during the war. In French. Requires RealPlayer or QuickTime player:
<http:// www.ina.fr/voir_revoir/algerie/>

U.S. Library of Congress general Web site on Algeria:
<http://lcweb2.loc.gov/frd/cs/dztoc.html>

Algeria Interface is maintained by Algerian and European journalists with many links to newspaper articles on contemporary and historical events in Algeria. In English and French:
<http://www.algeria-interface.com/>

PART II

Competing Voices

CHAPTER 4

Regional Languages in France: The Return of the Repressed?

It has been calculated that, in the mid-nineteenth century, about one-fifth of the population of France did not know any French; they spoke the patois of their local village or the dialect of their region.[1] This situation—understandable in a nation 80 percent of whose citizens were peasants and for whom school attendance was not mandatory—was unacceptable to those in charge of public education, who wished to create a truly national language. Breton, then spoken by almost two million citizens of France as a first (and often only) language, was especially targeted; in 1831 one of the prefects of northern and western Brittany wrote the following to the minister of public instruction: "We must, by any means possible, promote the weakening and corruption of the Breton language, to the point where, from one village to another, people do not understand each other. For in that way, the need to communicate will require that the peasant learn French. The Breton language absolutely must be destroyed" ("*[Il faut] par tous les moyens possibles, favoriser l'appauvrissement, la corruption du breton, jusqu'au point où, d'une commune à l'autre, on ne puisse pas s'entendre [. . .], car alors la nécessité de communication obligera le paysan d'apprendre le français. Il faut absolument détruire le langage Breton*").[2]

Today, in the town of Lorient as in other places in Brittany, students are learning Breton as early as kindergarten (*la maternelle*) in immersion programs in Diwan schools. Diwan, which means seed in Breton, is a linguistic and cultural movement dating from the mid-1970s. Almost 6,500 Breton children are taking most of their classes in this regional language in 135 schools in the five departments that make up Brittany.[3] Typically, Diwan schools are free and open to all students—not just those who are natives of Brittany—and aim as well to transmit a regional cultural identity that is one among many in France. The Breton language, two thousand years old and related to other Celtic tongues like Gaelic and Welsh, has thus been able to survive primarily through the efforts of those who believe in the benefits of bilingual education.

How did this reversal of policy come about? Is the French state now willing to preserve local languages? What elements came into play to bring about the necessity of creating groups to preserve local languages and cultures? What is the future of bilingual education in France? The answers to many of these questions can be found well before the modern era.

Background

The Ancient Regime: Toward Political and Cultural Unity

It has been pointed out that the union between state and language is particularly strong in France, so that it is even possible to say that the state was created through the French language.[4] The *Serments de Strasbourg,* a document sworn in ancient dialects of French and German by Charlemagne's two grandsons in 842 as they pledged mutual nonaggression, is the earliest instance of the use of French in the context of nation-building. Many centuries later, in the Edict of Villers-Cotterêts (1539), the king François I made French the official legal and judicial language of the realm.[5] While the edict was primarily directed at the use of French rather than Latin, regional languages were also targeted to disappear in favor of French. At the time, in fact, 99 percent of the population of France spoke no French, which was reserved to the city of Paris and to the aristocracy in the north of France.[6] In a sense, this edict of François I was also an act by which the state itself was founded, since it provided for the administration of royal justice through the publication of all official documents in French. Some ten years later, the poet Joachim Du

Bellay published his *Défense et illustration de la langue française* (*Defense and Illustration of the French Language*), a text in which he announced his intention to write his poetry in French instead of Latin. Du Bellay recommended as well the invention of new words and the use of terms derived from regional and foreign languages— all with the purpose of enriching literary language.[7] Throughout the sixteenth century, French continued to spread through the creation of universities (*collèges*) in which the teaching language was French.[8]

The Académie Française was created in the following century (1635) by Louis XIII and his minister Cardinal de Richelieu in part to defend the use and spread of the French language throughout the nation and to make certain that it remained uncorrupted by the importation of foreign or provincial words and expressions. The Académie was charged with overseeing the French language and with creating a dictionary as well as rules of grammar, rhetoric, and poetry. At this point in the nation's history, French was a language tied entirely to social origin; in this respect it belonged to the aristocracy and the bourgeoisie. Scholars estimate that perhaps only 5 percent of the population at this time spoke French.[9] Yet by the mid-eighteenth century the rest of Europe was coming to know French as well, primarily through the presence of French ministers, artists, engineers, and writers. In the courts of Germany and Italy, in Prussia and in Russia, French was the language of everyday conversation. It was reputed to be universal in its ability to, as the writer Voltaire claimed in his *Dictionnaire philosophique* (Philosophical Dictionary), "express with the most facility, clarity and delicacy all the topics of conversation of decent people" ("*La langue française est de toutes les langues celle qui exprime avec le plus de facilité, de netteté, de délicatesse tous les objets de la conversation des honnêtes gens*").[10]

The Revolution and Linguicide

In August 1790, the Abbé Grégoire, a deputy to the revolutionary National Convention, initiated a national survey on rural customs in order to support his intention to "stamp out local dialects and universalize the French language." His reasons were very clear, if one reads some of the questions that were asked: he particularly wanted to know what relationship might exist between the patois spoken in a region and the moral, religious, and political life of its speakers. Not surprisingly, he believed that the persistence of patois would harm the newly founded nation because these "vulgar idioms prolonged the childhood of reason as well as the old age of prejudice." Grégoire and the other revolutionaries reasoned that linguistic diversity would pose an obstacle to equality.[11] In order for citizens to understand "the true nature of the laws" as well as the nature of the powers that oppressed them under the ancien régime, it would be necessary for them to speak French, the "language of freedom."[12] Patriotism thus came to be extended to the domain of language; language and nation were officially associated for the first time. The new republic announced that it considered language to be an affair of the state: the masses were to be lifted up by public education in the language of that state, French. Since the nation was also considered to be one and indivisible, it was natural to believe that the cultural and linguistic particularism of the provinces could no longer be tolerated. The bourgeois who led the French Revolution thus "declared war on patois."[13]

Those who argued in favor of obliterating regional languages, dialects, and patois did not mince their words. Bertrand Barère, a member of the governing Committee on Public Safety and a deputy from the Ariège in southwestern France, where dialects of Occitan[14] were spoken, declared that "the monarchy might well resemble the tower of Babel; but in a democracy, to leave citizens ignorant of the national language, incapable of controlling power, is to betray the fatherland. In a free people, language must be one and the same for all" (*"La monarchie avait des raisons de ressembler à la tour de Babel; dans la démocratie, laisser les citoyens ignorants de la langue nationale, incapables de contrôler le pouvoir, c'est trahir la patrie. . . . Chez un peuple libre, la langue doit être une et la même pour tous"*). Barère went on to point out the high costs of translating the new republic's laws in the various idioms of France, and denounced the necessity of "maintaining these barbarous jargons and vulgar idioms that can only serve fanatics and counterrevolutionaries" (*"maintenir ces jargons barbares et ces idiomes grossiers qui ne peuvent plus servir que les fanatiques et les contre-révolutionnaires"*).[15] He added that "federalism and superstition speak low Breton; emigration and hatred of the Republic speak German; the counterrevolution speaks Italian; and fanaticism speaks Basque" (*"le fédéralisme et la superstition parlent bas Breton; l'émigration et la haine de la République parlent allemand; la contre-révolution parle l'italien et le fanatisme parle le basque"*).[16] In this way, Barère made it clear that continued tolerance of regional languages was tantamount to allowing all the enemies of the republic to undermine it from within.

Eventually, the word *langue* came to mean French alone, and everything that was not French was patois, or feudal idioms like Breton, Norman, Provençal, Basque, and others. The Decree of 2 Thermidor (July 20, 1794) specifically addressed the necessity for French to be the official language of the republic; all other languages would be forbidden. Some five decades later, the *Loi Falloux* (1850) stipulated that "French should be the sole language used in schools."[17] Instruction everywhere in France was to be conducted in French. Thus began a national linguistic policy whose effect was to repress and eventually eliminate all languages other than French.[18]

The Third Republic

This "linguistic terror," as some have called it, did not make local languages and dialects disappear, of course. Because it was difficult and expensive to train and send new teachers into all the corners of France, the status quo persisted, at least until the Third Republic (1870–1939) and its creation of a national system of education that would be free and mandatory for all. In the meantime, French was heard and spoken in the provinces, as many peasants became bilingual in order to understand the administrative laws that applied to them. The army also brought rural citizens into contact with French, which was the language spoken by officers and the *lingua franca* (shared language) of a military whose soldiers were made up of so many different patois speakers. Napoleon's creation of a meritocracy, in which citizens acceded to civil service jobs based upon their performance on exams, was also responsible for convincing those who spoke regional languages of the importance of being able to read and write in French.[19] Emigration from the countryside to the city toward the end of the nineteenth century likewise served to educate peasants in French.

The Third Republic also brought with it a number of other practices designed to ensure the *francisation* (Frenchification) of the peasantry, some of them barely imaginable today. For example, near the beginning of the twentieth century the Breton language was absolutely forbidden in both the classroom and the schoolyard. The expression "*Il est interdit de cracher par terre et de parler Breton*" (It is forbidden to spit on the floor and to speak Breton) is supposed to date from this time, and this injunction is said to have been posted in public places. Though no traces have ever been found of the original posters, this expression served for many years as a reminder to speakers of Breton that their language was somehow associated with an act that was socially prohibited.[20]

Many Breton authors speak as well of the humiliation they endured as children when they were caught speaking their native language in school. Most particularly, children were made to wear "*le symbole*" or the "*signum*,"[21] often a horseshoe-shaped object or perhaps a clog (*sabot*) that identified the wearer as backward; this was worn around the neck or pinned onto the child's clothing. Pierre-Jakez Hélias relates in his autobiography, *The Horse of Pride* (1978), that children were punished physically as well for sinning against the rule of speaking French, made to stand in the corner, or else asked to write out verb conjugations. Frequently, he notes, the punishment at school was followed by a worse one at home, since the child's parents saw the misbehavior as bringing disgrace onto the family.[22] Mastery of French was, after all, crucial to the child's social progress.[23]

Voices were occasionally raised against the official policy of stamping out regional languages, but these never succeeded in changing the minds of those responsible for educating French children. In an impassioned article published in the *Dépêche de Toulouse* in 1911, Jean Jaurès, the great socialist leader in the Assemblée Nationale, argued for study in school of regional languages. He reasoned that children would more easily learn about the Latin roots of French through a comparative study of the dialects of Occitan spoken in the Midi. And, not incidentally, children would discover the richness of their common heritage, lost to the political domination of the north of France.

Post–World War II Linguistic Policies

In 1951, however, the *Loi Deixonne* authorized the teaching of certain regional languages in the schools (Breton, Basque, Catalan, and Occitan). This change of heart may have come about for some of these regions as a result of their contribution to the French Resistance during World War II; it was thought to be good political strategy to recognize that these languages were spoken by those who had fought for France's freedom from her German occupiers. Postwar governments also formulated a policy to reunite the country after four years of the Vichy regime, which had encouraged decentralization. The change in policy was not actually put into place until the mid-1970s, when funds were authorized to encourage what constituted by then the relearning of these languages and cultures by children who had been thoroughly "*francisés.*"

The first Diwan *école maternelle* (Diwan kindergarten) was founded in 1976, following the passage of the *Loi Haby*, which mandated the offering of instruction in regional languages wherever there was demand. Gradually, the teaching of Breton was authorized at all levels (as an option) up through the university. In the Basque country in southwestern France, local Ikastola schools (some of which were founded as early as 1969) also offer immersion instruction in Euskara, the Basque language. Today it is possible to pass the baccalaureate exam in certain regional languages and to complete the CAPES degree in the teaching of these languages. The training of future teachers of regional languages will thus ensure their continuation in French culture.

But the way has not been smooth for the return of regional languages. Governments of the left and the right in France have systematically been lukewarm to the idea of encouraging students to learn these languages, and initiatives have been consistently underfunded. In 1982 the Giordan report urging the recognition and promotion of regional languages and cultures in the name of "the right to difference" ("*le droit à la différence*") brought no profound changes in the cultural policies of President Mitterrand.[24] One deputy pointed out, on the occasion of the debates on the ratification of the Treaty of Maastricht (for the European Union) in 1992, that if French children have to learn another language, "let's not waste their time with dialects they will only speak in their village; let's teach them as soon as possible an international language" ("*S'il faut apprendre une autre langue à nos enfants, ne leur faisons pas perdre leur temps avec des dialectes qu'ils ne parleront jamais que dans leur village: enseignons-leur le plus tôt possible une langue internationale!*").[25] He meant English, of course.

Even as late as 1994 the *Loi Toubon* (named for the then minister of culture) reminded the French that, by virtue of the Constitution, French is "the language of the Republic and is a fundamental element of the personality and heritage of France" ("*Langue de la République en vertu de la Constitution, la langue française est un élément fondamental de la personnalité et du patrimoine de la France*").[26] French was officially to be used in teaching, the workplace, and other public services, and would be the link among the countries of the French-speaking community. Toubon's law was, however, directed at the danger of an English language invasion of the French public sphere, rather than at regional languages.

Linguistic immersion students at the Collège Léon Còrdes in Montpellier show the Occitan flag, 1998. (© Andre Fernandez/Corbis Sygma).

A scholar of multiculturalism in France notes that there are no data available to let us know how many French people today speak or understand a regional language or dialect, since this information is not part of the national census, "a fact that reflects the traditional reluctance of the state to grant official recognition to these languages."[27] Estimates run as low as 10 percent and as high as 30 percent of the population, and of course the active speakers are usually older. Recent statistics indicate that overall only about 2 percent, or 320,000 of France's schoolchildren are receiving instruction in regional languages. The figures are much higher, though, in certain regions like Corsica and Brittany, and for the languages of southern France like Occitan and Catalan.[28]

Apart from their presence in some schools, regional languages can also be heard on radio and television. News broadcasts and other cultural programming exist in a number of regions, and quite a few newspapers run columns in regional languages as well. In general, such regional cultural programming is well supported by the French government, as are other forms of celebration of regional identity, such as folklore and music festivals.

The European Charter on Regional and Minority Languages

Now an important debate has arisen as a result of the European Council's promulgation of the Charter on Regional and Minority Languages, a document adopted by the council in 1992 and ratified by eighteen countries by 1998. The charter defines regional languages as "those spoken traditionally in an area of a nation by citizens who constitute a group that is smaller than the population of the state." This would refer to such languages as Breton, Corsican, and Alsatian, for example, among the seventy-five languages that have been identified as still existing in France.[29] Minority languages are those that may be traditionally spoken in a nation, but that are not associated with a specific region or a territory. These would seem to be the languages spoken by immigrants—but not all immigrants. For example, there are Italian and Portuguese immigrants in France, but their languages are already taught in the schools. Rather, this category would appear to apply to languages whose existence is threatened, such as Berber, in Spain or languages of peoples in diaspora.[30]

The aim of the charter is first of all to "protect and promote regional or minority languages insofar as they represent an aspect of European cultural patrimony whose existence is threatened" ("*protéger et promouvoir les langues régionales ou minoritaires en tant qu'aspect menacé du patrimoine culturel européen*").[31] The charter is also a consequence of the European Commission's desire to promote diversity among the "mosaic of cultures and languages" in the fifteen current members of the European Union. Though the charter wishes to defend languages that might be threatened with extinction, it does not "create individual or group rights for the speakers of those regional or minority languages."[32] However, the charter supports initiatives in the area of education, such as the promotion of bilingualism and trilinguilism. Such instruction would be available at all levels, from the *maternelle* to adult education. In addition, the charter proposes that important national legislative texts be published in regional languages, and that the electronic media be encouraged to broadcast in regional languages.

In 1999, after extended debate in the National Assembly and in the press, France signed only thirty-nine of the ninety-eight articles proposed by the charter, many fewer than other European countries. The primary concern is very clear; as we have seen, France is a nation for which the national language has been crucial in forming and maintaining national identity. This monolingual tradition is therefore extremely strong, and any challenge to it inevitably involves political issues. The government was especially careful to protect the terms of the Constitution of the Fifth Republic, by which no special protection or rights are to be given to minorities. The constitution ensures "the equality of all before the law and recognizes only the French people, composed of all citizens without regard for origin, race or religion." Article 2 of the constitution states plainly, "*La langue de la République est le français*" (the language of the republic is French).

As it happened, following the signing, the *Conseil constitutionnel* (a body that deliberates on the constitutionality of laws, treaties, procedures, and other acts of the legislature) immediately ruled that the document did not conform to the constitution, and the charter remains unratified and thus inapplicable in France. While Prime Minister Lionel Jospin proposed to President Jacques Chirac that the constitution be amended to allow for the ratification of the charter, the latter declined to do so (although he had been in favor of the charter some years before), citing the danger of threatening the indivisibility of the nation by encouraging "specific rights" for "linguistic communities."[33]

Most recently, there have been incidents involving both the financing of Diwan schools and the teaching of Corsican on the island of Corsica. In November 2001, the *Conseil d'Etat* (a body that advises the government with regard to proposed legislation) ordered the suspension of the process by which Diwan schools would be integrated into the system of public education, an initiative of then minister of education Jack Lang. Lang's plan was also to extend the teaching of foreign and regional languages to the elementary schools beginning in 2003. The *Conseil* seemed to be most disturbed by the immersion method embraced by Diwan schools (most of the courses are in Breton, which is also the language used outside of class); in their judgment, the use of Breton threatened the unity of the republic because the language of instruction in public education must be French. Bretons in favor of Lang's initiatives demonstrated in many cities in Brittany, calling for the government to pledge a modification of Article 2 of the Constitution of the Fifth Republic, and for the ratification of the European Charter on Regional and Minority Languages. The issue is very important to those who favor Diwan schools because they cannot progress and expand without public funding.

The Corsican question is a bit thornier, since it is related to a proposition for a law on the political status of Corsica, one of whose articles stipulates that the Corsican language will be taught to all pupils in the kindergartens and primary schools in Corsica. In fact, the Corsican regional council had voted for bilingualism in 1983, a decision that was reversed by the national government.[34] Deputies who debated the evolution of the island toward more autonomy once again saw in the proposal for the teaching of Corsican as a language with status equal to that of French a symbolic threat to the unity of the republic.

Predictably, the political debate about the charter found its way into the 2002 presidential elections, dividing the sixteen candidates roughly equally for and against, but not always according to left and right. For example, it is possible for a left-leaning Republican and a very conservative right-winger to oppose the charter, though not necessarily for the same reasons. The left wishes to avoid the creation of a "cultural mosaic of communities," along the Anglo-Saxon model,[35] while the right might insist on preserving the purity of French culture against the importation of minority languages and cultures.

Discussion

The teaching of regional languages should be supported.

Agree

Linguists point out that the learning of languages other than one's own has beneficial effects, especially if this learning takes place at an early age. It has been proved that students who are bilingual actually have better mastery of standard French than those who speak only French. The problem is that France, unlike the countries of northern Europe, does not have a tradition of learning second languages from kindergarten on. For this reason, bilingualism is the exception rather than the rule in France. This is unfortunate, because children who already have two languages find it easier to learn others.

Another extremely important consideration is the preservation of regional cultures at a time when the dissolution of national boundaries in the European Union might well be threatening diversity. The European Union could bring about the kind of unity that erases not only national differences, but also regional differences. Globalization will inevitably entail uniformity and standardization, and so it becomes more important to assert the traditions of one's own culture or ethnic group. A former minister of culture has pointed out the irony of the fact that the French government officially supports plurilingualism in Europe (as a way of defending against the "invasion" of American English), yet does not support it within France ("*Comment pourrions-nous militer pour le maintien du plurilinguisme en Europe si nous le refusions en France?*").[36]

Since it is impossible to consider oneself truly Alsatian, or Corsican, or Breton without knowledge of that regional language, it makes sense to support any initiatives that make this knowledge possible—such as Diwan schools, for example. Former minister of culture Jack Lang has argued that regional languages are an "element of the national patrimony," that consequently they "contribute to the diversity of cultural identities" and ought to be studied in all grades.[37] Even those who do not speak a regional language believe that such instruction should be available to those who want it.

It is sometimes argued that it is pointless to apply public funding to regional language instruction when such languages are disappearing. Yet the recent creation and success of regional language radio stations, television channels, and newspapers make it clear that there is a demand for such instruction.

Disagree

While it is the case that the teaching of regional languages may be desirable, there are other strategies that must take precedence. In the first place, such a policy requires diverting attention and funding from instruction both in French and in more strategically important languages, such as the major national languages of Europe. At the moment, for example, many students are having a difficult time mastering French as a native language (10 percent of students can barely read). The situation in the schools suggests that not enough energy or money has been invested in teaching the national language, particularly (though not exclusively) to children for whom French is a second language. In addition, enrollments in French schools in other national languages such as German and Russian have fallen considerably during the past few years. These languages are crucial if France is to maintain its leadership in the expanded European Union.

Furthermore, the importance of regional languages has been overestimated, especially if one considers the present number of speakers. In Brittany, for example, the two largest cities are French-speaking.[38] It is virtually impossible to estimate how many actual speakers of

Breton exist, because the published figures are all widely divergent. It is clear, though, that the numbers are not large and that the use of the language has been declining during the past decades.[39]

Finally, all too often the promotion of regional languages has been linked to separatism and the demand for regional autonomy, and even to terrorist acts associated with these separatist and autonomist movements. The French nation cannot tolerate these dangerous expressions of political activism.

France should sign the European Charter on Regional and Minority Languages.

Agree

Other countries in Europe have signed the charter; France should be willing to accept its very modest provisions. The image of France as a homogeneous nation is certainly no longer true, because France's cultural identity involves not only the diverse regional cultures, but also the many minorities who make up the population (in fact, about one-third of France's citizens are first- or second-generation immigrants). The charter does not mandate the teaching of regional or minority languages; it only indicates that where parents or students are interested, such instruction can be offered. This is indeed a minimalist approach that in no way threatens the status of French as the language of the republic.

Former prime minister Lionel Jospin has pointed out that the future of France lies in the signing of the charter. Linguistic and cultural pluralism can only be a healthy thing for the nation, and "fundamentalists" who persist in warning of "collective suicide" should France sign are exaggerating both the charter's charges and its effects.[40] The charter only recommends the teaching of regional languages as an option; it merely encourages the diffusion of regional languages in the media. Signing would not seem to imply an important change in the current linguistic policies followed by the French government. It does not seem likely, either, that regional languages, as a cultural phenomenon, really threaten French national unity. Finally, no one who recommends signing the charter has suggested that French should no longer be the national language. In fact, the defense of regional languages is a step toward preserving French, insofar as it is necessary to preserve the European linguistic diversity that is threatened by English. A vast majority of French people understand this fact, since a poll in 2000 indicated that 82 percent were in favor of ratifying the charter.[41]

Disagree

The ratification of the charter represents a danger to the unity of the republic because the link between the nation and the national language is so strong. The *Mouvement des citoyens,* which supported Jean-Pierre Chevènement for the presidency in 2002, argued that the republic is based on the existence of one language community, not on a mosaic of ethnic and cultural communities. The widespread teaching of regional and minority languages and the constitutional integration of such languages into French life could lead to the Balkanization[42] of the nation. The movement's proponents pointed out as well that the teaching of regional and minority languages poses a serious threat to francophonie (the continued presence of the French language and culture in France's former colonies) because it works against the integration of French speakers of foreign origin. As Georges Sarre, deputy to the National Assembly, said, "the citizen's nation and the French Republic were constructed thanks to a shared language, because no democratic debate can be possible among citizens who do not understand one another."[43] The issue is linked as well to other threats facing France's sovereignty, including its participation in the European Union, which may eventually hasten the death of nation-states.

In addition, the charter gives the same rights to minority languages as to regional ones, even though these are not even official languages in any country. The charter, by favoring certain languages and singling them out for special treatment, discriminates in favor of certain groups and proposes a communitarian vision of the nation, in which ethnic and linguistic minority identities take precedence over French identity. This is again specifically contrary to the principles of the republic.

Finally, what is the purpose in allowing students to waste their time learning languages that will have no usefulness outside of France? It makes more sense to encourage the study of another European language or English, rather than to spend money supporting bilingual education in regional languages. Since regional languages are already a fact of French life (on radio and in the press, primarily), there is no need to make their status official.

Questions and Activities

1. The seven regional languages of France are Basque, Breton, Catalan, Corsican, Occitan, Alsatian, and Flemish. Research these languages, and report to the class on the areas in which they are spoken and the history of their development. Good sources for this research include

Laroussi and Marcellesi, "The Other Languages of France"; Gaquin, *Peuples et langues de France*; and Ager, *Sociolinguistics and Contemporary French*, listed in the Bibliography and Resource Guide. Web sites include the following.

For Alsatian: <http://www.languages-on-the-web.com/links/link-alsatian.htm>

For Basque: <http://www.euskadi.net/euskara/indice800_c.htm>

For Breton: <http://www.breizh.net/ICDBL/saozg/nominoe.htm>

For Catalan: <http://www.ezresult.com/article/catalan_language>

For Corsican: <http://www.corsica-isula.com/language.htm>

For Flemish: <http://www.languages-on-the-web.com/links/link-flemish.htm>

For Occitan: <http://occitanet.free.fr/fr/index.html>

2. Can there be a cultural revival that does not depend on a linguistic one? What important links are there between language and culture? You may wish to interview speakers of languages other than English to get their viewpoints.

3. During the Middle Ages and the Renaissance, Occitania, or the area also known as the Languedoc, boasted a rich language and culture. Some authors who have written on the flowering and importance of Occitan ascribe its decline to certain measures undertaken by French governments over a period of hundreds of years. One author suggests that the republican school carried out colonialist policies in order to suppress regional identity,[44] and another refers to these policies as they applied to regional cultures everywhere in France as "cultural genocide."[45] Research the case of Occitania in particular, and report to the class on the events that brought about the demise of Occitan culture. A good starting point is Gaquin, *Peuples langues de France,* as well as the works of Robert Lafont, *Clefs pour l'Occitanie* and *La Revendication occitane*. The Web site at <http://www.languages-on-the-web.com/links/link-occitan.htm> supplies many helpful links.

4. Alphonse Daudet's short story *La dernière classe* (The Last Class) tells a tale of the linguistic and cultural consequences of the German occupation of Alsace during the Franco-Prussian War. The story appeared in Daudet's *Contes du lundi* (Monday Stories) (1873). Read this story and discuss it in class as an example of the triumph of French during the Third Republic.

5. Many in the United States believe that English should be the country's official language, and that immigrants should be taught in English, rather than encouraged to pursue bilingual education.

Debate the following statement: "Contrary to what is still wide-spread belief, making people feel guilty about the languages they speak, and destroying them, in an attempt to promote a single language, does not make for progress. It is the existence of a *common* language that is a necessary condition, but this need not mean the devaluing or wiping out of other languages."[46] Those who argue in favor of English only might consult one of these two Web sites: <http://www.us-english.org> or <http://www.englishfirst.org/>. Those who support preserving minority languages can consult <http://ourworld.compuserve.com/homepages/JWCRAWFORD/engonly.htm>.

6. Recently the French government proposed that the national educational system be decentralized in part—that is, that certain policy-making functions be turned over to the twenty-two regions of France. The proposal has met with a great deal of resistance on the part of teachers' unions, but with approval by some regional organizations. What reasons might each side have for its opinion? Consult <http://www.partibreton.org/> for information regarding the pro-decentralization perspective, and <http://www.fen.fr/~fen-ftp/Flash/02-03/TRACT%20DECENTRALISATION.Pdf> or <http://www.fen.fr/actualites.html> for the antidecentralization view.

7. Modern France has a strong centralizing history (Jacobinism) that has resisted regional autonomy or has granted it in limited fashion. Beyond demands for more local autonomy, certain regions like Corsica and Brittany have independence movements. Why would some regions in France have separatist movements? Form teams to investigate the question, using Corsica and Brittany as case studies. Do you think that Corsicans and Bretons should have official status for their languages or recognition as distinct nationalities? The main separatist group in Corsica is the FLNC (*Front de Libération National de la Corse*), which you should include in your investigation. See <http://www.ict.org.il/inter_ter/orgdet.cfm?orgid=85> or start with <http://www.guardian.co.uk/print/0%2c3858%2c4705334-103681%2c00.html> for an article on a recent constitutional poll in Corsica. For Brittany you might look at EMGANN (*Mouvement de la gauche indépendantiste*) at <http://www.chez.com/emgann/> or the UDB (*Union Démocratique Bretonne*) at <http://www.udb-bzh.net/>. Both of these are political organizations. A general overview of policy in France toward regional languages may be found in Hargreaves, "The Challenges of Multiculturalism," and in Ager, "Language and Power," especially 160–61 (see Bibliography).

8. As might be expected from what you have read about educational policy concerning regional languages in France, the French government makes no special provision for bilingual education for immigrants, who are expected to assimilate to the principles of French republicanism. That is, multiculturalism, insofar as it establishes separate communities within the nation, is rejected. Compare this attitude to legislation concerning bilingual education in the United States. For example, look up Proposition 227 in California (passed in 1998). A complete Web site on the issues involved can be found at <http://primary98.ss.ca.gov/VoterGuide/Propositions/227.htm>

9. During the nineteenth and early twentieth centuries, when people of many different nationalities emigrated to the United States, bilingual education was unknown, and students were expected to assimilate in English as quickly as possible. Why might the situation facing immigrants be different today?

10. Bilingualism is linked to biculturalism, that is, the preservation of one's native culture and traditions. How might this continuity be important to the social adjustment of children who are newly arrived immigrants?

Vocabulary/Vocabulaire

Nouns/Substantifs

Alsatian language	l'alsatien
autonomy	l'autonomie
Basque language	le basque
bilingualism	le bilinguisme
Breton language	le breton
Catalan language	le catalan
charter	la charte
community	la communauté
Corsican language	le corse
dialect	le dialecte
diversity	la diversité
ethnic group	l'ethnie (f.)
Flemish language	le flamand
immigrant	l'immigré (m.)
language (speech)	le langage

linguist	le linguiste
local dialect	le patois
mastery	la maîtrise
monolingualism	le monolinguisme
Occitanian language	l'occitan (m.)
patrimony	le patrimoine
plurilingualism	le plurilinguisme
policy	la politique
provision	l'article
separatism	le séparatisme
speaker	le locuteur
study	l'étude (f.)
teaching	l'enseignement
tongue (language)	la langue
unity	l'unité (f.)

Verbs/Verbes

decentralize	décentraliser
decline	diminuer
demand	réclamer
devalue	dévaloriser
oppose	s'opposer (à)
preserve	préserver
promote	promulguer
ratify	ratifier
require	exiger
sign	signer
support	soutenir

Adjectives/Adjectifs

bilingual	bilingue
cultural	culturel, culturelle
French-speaking	francophone
minority	minoritaire
monolingual	monolingue
optional	facultatif, facultative

regional	regional, -e
required	obligatoire

Notes

1. The distinction between language, dialect, and patois is not very clear. Indeed, the organization Terralingua suggests that since "there are no linguistic criteria for differentiating between a language and a dialect (or vernacular or patois)," one possible definition would be that "a language is a dialect promoted by elites," or "a language is a dialect with an army (and a navy)." See <http://www.terralingua.org/Definitions/DLangDialect.html>. In other words, designating one form of expression as a language and another as (an inferior) dialect or patois depends on the political power being exercised by the speaker of the language. For the purposes of this chapter, we will use *dialect* to refer to a regional variety of a language, whereas the term *patois* will be used to describe a local variant. See Robert Lafont, *Langue dominante, langues dominées* (Paris: Edilig, 1981), for a discussion of the confusion of terms. See also Roger Hawkins, "Regional Variation in France," in *French Today: Language in Its Social Context,* ed. Carol Sanders (Cambridge: Cambridge University Press, 1993), 55–84, for information on the difference between standard French and its regional variants.

2. Jacques Leclerc, "Histoire du français, Sec. 9: Le français contemporain," *L'aménagement linguistique dans le monde,* Québec, TLFQ, Université Laval, 10 juillet 2003, <http://www.tlfq.ulaval.ca/axl/francophonie/HIST_FR_s9_Fr-contemporain.htm> (accessed August 12, 2003).

3. It has been estimated that in the late 1980s, there were somewhere around six hundred thousand Breton speakers. See Denetz, quoted in Foued Laroussi and Jean-Baptiste Marcellesi, "The Other Languages of France: Towards a Multilingual Policy," in *French Today: Language in Its Social Context,* ed. Carol Sanders (Cambridge: Cambridge University Press, 1993), 88.

4. Bernard Cerquilini, "Le Monolinguisme, une idéologie française," interview with Béatrice Vallaeys. *Libération* 10–11 novembre 2001.

5. For further information on the articles of the Edict of Villers-Cotterêts, see <http://www.tlfq.ulaval.ca/axl/francophonie/Edit_Villers-Cotterets.htm>.

6. Jacques Leclerc, "Histoire du français, Sec. 5: La Renaissance," *L'aménagement linguistique dans le monde,* Québec, TLFQ, Université Laval, 10 juillet 2003, <http://www.tlfq.ulaval.ca/axl/francophonie/HIST_FR_s5_Renaissance.htm> (accessed August 15, 2003).

7. See <http://www.tlfq.ulaval.ca/axl/francophonie/Du_Bellay.htm> for the text of Du Bellay's pamphlet.

8. Anne Judge, "French: A Planned Language?" in *French Today: Language in Its Social Context,* ed. Carol Sanders (Cambridge: Cambridge University Press, 1993), 12.

9. Jacques Leclerc, "Histoire du français, Sec. 6: Le français au Grand Siècle," *L'aménagement linguistique dans le monde,* Québec, TLFQ, Université Laval, 10 juillet 2003, <http://www.tlfq.ulaval.ca/axl/francophonie/HIST_FR_s6_Grand-Siecle.htm> (accessed August 10, 2003).

10. Quoted in Jacques Leclerc, "Histoire du français, Sec. 7: Le Siècle des Lumières," *L'aménagement linguistique dans le monde,* Québec, TLFQ, Université Laval, 10 juillet 2003, <http://www.tlfq.ulaval.ca/axl/francophonie/HIST_FR_s7_Lumieres.htm> (accessed August 10, 2003).

11. Judge, "French," 13.

12. Dennis Ager, *Language Policy in Britain and France: The Processes of Policy* (New York: Cassell, 1996), 42.

13. Jacques Leclerc, "Histoire du français, Sec. 8: La Révolution française," *L'aménagement linguistique dans le monde,* Québec, TLFQ, Université Laval, 9 juillet 2002, <http://www.tlfq.ulaval.ca/axl/francophonie/HIST_FR_s8_Revolutionl789.htm> (accessed August 12, 2003).

14. Occitan was the primary language of the southern third of France—from the Atlantic coast to the Italian border—until well into the twentieth century. Composed of a number of regional dialects and local patois, Occitan is close to Catalan (a language of northeastern Spain), and resembles French, Spanish, and Italian, all of which are Romance languages. The word *occitan* is derived from the *langue d'oc,* as distinct from the *langue d'oïl,* those languages derived from *francien* (the language of Paris and the Ile de France) and spoken in northern France. *Oc* and *oïl* meant yes in their respective languages, from the Latin *hoc ille.*

15. Leclerc, "Histoire, Sec. 8: La Révolution française."

16. Quoted in Michel de Certeau, *Une politique de la langue* (Paris: Gallimard, 1975), 10–11.

17. Laroussi and Marcellesi, "The Other Languages of France," 110.

18. Ibid., 96.

19. Ager, *Language Policy,* 45.

20. Fanch Broudic, "Il est interdit de cracher par terre et de parler Breton," <http://perso.wanadoo.fr/fanch.broudic/PAJENN/Interdiction.1902.html> (accessed August 15, 2003).

21. Laroussi and Marcellesi, "The Other Languages of France," 96.

22. Pierre-Jakez Hélias, *The Horse of Pride* (New Haven: Yale University Press, 1978), 147–48.

23. Antoine Prost, "Immigration, Particularism, and Republican Education," *French Politics and Society* 16, no. 1 (1998): 18.

24. Laroussi and Marcellesi, "The Other Languages of France," 98.

25. Robert Pandraud, quoted in Leclerc, "Histoire, Sec. 9: Le Français contemporain."

26. The full text of the *Loi Toubon* (1994) is available at <http://www.culture.gouv.fr:80/culture/dglf/lois/loi-fr.htm>.

27. Alec Hargreaves, "The Challenges of Multiculturalism: Regional and Religious Differences in France Today," in *Contemporary French Cultural Studies,* ed. William Kidd and Siân Reynolds (New York: Oxford University Press, 2000), 98.

28. Ibid. See also Catherine Trautmann, "La France et ses langues," *Le Monde* 31 juillet 1999.

29. According to Laroussi and Marcellesi, "The Other Languages of France," 85: "France has the most varied linguistic profile" in Western Europe.

30. "La charte européenne sur les langues régionales," *Europe et Liberté Magazine,* September 2000, <http://www.eurolibe.com/pages/pagesbiblio/articles/Lacharte.htm>.

31. Quoted in Cerquiglini, "Le Monolinguisme."

32. Ibid.

33. "Le chef de l'Etat réclame une loi-programme sur les langues régionales," *Les Echos* 6 juillet 1999.

34. Laroussi and Marcellesi, "The Other Languages of France," 89.

35. Dennis Ager, "Language and Power," in *Structures of Power in Modern France,* ed. Gino Raymond (New York: St. Martin's Press, 2000), 162.

36. Trautmann, "La France et ses langues."

37. Nathalie Guibert, "Jack Lang installe les langues régionales dans le service public de l'éducation," *Le Monde* 27 avril 2001.

38. S. Gemie, "The Politics of Language: Debates and identities in Contemporary Brittany," *French Cultural Studies* 13 (2002): 146.

39. Ibid., 159.

40. "M. Jospin et M. Chirac pris dans la polémique sur les langues régionales," *Le Monde* 19 juin 1999.

41. Gemie, "The Politics of Language," 155.

42. The term refers to the former Yugoslavia, where regional ethnic rivalries have created unstable political situations for more than a century.

43. Georges Sarre, Mouvement Républicain et Citoyen, MDC Communiqué, 4 avril 2001, <http://mrc-france.org/lr57>.

44. Robert Lafont, quoted in Audrey Gaquin, *Peuples et langues de France* (Lanham, MD: University Press of America, 1996), 514.

45. Manex Goyhenetche, "Pays Basque Nord, un people colonisé," in *Peuples et langues de France,* ed. Gaquin, 14.

46. Laroussi and Marcellesi, "The Other Languages of France," 96.

Bibliography

Ager, Dennis. "Language and Power." In *Structures of Power in Modern France.* Edited by Gino Raymond, 146–64. New York: St. Martin's Press, 2000.

————. *Language Policy in Britain and France: The Processes of Policy.* New York: Cassell, 1996.

————. *Sociolinguistics and Contemporary French.* Cambridge: Cambridge University Press, 1990.

Broudic, Fanch. "Il est interdit de cracher par terre et de parler Breton." <http://perso.wanadoo.fr/fanch.broudic/PAJENN/Interdiction .1902.html> (accessed August 15, 2003).

Cerquiglini, Bernard. *Les langues de la France. Rapport au Ministre de l'Education Nationale, de la Recherche et de la Technologie.* Avril 1999. <http://www.culture.fr/culture/dglf/lang-reg/ rapport_cerquiglini/langues-france.html>.

————. "Le Monolinguisme, une idéologie française." Interview with Béatrice Vallaeys. *Libération* 10–11 novembre 2001.

Certeau, Michel de. *Une politique de la langue.* Paris: Gallimard, 1975.

"La charte européenne sur les langues régionales." *Europe et Liberté Magazine,* September 2000. <http://www.eurolibe.com/pages/ pagesbiblio/articles/Lacharte.htm>.

"Le chef de l'Etat réclame une loi-programme sur les langues régionales." *Les Echos* 6 juillet 1999.

Gaquin, Audrey, ed. *Peuples et langues de France.* Lanham, MD: University Press of America, 1996.

Gemie, S. "The Politics of Language: Debates and identities in Contemporary Brittany." *French Cultural Studies* 13 (2002): 145–64.

Goyhenetche, Manex. "Pays Basque Nord, un people colonisé." In *Peuples et langues de France.* Edited Audrey Gaquin, 9–14. Lanham, MD: University Press of America, 1996.

Guibert, Nathalie. "Jack Lang installe les langues régionales dans le service public de l'éducation." *Le Monde* 27 avril 2001.

Hargreaves, Alec G. "The Challenges of Multiculturalism: Regional and Religious Differences in France Today." In *Contemporary French Cultural Studies.* Edited by William Kidd and Siân Reynolds, 95–110. New York: Oxford University Press, 2000.

Hélias, Pierre-Jakez. *The Horse of Pride.* New Haven: Yale University Press, 1978.

Judge, Anne. "French: A Planned Language?" In *French Today: Language in Its Social Context.* Edited by Carol Sanders, 7–26. Cambridge: Cambridge University Press, 1993.

Laroussi, Foued, and Jean-Baptiste Marcellesi. "The Other Languages of France: Towards a Multilingual Policy." In *French Today: Language in Its Social Context.* Edited by Carol Sanders, 85–104. Cambridge: Cambridge University Press, 1993.

Leclerc, Jacques. "Histoire du français, Sec. 5: La Renaissance." *L'aménagement linguistique dans le monde,* Québec, TLFQ, Université Laval. 21 janvier 2003. <http://www.tlfq.ulaval.ca/axl/francophonie/ HIST_FR_s5_Renaissance.htm> (accessed August 15, 2003).

———. "Histoire du francais, Sec. 6: Le français au Grand Siècle." *L'aménagement linguistique dans le monde,* Québec, TLFQ, Université Laval. 24 février 2003. <http://www.tlfq.ulaval.ca/axl/francophonie/HIST_FR_s6_Grand-Siecle.htm> (accessed August 10, 2003).

———. "Histoire du francais, Sec. 7: Le Siècle des Lumières." *L'aménagement linguistique dans le monde,* Québec, TLFQ, Université Laval. 24 février 2003. <http://www.tlfq.ulaval.ca/axl/francophonie/HIST_FR_s7_ Lumieres.htm> (accessed August 10, 2003).

———. "Histoire du français, Sec. 8: La Révolution française." *L'aménagement linguistique dans le monde,* Québec, TLFQ, Université Laval. 9 juillet 2002. <http://www.tlfq.ulaval.ca/axl/francophonie/ HIST_FR_s8_Revolutionl789.htm> (accessed August 12, 2003).

———. "Histoire du français, Sec. 9: Le français contemporain." *L'aménagement linguistique dans le monde,* Québec, TLFQ, Université Laval. 10 juillet 2003. <http://www.tlfq.ulaval.ca/axl/francophonie/HIST_FR_s9_Fr-contemporain.htm> (accessed August 12, 2003).

"M. Jospin et M. Chirac pris dans la polémique sur les langues régionales." *Le Monde* 19 juin 1999.

Prost, Antoine. "Immigration, Particularism, and Republican Education." *French Politics and Society* 16, no. 1 (1998): 13–22.

Sarre, Georges. Mouvement Républicain et Citoyen, MDC Communiqué, 4 avril 2001, <http://mrc-france.org/lr57>.

Simons, Marlise. "In New Europe, a Lingual Hodgepodge." *New York Times,* October 17, 1999, sec. 1.

Trautmann, Catherine. "La France et ses langues." *Le Monde* 31 juillet 1999.

Vallaeys, Béatrice. "La France délie ses langues." *Libération* 8–9 mai 1999.

Resource Guide

Further Reading

Hawkins, Roger. "Regional Variation in France." In *French Today: Language in Its Social Context.* Edited by Carol Sanders, 55–84. Cambridge: Cambridge University Press, 1993.

Lafont, Robert. *Clefs pour l'Occitanie.* Paris: Seghers, 1971.

———. *Langue dominante, langues dominées.* Paris: Edilig, 1981.

———. *La Revendication occitane.* Paris: Flammarion, 1974.

Landick, Marie. "French Courts and Language Legislation." *French Cultural Studies* 11 (2000): 131–48.

Reece, Jack. *The Bretons against France.* Chapel Hill: University of North Carolina Press, 1977.

Sanders, Carol, ed. *French Today: Language in Its Social Context.* Cambridge: Cambridge University Press, 1993.

Weber, Eugen. *Peasants into Frenchmen: The Modernization of Rural France 1870–1914.* Stanford, CA: Stanford University Press, 1976.

Newspaper and Journal Articles

In 1994 (at the time of the passage of the *Loi Toubon*) and again in 1999 (at the moment of debate on the ratification of the European Charter on Regional and Minority Languages), there was a great deal of discussion concerning the implications of both measures. Articles in *Le Monde, Libération,* and *Le Figaro,* to name just three newspapers, can be researched in Lexis-Nexis under such rubrics as *francophonie, anglicismes, langues régionales, charte européenne,* and *pluralisme linguistique.* A good source for journal articles as well as books is the OCLC First Search database. Check to see whether these databases are available in your school library or in a nearby public or college library.

Web Sites

There are a number of rich Web sites containing information on all aspects of the question of regional languages and the preservation of French national identity. The following site gives a great deal of information about the history of regional languages in France, and includes interviews with the author Danièle Sallenave:

<http://languefrancaise .free.fr/pratique/galerie_dialecte.htm>

Arguments in favor of bilingualism in France:

<http://www.lemondebilingue.asso.fr/france.html>

Map of the important dialects of France:

<http://www.tlfq.ulaval.ca/axl/europe/France-Parkvall-map.htm>

Information on the defense of the French language:

<http://languefrancaise.free.fr/promotion/dlf_texte.htm>

Full text of the European Charter on Regional and Minority Languages:

<http://conventions.coe.int/treaty/en/Treaties/Html/148.htm>

Overview of the debate on the ratification of the European Charter:

<http://www.flarep.com/presse/#_Toc456437305>

<http://www.tlfq.ulaval.ca/axl/europe/france_politik_minorites .htm>

Useful sites about Diwan:

<http://www.diwanbreizh.org/>

<http://diwan.an.oriant.free.fr/diwan/>

CHAPTER 5

The Headscarf Affair:
Multiculturalism in Debate

Like many countries in Europe, France is struggling with tensions that have been created by the need to integrate newcomers of different faiths into a largely secular society. The Muslim immigrants who have been arriving in France from North Africa (*les Maghrébins*)[1] since decolonization in the 1950s and 1960s have been the object of special concern. Many French people believe that Muslim immigrants do not wish to assimilate into French society, and that they will resist efforts to encourage them to embrace French culture and traditions. Such resistance may lead to the creation of separate communities within the nation, a notion that is intolerable to those who believe in the ideal of egalitarian and republican France, where all ethnic and religious distinctions are erased. Others affirm that hostility to Muslims is based on many misconceptions of how best to integrate Muslim youth, and on the exaggeration of the influence of fundamentalist doctrine on young people. These tensions crystallized in the late 1980s around a matter concerning the separation of church and state: the wearing of the Muslim headscarf in public schools. The issue has not yet been resolved; indeed, it continues to highlight the conflict between guarantees of freedom of conscience and the demands of the secular public sphere in France.

Background

When the French public educational system was founded by the Third Republic's Jules Ferry laws in March 1882, its principles seemed clear: instruction would be free, mandatory, and secular (*gratuit, obligatoire, et laïc*). *Secular* was understood in France to mean that education would be neutral with regard to philosophical, religious, and political beliefs. It was agreed that this concept of secularism (*laïcité*) would entail the separation of religious instruction from general education. To this end, religious teaching personnel were obliged to leave the schools; they were replaced by a new corps of republican teachers (*les hussards de la République*).

The Ferry laws represented the final attempt to weaken the Catholic Church's influence in the education of French children. Although the French Revolution in 1789 had launched the long process of the secularization of the French state, by the mid-nineteenth century there had been two attempts to guarantee the continued existence of religious education: the *Loi Guizot* (1833), which recognized both public and private primary education, and the *Loi Falloux* (1850), which allowed the Church to create self-financing private secondary schools. These two laws had ensured that local primary education remained essentially under the authority of the village priest (*curé*), who made certain that children had both moral and religious instruction.[2]

The Ferry laws under the Third Republic thus set up a system that could inculcate in French children a new allegiance to the nation rather than to the Church. In this respect, *laïcité* was intended not only to put an end to Catholic involvement in education, but also to disseminate "a left-dominated Republican ideal intended . . . to provide a new unifying social and political focus for France's citizens."[3]

This secular mandate was further reinforced by the separation of church and state in 1905. Under the terms of this law, religious instruction would no longer be required, no religious ceremonies would be permitted in the public schools, and symbols or emblems of religion would be banned as well. By the same token, the state guaranteed freedom of religious belief and expression, as long as these are "confined to the private domain and in no way impinge on public life or intervene in the affairs of State."[4] The Popular Front government in 1937 reasserted school neutrality by banning any form of proselytizing, whether religious or political. Most importantly, the directive of 1937 forbade the wearing of any religious or political symbols that might provoke counterdemonstrations (*"tout objet dont le port serait susceptible de provoquer des manifestations en sens inverse"*).[5] The concept of *laïcité* has further been inscribed in the French constitution since the Fourth Republic (1946–1958).

Because of, or perhaps in spite of, these edicts, for decades after the Ferry laws, French popular culture continued to make much of the village priest's disagreements with the local schoolteacher about who had the primary responsibility for the education of the child; indeed, this is often the first image to come to mind when the concept of *laïcité* is discussed. But a number of incidents in the late 1980s and 1990s in France raised very serious new questions about the relationship between religion and the secular state. These included the headscarf affair, which we will study more closely below; the visit of the Pope to the city of Reims during the 1500th anniversary of the crowning of Clovis and the founding of the Merovingian royal dynasty; and socialist ex-president François Mitterrand's surprising choice of a religious funeral.

The Origins of the Headscarf Affair

In September 1989, at the college Gabriel-Havez in Creil, a suburb to the northeast of Paris, three students of North African (*maghrébin*) background were refused entry to their school because they persisted in wearing their headscarves to class. A year earlier the three young Muslim girls, two from Morocco and one from Tunisia, had been authorized to wear their scarves in the schoolyard and in the halls, but had been forbidden to attend class with their heads covered. The principal of the school, Ernest Chenière, a native of Martinique in the Caribbean, argued that his decision was not racist. He instead invoked the principle of *laïcité* to defend his decision. The school's 850 students were of twenty-five different nationalities, and almost 400 of them were Muslim. Chenière stated that "the veil [sic] put undue ideological pressure on the other students and disturbed relations with the teachers."[6] Chenière denied that he had singled out Muslim students for punishment, saying that he had only acted in this matter following similar demands for special treatment by students of other faiths in his school. Some Jewish students, for example, had declined to attend school on Saturdays.

Thus began the headscarf affair, a long-running drama in the French educational system that has yet to be resolved to the satisfaction of all the parties concerned, from the Ministry of Education to the young women involved. But most important of all, the headscarf affair has provoked questions about the very nature of the mission of

Demonstration in favor of the wearing of the Muslim headscarf, Ile-de-France, 1994. (© Vincent Leloup/Corbis Sygma)

the French educational system. Most notably, one scholar asks, "Is the rather egalitarian and uniform republican system of education moving toward some kind of multiculturalism?"[7] Perhaps even more importantly, the controversy has raised issues concerning the integration of Muslims into French society and the role of ethnic communities in the fabric of the republic.

The wearing of the headscarf in French schools was actually not a novelty in 1989; in fact, earlier in the 1980s, students dressed in this way were permitted in class, and no principal had thought to exclude them. They represented a very tiny minority of the 6 or so percent of students of Muslim origin in the French public schools. What, then, might explain the reaction of the principal in Creil and the many debates that continue to surround the Muslim scarf? Clearly, during the 1980s something occurred to make the presence of an article of clothing associated with the Islamic religion intolerable in French schools, at least for some.

94

Public Reaction 1989–1994

When Chenière negotiated a settlement with the families so that the three young women removed their scarves in class, the events in Creil were resolved rather quickly. But by that point, the "*affaire du foulard*," or the "*affaire du tchador*," as it came to be known, had come to public attention and entered into public debate.[8] Rapidly, other headscarf affairs followed, as students were excluded from other elementary schools and *lycées*. Both the MRAP (*Mouvement contre le racisme et pour l'amitié entre les peuples*) and SOS-Racisme called upon Lionel Jospin, then minister of education, to ensure that such sanctions as excluding students would not be applied in future cases. Politicians on the left and the right gave their opinions. One, Jean-Pierre Chevènement (later secretary of state under Lionel Jospin when the latter became prime minister in the late 1990s), claimed that "Islam has no place in the republican school."[9] Jospin himself, while reiterating that the republican school is a place of "religious neutrality," responded nevertheless that he opposed the exclusion of students wearing the headscarf and asked that parents, teachers, and administrators negotiate each case individually. He supported the role of the French school system in carrying out the *projet républicain*, that is, the integration of ethnic and religious communities in the formation of French citizens.[10]

In order to avoid further repetitions of the Creil affair, Jospin called for the *Conseil d'Etat* to rule on the wearing of the headscarf in class. The *Conseil*, which acts as a deliberative body for proposed laws and ordinances and advises the government on issues that pose legal or administrative difficulties, announced its judgment in November 1989. It endorsed the compromise proposed by Jospin. While reasoning that neutrality is guaranteed by the separation of church and state, it judged illegal any discrimination on the basis of religion in access to education. The Conseil stated that students were guaranteed freedom of conscience if they chose to demonstrate their belief in any religion, as long as that demonstration did not constitute an act of provocation, propaganda, or proselytizing (the attempt to persuade others of the virtues of a particular ideology or religion) that might disturb other members of the educational community or interfere with teaching and other school activities.

Thus the *Conseil* ruled on the headscarf debate without actually solving any of the fundamental issues raised by the Creil affair. For example, the question of whether a redefinition of *laïcité* might be needed in order to account for a more multicultural student body was not specifically addressed. In addition, the *Conseil* left it up to school officials to decide whether to discipline students who wore the headscarf. Some chose to exclude students; others, seeking to avoid confrontation, elected to negotiate the issue with the student's family. No ban on the headscarf was proposed, and the creation of a law to deal with the issue was deemed to be inadvisable at the time, because the *Conseil* reasoned that such an action might interfere with the student's freedom of expression.[11]

As a result of this rather vague resolution, the battle lines continued to be drawn. There were demonstrations in favor of the wearing of the headscarf, noting that it was the case, for example, that other ethnic communities were not subject to dismissal for wearing their own symbols (such as the Jewish *yarmulke* or *kippa*, or Christian crosses). Many Muslim associations felt that children of their faith were being singled out for special disapproval, and that the attitude of those who opposed headscarves was another demonstration of France's anti-Islamic attitudes. Indeed, many French citizens, when asked about their image of Islam, responded that they associated the religion with violence; many others viewed Islam as antiprogressive or fanatical.[12] No wonder that in 1989, at the time of the Creil affair, more than 80 percent of French citizens questioned in an opinion poll stated that they were opposed to the wearing of the headscarf in state schools.[13]

Many French people simply assumed that the young women who insisted on wearing headscarves to school were expressing extremist or fundamentalist views. It was routinely asserted—generally without proof—that the young women in question were being pressured to wear their scarves by their fathers and brothers, and that the next step might also be the appearance of veiled teachers in the classrooms. It was pointed out by those who claimed that young women were being manipulated by fanatics that the wearing of the scarf or veil is a matter of debate even in a number of Muslim countries. For example, the *hidjeb* (scarf) is forbidden in schools in Tunisia. Likewise, Turkey's secular state recently refused to allow a newly elected Muslim female member of parliament to take the oath of office while wearing a headscarf. Those who held these opinions pointed out as well that Muslim parents were preventing their children from attending certain classes (sex education, physical education) for religious reasons, and that they were demanding special options in a number of other areas, like cafeteria menus.

The North African community in France was actually very divided on the notion of the headscarf in school, though it was often mistakenly assumed that Muslims spoke in one voice in favor of the wearing of the headscarf. Muslims living in France were asked their opinions at the time of the Creil affair, and a majority were opposed, as they were again when polled several years later. Some North Africans believed that the headscarf was a symbol of those in the Muslim community who preferred ethnic ghettoes to full integration into French society. Many Muslim women argued that the veil was itself a sign of exclusion in that it denoted gender inequality. Hanifa Cherifi (herself an immigrant from Algeria) has served for many years as the mediator between the Ministry of Education and Muslim families. She argues that there is only a "difference of degree" between the Afghan *burqa* (which covers women from head to toe) and the headscarf. Behind the veil, she reasons, are practices that run counter to egalitarian ideals in French society, such as forced marriages, exclusion from participation in public life, and other aspects of what she terms reactionary currents in Islam.[14]

Many of those who favored inclusion rather than exclusion reasoned that a tolerant attitude toward the headscarf might be the ideal way to deal with what they perceived to be gender inequalities and the subjugation of women in Islam. Claude Allègre, who would become minister of education in the mid-1990s, stated that when Muslim women are allowed entry to French schools, they can "learn, compare, understand and finally decide for themselves. That is to say, to remove the veil."[15] Thus, those who defended the right to be different (*"le droit à la différence"*) argued that integration and assimilation of France's Muslim community could better take place as the result of an attitude that encouraged education and open-mindedness. In some respects, it could be concluded that both sides favored the same assimilationist goals, but defended completely different paths toward achieving those goals.

The Second Wave

The events of 1989 were followed by a number of other incidents resulting in the exclusion of students that were occasionally brought to the courts, but often ended in contradictory rulings. Finally, in October 1993 and again in September 1994, faced with what many believed to be a worrisome expansion of the headscarf movement (although by that date only a few hundred Muslim students were wearing headscarves in school), François Bayrou, minister of education under François Mitterrand, published two directives (*circulaires*) that addressed the question squarely. In the first, he reminded the nation of the role of the school in promoting integration rather than division, with regard for the principle of *laïcité*. Yet the second directive seemed to go beyond the tolerant nature of the first. It reminded the public that, while the republic was "respectful of all religious and political convictions" as well as "cultural traditions," it also excluded the idea of a France made up of separate communities (*le communautarisme*). In his second directive, Bayrou stated explicitly (without evoking the principle of *laïcité*) that there was a distinction between "discreet" and "ostentatious" religious symbols. The effect of the latter, he asserted, was to "separate certain pupils from the rules of communal school life" and constituted in themselves "elements of proselytism."[16] He once again asked administrators to make every effort to mediate with families who did not respect this edict. Although Bayrou did not mention the headscarf, it seemed clear to most French people that this article of clothing was being targeted, a perspective that had the effect of singling out Islam for discriminatory treatment. Bayrou also created the position of a national mediator for questions relating to the Islamic headscarf, a person who was called upon to intervene in any conflicts that arose between a school and a Muslim family.

The consequences of Bayrou's second directive were fairly concrete. Though it did not have the force of a law, the directive nevertheless functioned as a guide to those in charge of educational establishments. Predictably, there were several instances of exclusion, and cases were brought before administrative courts. The directive was never vacated, but other courts continued to rule either for or against exclusion of students. By and large, during the 1990s, then, school directors were allowed to decide for themselves whether or not to exclude young women who wore the headscarf.

The Consequences

Why did the government reject the idea of a law that would decide once and for all the right of students to express their consciences in a manner suited to their faith? In 1994 Bayrou told the weekly *Le Nouvel Observateur* that he had studied this idea with other ministers. They were especially concerned by the growing number of manifestations of fundamentalism in the schools—and not only on the part of Muslims. Bayrou cited a case of students refusing to attend French class because they judged the authors (Rabelais and Ronsard) to be impious. He also noted that elsewhere students had asked for rooms reserved for prayer or special dining facilities.[17] Nevertheless, the ministers had decided that public discussion of such a proposed law in an atmosphere that was already heated risked giving the impression that the government was opposed to freedom of conscience or religious expression. He hoped that the directive would be sufficient.

The situation continued, however, to pose difficulties through the end of the 1990s. In many schools where the principals favored *le droit à la différence*, or the expression of diversity, every attempt was made to compromise and negotiate with the families of the young women, and no one was excluded for wearing a headscarf. In others, a harder line was often the case. For example, at one point in 1999, a high school in the town of Tourcoing in northeastern France had adopted a policy of nonintervention with students wearing headscarves. Instead, the principal chose to negotiate the issue with parents and students. At the same time, in the town of Flers in Normandy, an elementary school decided to exclude two young Turkish girls who had chosen to wear scarves and who had missed several classes in physical education. Most of the teachers sided with the school's disciplinary council and went on strike to make sure their point of view would be respected. Just three years later, in the Parisian suburb of Tremblay, after a young woman was suspended from high school classes for wearing a black headscarf and for "proselytizing behavior," the *Conseil d'Etat* ruled against her expulsion and ordered her reinstated. The teachers called a strike and refused to return to work unless a solution was found. The school eventually decided that the student could keep wearing the headscarf, as long as it was in a color other than black. During the presidential elections of April-May 2002, the issue of the headscarf was not forgotten, and several candidates on the left and the right made their supporting or opposing views known, even integrating the issue into their electoral platforms.

It would seem, then, that the wearing of the headscarf in schools and the strong reactions this practice generates have become a kind of permanent fixture in French public debate. Indeed, this is to be expected, given the fact that since the mid-1990s, following a spate of terrorist actions in Paris and in Algeria and the widespread impression that *insécurité* (crime) is associated especially with immigrants from the Maghreb and their children (*les Beurs*),[18] the integration of Muslims in France has itself been the object of enormous media attention. In this respect, the headscarf is only a symbol of the wider question of how ethnic minorities assimilate into the social fabric of the French republic. A look at some of the issues involved with immigration and citizenship can help us understand how the headscarf affair fits in with the controversy over integration.

Maghrebi Immigration and the Citizenship Debate

It was during the 1980s that the question of the integration of immigrants into French society came to the fore, fueled to some degree by a debate on the obtaining of citizenship by young people primarily of Maghrebi origin. Immigrants largely from Algeria, and to some extent from Morocco and Tunisia, had been coming to France since the 1950s. They contributed to the reconstruction of France after the Second World War by serving in the workforce, often performing difficult, dangerous, and repetitive jobs for very low salaries. It was generally expected that once France had regained her prewar economic status, these visitors from the Maghreb would return home. As it happened, the workers chose to stay and eventually were able to bring their families to France as well.

Faced with an economic recession provoked by the oil crisis in 1973–1974 and rising unemployment among French workers, France took strong measures to curb immigration. The government attempted to persuade immigrants to return to their home countries, even offering financial incentives—and when this failed, by proposing forced repatriation. Still, family reunification continued.[19] Throughout the 1970s Maghrebi immigrants began to cluster in the suburbs of large French cities, often living in large and dilapidated housing projects (*habitations à loyer modéré*) that had been built after the Second World War. Because they were culturally distinct from the French (by both physical features and religious practices), it was difficult for Maghrebis to achieve the same degree of assimilation into French society achieved by earlier generations of immigrants from western Europe, such as the Portuguese and the Spanish. By the end of the 1970s and the early 1980s, therefore, public opinion began to perceive North Africans as a threat to the French social fabric.[20]

By the mid-1980s, the perception of Maghrebi immigrants as a group that could not be readily assimilated into French society had reached a high point, and not coincidentally legislation was introduced into the French parliament to reform the process by which immigrants and their children became citizens (*le Code de la nationalité*). Traditionally, the children of immigrants born on French soil automatically became French through a concept known as *le droit du sol* (literally, the right to the land, or a territorial right).[21] The new law that took effect in 1993 (the *Loi Méhaignerie*, named for a minister serving in the government of Prime Minister Jacques Chirac) no longer extended the right of automatic citizenship to the children of immigrants. Instead, these young people were expected to make an explicit request for citizenship after their sixteenth birthday, and in so doing demonstrate their allegiance to the French state. It was argued, on both the left and the right, that this reform of the *Code de la nationalité* would ensure that French identity would not be conferred routinely, but would rather be earned as an expression (though perhaps only symbolic) of choice and the commitment to republican values. While children of immigrants of all nationalities were affected by the new law, it was clear to most French citizens that the primary target of the reform was the second generation of Maghrebi immigrants, *les Beurs*.

The reform of the nationality law lasted only five years, however. In 1997 minister of the interior Jean-Louis Debré proposed curbing illegal immigration by, among other things, requiring French citizens to report foreigners who overstayed their visas. The proposal provoked petitions, demonstrations in Paris, and other expressions of moral outrage at the idea that the French should denounce or inform on illegal visitors. Those opposed to the *Loi Debré* viewed it as contrary to the universal values of human rights. The opposition won the day, and shortly afterward, when the Socialists regained a majority in parliament, a revised law (the *Loi Guigou*, named for the new minister of justice under Prime Minister Lionel Jospin) restored the *droit du sol*, doing away with the attempt to single out any groups for special treatment.[22] Nevertheless, it is to be expected that France will continue to debate the issue of how citizenship is granted and the necessity for new citizens to assimilate into the national community.

The question of national identity is thus bound up with many different kinds of considerations. Are immigrants and the children of immigrants, when they are of non-European or nonwestern descent, essentially unassimilable in France? The French republic understands the position of the citizen to be unitary: that is, as one scholar states, there is an "unmediated relation of the individual with civil society, a relation initiated from above by the state and not from below by the community."[23] This means that community identity (ethnic or religious, for example) must always be secondary to national identity.

The French school system, in the face of the weakening of other institutions that used to help immigrants assimilate—such as the Catholic Church, the army, the Communist Party and trade unions[24]—bears virtually alone the primary responsibility for integrating the children of immigrants into French culture and of forming citizens who embrace the republican values cited above. While the inculcation of civic values has always been the ideal of French education, the headscarf affair indicates that the traditional definition of secularism that is part and parcel of civic education is finding itself under siege.

The Third Wave

Most recently, President Jacques Chirac appointed a commission to study the application of the principle of *laïcité* in the republic. This group, under the direction of former minister Bernard Stasi, spent many months listening to testimony from various groups arguing for and against the reaffirmation of a strict definition of secularism. They were charged with considering the case of the headscarf and other religious symbols in the schools as well as with weighing the problems that have arisen in other areas of French life where religious beliefs and practices prove incompatible with the operation of public services.

The Stasi commission published its report in early December 2003. In its very first paragraphs it reminded French citizens that although many Western democracies respect freedom of conscience and the principle of nondiscrimination, France is the only country that has made secularism a founding value *("la France a érigé la laïcité au rang de valeur fondatrice")*.[25] The commission went on to note that secularism, as the cornerstone *("pierre angulaire")* of the republican contract, guarantees equality of spiritual and religious choice, but also that political power must not be influenced by religious faith. In this way, *laïcité* is related to the notion of the common good.[26] The commission's reaffirmation of the secularist nature of the republic thus discreetly reminded French citizens that the notion of *laïcité* as expressed in the nineteenth century and reaffirmed with the separation of church and state in 1905 was inextricably linked to the long tradition of the abuse of religious power in French history. Republican secularism thus put an end to the Catholic Church's "power to oppress minorities and make law."[27]

The Stasi commission went on to make a number of recommendations concerning *laïcité*, including the necessity of creating a law to settle once and for all the question of the presence of religious symbols in the schools. It was proposed that the law exclude very visible (*"ostensible"*) religious signs and dress (such as large crosses, the headscarf, or the *yarmulke*) in the public schools, while at the same time tolerating discreet signs such as medals, small crosses, stars of David, hands of Fatima, or small Korans.[28] The government of Jacques Chirac wasted little time in approving the idea of a law concerning religious symbols and promised to ensure that the new regulations would be in place by September 2004.

As might be expected, the report of the Stasi commission raised as many questions as it purported to solve, not the least of which was the problem of certain French regions and overseas departments that either benefit from special status regarding the practice of religion in the schools (Alsace and Lorraine, for example) or that have overwhelmingly Islamic populations—such as the island of La Mayotte in the Indian Ocean. Teachers and school principals were understandably in favor of a law by a wide majority, since it would largely relieve them of the burden of deciding whether a student should be excluded from classes for wearing an article of religious clothing or a religious emblem. On the other hand, many thousands of Muslims demonstrated against the passage of a law in winter 2004. The political parties were themselves split on the question, and there were often disagreements within parties as to the best strategy to adopt. Even the meaning of the word *ostensible* as it appeared in the proposed law created a furor, since even small or discreet signs can be visible.

Conclusion

To sum up, the headscarf affair, with its assault on *laïcité*, reflects the "crisis of universalism"[29] that French society has undergone for the past few decades. At present, there would seem to be two opposing scenarios for France's future, one that proposes radical change and the other that counsels adherence to republican tradition. The first suggests that France accept a new communitarian image in which the nation is made up of "religious and ethnic communities living according to their own rules, constituting different ghettos in society, a state within a state."[30] Or, on the other hand, France can remain "faithful" to its history and ask that Muslims who wish to become French citizens accept the fact that their minority religion must make the same concessions to secularism that Catholicism had to make in the past.[31] In other words, according to those who embrace the idea of France as a true melting pot in which all ethnic differences might be dissolved, the nation may preserve its universalist, egalitarian, and republican tradition, or (which is perhaps unlikely) it may evolve toward the particularist British and U.S. model, which seeks to recognize and even privilege ethnic diversity.[32]

Discussion

While it is probably difficult for Americans to understand all the issues and nuances involved in the headscarf affair because we do not have such strict limitations on the expression of conscience in the public schools, there are nevertheless fairly clear-cut sides to the question, and these broadly involve whether one believes that the concept of *laïcité* should be defined as neutrality, or whether it should be understood as meaning tolerance of difference.

Secularism (*la laïcité*) guarantees the tolerance of difference.

Agree

Many French citizens support the right to wear the headscarf in school and back the idea that the notion of *laïcité* was never meant to exclude, but rather to guarantee the tolerance of difference. In fact, they argue, the concept of secularism does not mean that children may not wear signs of their religious belief, which is why French schools have always tolerated symbols of the Christian and Jewish religions. One commentator has pointed out, rereading the Ferry laws, that only the *teachers* are required to be religiously neutral in the schools; children are not obliged to observe strict secularism.[33] Along these lines, those who believe that the wearing of the headscarf does not in and of itself constitute proselytizing argue generally in favor of the idea that France has become a multicultural society, and that it is only normal that *laïcité* be reinterpreted to mean the right to be different. In this view, representatives of different cultural groups can coexist within the neutral grounds of the school, and this might in fact hasten the integration of France's Muslim community into the nation. In addition, it would seem to be a more fruitful tactic to instruct a child in the ideals of integration and citizenship, rather than to exclude that child and thereby ensure that she will never be exposed to republican ideals.

Others, also on the side of tolerance, point out several instances where Muslims are treated unequally in the schools. For example, under the provisions of the 1905 law of separation of church and state, French schools must make a place for a chaplain's office (*aumonerie*), defended by some as being traditionally authorized in public institutions for representatives of the Catholic, Protestant, and Jewish faiths. Nevertheless, it is not yet the case that Muslim representatives have been welcomed into state schools. There are counterexamples of special treatment, however. Some schools with Muslim pupils regularly offer several lunch menus so that children may avoid eating pork. In addition, as with other religions, student absence for certain holidays is tolerated.

While it may have been the case that Jules Ferry and the original framers of the republican school were primarily interested in making certain that education remained neutral, and that all expressions of ideology stop at the doors of the school, it is true that the principle of neutrality has never been evenly applied. For example, Catholic and Jewish students are not asked to remove the symbols of their religions that they have chosen to wear in school. Is this a double standard? Why ask young Muslim women to remove an article of clothing that fulfills the same function as a cross or a *yarmulke*? It appears that behind the denial of the right to wear the headscarf in school there is racial or anti-Islamic bias.

A further example of standards unevenly applied is Alsace-Lorraine (today the departments of the Bas-Rhin, the Haut-Rhin, the Vosges, the Moselle, the Meuse, and Meurthe-et-Moselle). Because this northeastern region was annexed by Germany during the Franco-Prussian War of 1870–1871 and remained under German control until after World War I, schools did not operate under the same laws of secularism. In Alsace today there are still crucifixes on the walls of classrooms, and chaplains paid by the state offer religious instruction.

Disagree

For those who oppose the wearing of the headscarf in the name of *laïcité*, it is clear that schools must remain absolutely neutral and that the display of any religious symbols constitutes an attack on the fundamental principles of education in France. Shortly after the

Creil affair, a group of important leftist intellectuals called upon public school teachers not to capitulate to the demands of "fanatics," and to defend the principles of the republic. They argued that excluding a child who violated the rules was a disciplinary action, not a discriminatory one. Their point of view was that school must be a place of emancipation, one in which children have the freedom to "forget about their community of origin and think about something other than what they are in order to be able to think for themselves" (*"oublier leur communauté d'origine et [. . .] penser à autre chose que ce qu'ils sont pour pouvoir penser par eux-mêmes"*).[34] In other words, the function of school is to educate students in freedom of choice. For this reason, schools must welcome all students, but do not have the obligation to welcome as well the religion of the parents of those students. Tolerating the Islamic headscarf, according to this perspective, is tantamount to opening the door to young women who have had no freedom of choice, and of asserting that there is no difference between the school and the home. Those who agree with this position argue for maintaining the nineteenth-century definition of *laïcité* as ensuring that particular ideologies would not be welcome in the state schools, even if these ideologies are not verbally expressed.

In addition, the headscarf, as it is worn by many young Muslim women, is not simply an expression of religious belief. Some might interpret it as a sign that the wearer does not wish to belong to the nation, or that the wearer is proclaiming the superiority of her religion. In this respect, the headscarf should not be compared to the cross or the *yarmulke*, both of which manifest only respect for God and do not intend to proselytize. Those students who feel that their religion is important enough that they must manifest their beliefs in public, at the risk of disturbing other pupils who do not share these beliefs, ought to choose private school, where there are no restrictions on their freedom of expression. The *école libre* (private school, usually religious) exists primarily for this reason. Parents who wish to ensure that their children are schooled in different cultural values and beliefs therefore have the option to withdraw their children from the public system.

Questions and Activities

1. Do you think that the debate over the wearing of the headscarf might be a reflection of an opinion held by many French people

that Muslims, as distinct from other immigrants to France in the last century, represent a special threat to a society that believes in the assimilation of newcomers? Is this opinion based on belief that there is a clash of civilizations between Muslims and those of the Judeo-Christian tradition? Explain your point of view.

2. The extreme right in France, as represented primarily by the *Front National* political party of Jean-Marie Le Pen, has been vocal with regard to what are perceived as special demands being made by certain elements in the Muslim population, both newly arrived immigrants and others who have been living in France for two or three generations. Look up the *Front National* online at <http://www.frontnational.com/> and report back to the class on this party's stance with regard to Arab immigration in particular.

3. What strikes you as being the primary difference between French attitudes toward multicultural diversity, as they are expressed by some of the perspectives you've studied in the headscarf affair, and American attitudes? Do you think it is fair to generalize in this way about cultures? Debate this question in class.

4. Where do you stand on the question of whether to create a law dictating once and for all which religious symbols (if any) are acceptable in the public schools, and which are not? Passage of a law on the wearing of articles of clothing or other symbols of one's religion might ensure that in every school all students' rights were being respected. There would be uniformity throughout the French school system, and principals would not have to negotiate every case individually. A law would also put an end to the many teachers' strikes that have occurred in response to disagreement with individual school policies. On the other hand, such a law might be found to be unconstitutional because it might have the effect of excluding some students who do not conform, and so deny their right to public education. Those who are opposed to a law banning the Islamic headscarf would prefer instead to legislate a new definition of secularism. Imagine that you are an adviser to the French minister of education. Prepare a memorandum in which you suggest a solution to the problem of the wearing of religious insignia in the schools. You might consult the following articles: "M. Ferry annonce une loi sur la laïcité à l'école," *Le Monde* 22 avril 2003; Paul Quinio and Vanessa Schneider, "Loi ou pas loi? Le foulard brûle," *Libération* 4 juillet 2003: 3; and Michel Delberghe, "Des sénateurs se déclarent hostiles à une loi sur le foulard islamique," *Le Monde* 28 mars 1997. For a discussion of the Socialist Party's proposed law, see "Le PS va présenter une proposition de loi sur la laïcité," *Libération*, 12 novembre 2003. You might also want to consult the Stasi Com-

mission Report, published in *Le Monde* on 12 décembre 2003. All these articles and texts are available on Lexis-Nexis.

5. It has been argued that some Muslim young women do not choose to wear the headscarf purely as an expression of their faith, but rather as an indication that while they wish to be integrated into French society, they do not want to be assimilated—that is, they prefer to keep both identities, Muslim and French.[35] In general, do you think it is possible to retain two identities in this manner? What obstacles or pressures might make this difficult?

6. In 1984, when minister of education Alain Savary (in the Socialist government of François Mitterrand) proposed reforming the schools by unifying the public and private systems (*l'école libre*), hundreds of thousands of French citizens around the country demonstrated against the plan. Mitterrand was forced to withdraw it, and Savary resigned shortly thereafter. Many French parents choose to send their children to private schools (most of which are associated with a religious denomination) not for religious reasons, but because of other advantages private schools offer, such as smaller classes. They are therefore in favor of keeping the public and private systems separate. Somewhat surprisingly, in 1993, when the center-right government of Jacques Chirac proposed extending state funding to the private sector, there again were demonstrations, but this time in favor of limiting state funding only to the public schools. Debate the merits and disadvantages of a single, integrated (public and private) state-funded school system. For comparative purposes, you may want to consider the proposals for vouchers that have been made recently in the United States. A good Web site to consult in this regard is <http://www.iedx.org/>. Search under "vouchers."

7. France is alone among its European neighbors with regard to the exclusion of religious expression in the public schools. In the United Kingdom, for example, not only are students permitted to pray in the schools, but the wearing of traditional clothing and special dispensation from physical education, music, and dance classes is authorized. In Germany, the teaching of Catholicism and Protestantism is required in the public schools, unless parents request otherwise. In some elementary schools, students who wish to study the Koran (Islam's holy text) are permitted to do so. Should France legislate against wearing the headscarf, it is likely that this policy will run counter to European Union treaties permitting the wearing of religious symbols. Imagine that you are a delegate from France to the European Union. How would you justify France's position on the matter of religious expression in the public schools? You might consult some of the sources in the

Resource Guide to help prepare your argument, or the Chadwick and Costa-Lascoux articles listed in the Bibliography.

8. There have been many cases in the United States of disputes involving the teaching of religious beliefs in the public schools. The most famous is no doubt *Tennessee* v. *John Scopes* (1925) (see <http://xroads.virginia.edu/%7EUG97/inherit/1925home.html>). More recently, there have been *Edwards* v. *Aguillard* (1987) (see <http://www.law.umkc.edu/faculty/projects/ftrials/conlaw/edwards.html>); *Santa Fe Independent School District* v. *Doe* (2000) (see <http://supct.law.cornell.edu/supct/html/99-62.ZS.html>); and *Adler* v. *Duval County School Board* (Case No. 01-287) (see <http://www.edweek.org/ew/newstory.cfm?slug=16scotus.h21>. Form groups of two or three students, choose one of these cases, and discuss how the issues reflect American cultural attitudes. How were these issues resolved? Do they remain contentious? How can they be related to the headscarf debate in France?

9. Quite recently, the issue of dress for Muslim women and its relationship to secularism has arisen again with regard to the full-face photographs that are necessary for French identity cards. The French government has decided not to permit women to wear veils or headscarves. Here, we can draw a parallel with the United States, since equally recently the issue has come up with respect to photographs on driver's licenses. Debate in class whether or not the law should protect the right of the citizen to wear a veil or a headscarf when such photographs are taken.

10. In spite of the separation of church and state in France, under certain circumstances the government provides subsidies to private religious schools. Schools that sign contracts with the state (*contrats d'association*) agree to allow the government to exercise some control in the areas of pedagogy and hiring qualified teachers, in return for which they receive funding. The question of public funding of religious education has come under scrutiny in the U.S. Supreme Court. Recently in Michigan a college student was denied state scholarship aid when she declared a major in theology. She sued, and a case similar to hers in the state of Washington has been decided by the Supreme Court. (See "Courts Weighing Rights of States to Curb Aid for Religion Majors," *New York Times,* August 10, 2003 and "Court Says States Need Not Finance Divinity Studies," New York Times, February 26, 2004.) If you were a Supreme Court justice, how would you have ruled on the question of state financing for religious education?

11. In 1992, *Le Nouvel Observateur,* fearing a "shattered France," asked a number of historians and sociologists the following ques-

tion: "Are we in danger of gradually sliding towards an American model?" (12–18 octobre 1992). The question assumed that national unity was being threatened by the example of the American melting pot. Reflect on this model of national integration: Is the United States of America actually a melting pot? Or is another analogy more appropriate, such as beef stew or mixed salad? Defend your position with examples.

Vocabulary/Vocabulaire

Nouns/Substantifs

advantage	l'avantage (m.)
assimilation	l'assimilation (f.)
badge, insignia	l'insigne (m.)
choice	le choix
citizenship	la citoyenneté
clothing	l'habit (m.)
cross	la croix
culture clash	le choc des cultures
disadvantage	le désavantage
driver's license	le permis de conduire
faith	la foi
far right	l'extrême droite (f.)
freedom of conscience	la liberté de conscience
headscarf	le foulard
identity	l'identité (f.)
ideology	l'idéologie (f.)
integration	l'intégration
law	la loi
melting pot	le creuset
model	le modèle
multiculturalism	le multiculturalisme
neutrality	la neutralité
political party	le parti politique
prayer	la prière
principle	le principe

private school	l'école libre (f.)
religion	la religion, la confession
right to be different	le droit à la différence
secularism	la laïcité
strike	la grève
symbol	le symbole
tolerance	la tolérance
trial	le procès
uniformity	l'uniformité (f.)
veil	le voile
yarmulke	la kippa

Verbs/Verbes

assimilate	s'assimiler
authorize	autoriser
conform	se conformer
display	afficher
exclude	exclure
express	exprimer
integrate	s'intégrer
pass a law	légiférer
pray	prier
proselytize	prosélytiser
show	manifester
threaten	menacer
wear	porter

Adjectives/Adjectifs

Catholic	catholique
Jewish	juif, juive
Muslim	musulman, -e
North African	maghrébin, -e
Protestant	protestant, -e
secular	laïc, laïque

Notes

1. The Maghreb is the name given to the region of North Africa that includes the countries of Morocco, Tunisia, and Algeria.

2. Kay Chadwick, "Education in Secular France: (Re)defining *Laïcité*," *Modern and Contemporary France* 5, no. 1 (1997): 49.

3. Ibid. Religious schools (*écoles libres*) did not disappear with the advent of the public school system. In fact, as Chadwick points out (51), Catholic education expanded after the Ferry laws in areas that were traditionally more practicing than others, such as the provinces of Brittany and Alsace-Lorraine.

4. Ibid., 47.

5. Communication by Jean-Michael Dubernard, Président de la commission des Affaires culturelles, familiales et sociales, on the occasion of an information meeting of the Assemblée Nationale on June 3, 2003. See <http://www.assemblee-nat.fr/12/dossiers/laicite_CR.asp>.

6. Raphaëlle Rérolle, "Trois foulards contre la 'sérénité laïque,'" *Le Monde*, 7 octobre 1989, 13b.

7. Antoine Prost, "Immigration, Particularism, and Republican Education," *French Politics and Society* 16, no. 1 (1998): 13.

8. The question of what term to use for the headscarf has been studied by Yvan Gastaut, who points out that the choice of word in writing about the subject—*voile* (veil), *foulard* (scarf), *hidjeb, tchador*—very much depends upon the ideological perspective of the author. Generally, the use of the word *headscarf* is more neutral than the choice of either an Arabic term or a French term denoting a more religious article of clothing. See Yvan Gastaut, *L'Immigration et l'opinion en France sous la Ve République* (Paris: Seuil, 2000), 570ff.

9. Pierre Tévanian, "Foulard: Que s'est-il passé en vingt ans?," Collectif Les mots sont importants, October 10, 2001, <http://www.ornitho.org/numero17/invite/foulard.html>.

10. "La laïcité ne peut être négociée," *Le Monde*, 1er décembre 1989, 16a.

11. Jacqueline Costa-Lacoux, "Les Arabesques de l'Islam dans l'architecture laïque," *Confluences Méditerranée* No. 32 (hiver 1999–2000), 1–8, May 22, 2002, <http://www.ifrance.com/Confluences/Textes/32costa.htm> (accessed July 30, 2003).

12. Leïla Sebbar, "Pourquoi cette peur?" *Le Monde*, 24 octobre 1989, 2.

13. David Beriss, "Scarves, Schools, and Segregation: The *Foulard* Affair," *French Politics and Society* 8, no. 1 (1990): 6.

14. "Non aux femmes voilées," August 13, 2003, <http://www.sos-sexisme.org/infos/voilees.htm>.

15. Claude Allègre, "La Meilleure Façon d'enlever le voile," *Le Nouvel Observateur*, 9–15 novembre 1989, 33.

16. The text of the directive stated specifically that "the wearing of discreet signs of religious conviction is admissible in state schools. But ostentatious signs, which constitute in themselves elements of proselytism or discrimination, are forbidden" ("*Le port par les élèves de signes discrets,*

manifestant leur attachement à des convictions notamment religieuses, est admis dans l'établissement. Mais les signes ostentatoires, qui constituent en eux-mêmes des éléments de prosélytisme ou de discrimination, sont interdits").

17. Elisabeth Schemla and Carole Barjon, "Foulard islamique: Bayrou se fâche," *Le Nouvel Observateur*, 3 novembre 1994, 43–44.

18. The term *beur* originates in verlan, a form of slang in which syllables are inverted. Thus, *beur* comes from an inversion of the French *arabe*.

19. Alec Hargreaves, *Immigration, 'Race' and Ethnicity in Contemporary France* (London: Routledge, 1995), 16.

20. One of the primary motors of this hostile attitude was the *Front National*, Jean-Marie Le Pen's extreme right-wing political party, which began to gain voters at the end of the 1970s, and continued to grow in the last quarter of the twentieth century. A key element of Le Pen's platform was the repatriation of immigrants, particularly those from North Africa, on the pretext that their presence was causing unemployment among native French-born citizens.

21. Children of French natives have French nationality by birth (*le droit du sang*, literally the right of blood, or a biological right).

22. An exception to this is the case of Algerians. Since 1968 some Algerians have benefited from double *jus soli*, which means that a child born in France is automatically both French and Algerian if one parent was born in Algeria before 1962 (the year Algeria gained independence).

23. Georges Salemohamed, "The State and Religion: Rethinking *Laïcité*," in *Structures of Power in Modern France*, ed. Gino G. Raymond (New York: St. Martin's, 1999), 140.

24. Jean Daniel, "Je choisis la République française," *Le Nouvel Observateur*, 13–19 mai 1993, 22.

25. "Le Rapport de la Commission Stasi sur la laïcité," *Le Monde*, 12 décembre 2003.

26. Ibid.

27. Guy Coq, "Scarves and Symbols," *New York Times*, January 30, 2004.

28. "Le Rapport de la Commission Stasi sur la laïcité."

29. Naomi Schor, "The Crisis of French Universalism," in *France/USA: The Culture Wars*, ed. Ralph Sarkonak, *Yale French Studies* 100 (2001), 50.

30. Michael Winock, quoted in Maxim Silverman, *Deconstructing the Nation: Immigration, Race and Citizenship in Modern France* (London: Routledge, 1992), 113.

31. Ibid.

32. Silverman, *Deconstructing the Nation*, 111.

33. Guy Sitbon, "La Laïcité a bon dos," *Le Nouvel Observateur*, 9–15 novembre 1989, 35.

34. Elisabeth Badinter, Régis Debray, Alain Finkielkraut, Elisabeth de Fontenay, and Catherine Kintzler, "Profs, ne capitulons pas!," *Le Nouvel Observateur*, 2–8 novembre 1989, 30.

35. Françoise Gaspard, and Farhad Khosrokhar, *Le Foulard et la République* (Paris: Editions La Découverte, 1995). Quoted in N. Schor, "The Crisis of French Universalism," 53.

Bibliography

Allègre, Claude. "La Meilleure Façon d'enlever le voile." *Le Nouvel Observateur* 9–15 novembre 1989: 33.

Badinter, Elisabeth, Régis Debray, Alain Finkielkraut, Elisabeth de Fontenay, and Catherine Kintzler. "Profs, ne capitulons pas!" *Le Nouvel Observateur* 2–8 novembre 1989: 30–31.

Beriss, David. "Scarves, Schools, and Segregation: The *Foulard* Affair." *French Politics and Society* 8, no. 1 (1990): 1–13.

Chadwick, Kay. "Education in Secular France: (Re)defining *Laïcité*." *Modern and Contemporary France* 5, no.1 (1997): 47–59.

Costa-Lacoux, Jacqueline. "Les Arabesques de l'Islam dans l'architecture laïque." *Confluences Méditerranée* No. 32 (hiver 1999–2000): 1–8. May 22, 2002. <http://www.ifrance.com/Confluences/Textes/32costa.htm>.

Daniel, Jean. "Je choisis la République française." *Le Nouvel Observateur* 13–19 mai 1993: 22-23.

Etienne, Bruno. "Pour un Islam français." *L'Express* 19 mai 1989: 41–44.

Gastaut, Yvan. *L'Immigration et l'opinion en France sous la Ve République.* Paris: Seuil, 2000.

Hargreaves, Alec. *Immigration, 'Race' and Ethnicity in Contemporary France.* London: Routledge, 1995.

"La laïcité ne peut être négociée." *Le Monde* 1er décembre 1989: 16a.

"Non aux femmes voilées." August 13, 2003. <http://www.sos-sexisme.org/infos/voilees.htm>.

Prost, Antoine. "Immigration, Particularism, and Republican Education." *French Politics and Society* 16, no. 1 (1998): 13–22.

Rérolle, Raphaëlle. "Trois foulards contre la 'sérénité laïque.'" *Le Monde* 7 octobre 1989: 13b.

Salemohamed, Georges. "The State and Religion: Rethinking *Laïcité*." In *Structures of Power in Modern France.* Edited by Gino G. Raymond. New York: St. Martin's, 1999.

Schemla, Elisabeth, and Carole Barjon. "Foulard islamique: Bayrou se fâche." *Le Nouvel Observateur* 3 novembre 1994: 43–44.

Schor, Naomi. "The Crisis of French Universalism." In *France/USA: The Culture Wars.* Edited by Ralph Sarkonak. *Yale French Studies* 100 (2001): 43–64.

Sebbar, Leïla. "Pourquoi cette peur?" *Le Monde* 24 octobre 1989: 2.

Silverman, Maxim. *Deconstructing the Nation: Immigration, Race and Citizenship in Modern France.* London: Routledge, 1992.

Sitbon, Guy. "La Laïcité a bon dos." *Le Nouvel Observateur* 9–15 novembre 1989: 35.

Solé, Robert. "Dieu et la République." *Le Monde* 11 décembre 1997.

Tévanian, Pierre. "Foulard: Que s'est-il passé en vingt ans?" Collectif Les mots sont importants. October 10, 2001. <http://www.ornitho.org /numero17/invite/foulard.html>.

Walter, Emanuelle. "C'est quoi un foulard ostentatoire?" *Le Nouvel Observateur* 2002/2003. August 13, 2003. <http://www.parisobs .com/articles/p71/a15169.htm>.

Resource Guide

Further Reading

Baubérot, Jean. *Vers un nouveau pacte laïque.* Paris: Seuil, 1990.

Ben Jelloun, Tahar. *Hospitalité française: racisme et immigration maghrébine.* Paris: Seuil, 1984.

Coq, Guy. "Querelle autour d'un voile." *Les Collections de l'Histoire* No. 6 (1999): 98-99.

Feldblum, Miriam. *Reconstructing Citizenship.* Albany: State University of New York Press, 1999.

Gaspard, Françoise, and Farhad Khosrokhar. *Le Foulard et la République.* Paris: Éditions La Découverte, 1995.

Jaccomard, Hélène. "French against French: The Uneasy Incorporation of Beurs into French Society." *Mots Pluriels* 1.2 (1997). October 10, 2001. <http://www.arts.uwa.edu.au/MotsPluriels/ MP297hj.html>.

Noiriel, Gérard. *Le Creuset français: histoire de l'immigration XIX-XXe siècle.* Paris: Seuil, 1988.

Ozouf, Mona. *L'Ecole, l'Eglise et la République 1871–1914.* Paris: Seuil, 1982.

Schor, Ralph. *Histoire de l'immigration en France de la fin du XIXe siècle à nos jours.* Paris: Armand Colin, 1996.

Solé, Robert. "L'Islam dans l'école de la République." *Le Monde* 7 octobre 1989.

Toner, Fred. "Multiculturalism in Debate: The Immigrant Presence as Social Catalyst in Contemporary France." In *France at the Dawn of the Twenty-first Century.* Edited by Marie-Christine Weidmann Koop. Birmingham, AL: Summa Publications, 2000.

Newspaper and Journal Articles

Hundreds of articles concerning the headscarf affair have appeared since 1989, both in French and in English. If you have access to microfilm and microfiche collections, research *Le Monde* and *Le Nouvel Observateur*

115

beginning in October 1989. For more recent articles (the past ten years), Lexis-Nexis is an excellent source for online searching of newspaper articles in both languages. You might use such key words in French as *voile, tchador, foulard,* and *laïcité.* A good source for journal articles as well is the OCLC First Search database. Check with your school librarian as to availability in your school or at a nearby college or university.

Web Sites

The group known as *Les mots sont importants* publishes a Web site that contains a number of documents relating to the question of the headscarf in school:
<http://www.laicite-republique.org/documents/foulard/>
<http://lmsi.net/article.php3?id_article=41>
Feminist view of the issue:
<http://www.refractaires.org/resistance-feminine/index-en.htm>
General source on the veil and racism in France: <http://www.unc.edu/depts/europe/conferences/Veil2000/intro.htm>
Excellent bibliographical source for documents concerning immigration and the various laws that were proposed or passed during the 1990s:
<http://www.uni-muenster.de/Romanistik/Lacouriere/Page_Dossier_Immigres.htm>
General information on the meaning and history of the concept of *laïcité* in the French schools:
<http://www.ac-bordeaux.fr/Pedagogie/ECJS/Premiere/accomptheme3ficheres2.htm>
Recent poll on French values and *laïcité*: <http://www.bva.fr/>

CHAPTER 6

The Power of Language and Culture in Quebec

Unless they are particularly attuned to Canadian affairs, most people in the United States are only marginally aware of the ethnic and cultural issues at the heart of the periodic constitutional crises that have erupted in Canada over the past thirty years. Although the Canadian situation may not exactly parallel what one finds in the United States, we live in a world in which ethnic and cultural issues are becoming at least as important as economic and political ones. It is obvious that questions of ethnicity and language are of great importance to U.S. society as it evolves. These issues are particularly poignant in Canada because they are taking place in a country that has been called "improbable" not only because of its varied geography and harsh climate, but also because of its diverse ethnicities and the underlying tensions that have existed between its English- and French-speaking cultures. Consequently, in order to understand our neighbor to the north, no less than to compare its affairs to ours, we must first review the history of Canada's leading minority culture.

Background

Early History of Quebec

During the age of exploration that began in the Renaissance, Jacques Cartier set out from Saint-Malo, France, to find fabled isles of riches by locating a passage, as others had attempted, through North America to East Asia. Cartier sailed to the gulf of the Saint Lawrence River in 1534, making contact with Micmac and Huron Indians. By 1536 he had mapped the Saint Lawrence, traveling as far as present-day Montreal. After Cartier's last trip in 1541–1542, with the passage to riches remaining as elusive as ever, France turned its attention elsewhere.

The next stage of exploration began at the end of the sixteenth century, when fur became the fashion among the wealthy of Europe. For the next three hundred years, beaver fur hats were the rage in Europe, to the extent that local animals became almost extinct. The North American fur trade developed, fostering the establishment of trading counters and permanent settlements. The explorations of Samuel de Champlain in 1608 led to the founding of the city of Quebec. In order to protect the French trading system, the young French King Louis XIV sent military expeditions to quell the Iroquois, who were the rivals of the French-allied Hurons. Louis XIV encouraged development of the French presence in North America, making New France (*La Nouvelle France*) a royal colony in 1663. The French population of the colony numbered about three thousand. This is the period of the fabled *coureur des bois* or *voyageur*, the trapper-hunter who could cover forty miles a day on foot, who lived among the local tribes, and who spoke the Amerindian languages.

French exploration continued as René Robert Cavelier, Sieur de LaSalle, descended the Ohio River in 1669 while Louis Joliet and Jacques Marquette led a French expedition down the Mississippi in 1673, reaching the mouth of the Arkansas River. Their explorations led to the events that gave the French possession of Louisiana. Nonetheless, by 1670 French control over North America was being challenged by the English with the founding of the Hudson Bay Company, representing a threat to French dominance in the fur market. In spite of French exploration as far west as present-day Montana and North and South Dakota, its holdings could not resist increasing English expansionism in North America.

During the 1750s England and France came to blows in the Ohio Valley. The strategy of William Pitt, the British prime minister, was to reinforce the English forces in North America, while the Prussians pinned down the French in Europe during the Seven Years' War. Between 1758 and 1760 the French were defeated on several occasions, culminating in a victory by British forces under General James Wolfe over the forces of French General Louis-Joseph de Montcalm on the Plains of Abraham, outside the city of Quebec, in 1759. With the surrender of Quebec and the fall of Montreal a year later, it was just a matter of time before the British controlled North America. The Treaty of Paris, signed in 1763, surrendered Canada to the British along with French possessions east of the Mississippi. When New France became a British colony in 1763, its population numbered between seventy thousand and eighty thousand French-speaking people who were already bordered by one and a half million English-speaking inhabitants of the thirteen American colonies. Immigration from France to New France ceased at this point, although immigrants continued to arrive elsewhere in Canada from Britain.

Quebec in the Eighteenth and Nineteenth Centuries

The unpopular royal proclamation of 1763 created a colony like the other British crown colonies. It was to be governed by British common law. Catholics could not hold public office. However, the threat of an American revolution led the British to come to an understanding with leaders in Quebec. The Quebec Act of 1774 permitted Catholics to hold office, freer operation of the Catholic Church, and the reinstatement of French civil law. Still, pressure from Loyalists led to the proclamation of the Constitutional Act of 1791, dividing the colony into two provinces, Lower and Upper Canada (le *Bas Canada* and *le Haut Canada*). Upper Canada included present-day Ontario, which was bolstered by immigration of British loyalists after the American Revolution as well as by continued English immigration. Lower Canada remained populated by French speakers. Two ethnic entities had been created, each having its own religious practice and language. Of the 160,000 inhabitants of *le Bas Canada*, only 20,000 were English-speaking.[1]

Within Lower Canada, divisions began to appear. The province was divided by opposing political coalitions. Wealthy commercial interests favored British influence along with Protestant religious culture. The middle class favored popular rule, governance under French law, and Catholic religious culture. Louis-Joseph Papineau (1786–1871), leader of the Patriot Party and champion of French-Canadian nationalism, inspired the 92 Resolutions, a listing of French-Canadian demands and grievances subsequently rejected by the British. Papineau's speeches fostered the idea that noncooperation with the English and the creation of a separate state in Quebec would be the only way to preserve French heritage and culture in the face of British political authority. Although Papineau favored a moderate political strategy, others who were more radical rose up in arms. Conflict broke out in 1837 and 1838 (*la rébellion des Patriotes*). The insurgents against British rule issued a *Déclaration d'indépendance du Bas-Canada* inspired by the American Declaration of Independence, but they were crushed.[2] Many of them sought refuge in the United States, while others were imprisoned, deported, or hanged.

Named to head an investigatory commission, Lord John George Durham recommended in 1839 that peace would be restored only by anglicizing all Canadians and by improving the colonial relationship between the mother country and the colony. Responding to the idea that assimilation of the French-speaking population would bring calm and stability, the British proceeded to subordinate French Canadians politically through the Union Act of 1841, in which the colonial assembly would be dominated by English speakers, English interests would decide on which laws to use, while no guarantee was given to the use of French in government or law. This was immediately perceived in Quebec as an act of repression and a new conquest by the English. The Union Act marks the beginning of *Québécois* solidarity. Now the question of a surviving French Canada was real. Under the Union Act, Upper and Lower Canada (corresponding roughly to the present-day provinces of Ontario and Quebec) were unified and administered by a single government headed by a governor answerable to the British Parliament. English was decreed to be the only official language of the country. French- and English-speaking areas were allowed the same number of representatives, although the French-speaking population was more numerous. Under continuing strong protests, however, England recognized the use of French in 1848.

During the 1860s a federation movement to unify all of Canada's colonies arose in answer to economic problems, questions of national defense, and international prestige. Federalists agreed in principle that French Canada would retain its administration, French civil law, the French language, and religious and cultural heritage, and that it would have representation within the federation equal to its population.[3] The Quebec government was to retain control of legislation affecting cultural and social matters, particularly education and health. The British House of Commons approved federation, as did Queen Victoria. The Canadian Confederation came into being on July 1, 1867, with the hope that a federal system of government would be the way to create a modern country capable of satisfying the needs and aspirations of two linguistic entities.

Twentieth-Century Transformations

A snapshot of Quebec at the time of confederation would have revealed a population of 1.1 million people, 75 percent of whom spoke French and 85 percent of whom lived in rural areas, mostly at subsistence levels. The underdeveloped economy and few resources at the disposal of the provincial government assured a wave of emigration in which many French Canadians left for the United States in the second half of the nineteenth century. Still, by the end of the nineteenth century, demands for paper and electricity in the United States were making Quebec's resources attractive. The heretofore moribund Quebec economy was transformed between the two world wars, so that new industries dependent upon Quebec's resources in copper, nickel, and aluminum fabrication came into prominence. By the outbreak of World War II, agriculture represented only 10 percent of Quebec's economic activity, while manufacturing represented 64 percent. As might be expected, urbanization proceeded apace. While 60 percent of the population was rural at the turn of the twentieth century, by 1941 that figure had fallen to 37 percent. Although Quebec's economy was being transformed, most of its capital was still coming from the United States and Britain.[4]

Since the 1880s the vision of the Catholic Church had been centered on an agrarian economy within which French and Catholic culture could flourish. Called *le clérico-nationalisme* (clerical-nationalism), this perspective stood against increasing disparities between rich and poor and the negative effects of industrialization, and for the necessity of an alliance between practitioners of the faith and the Church hierarchy in order to protect French-Canadian minority rights. The Church became one of the strongest advocates of French-Canadian *francophonie* in opposition to cultural dominance by the English-speaking culture of Canada and the United States. During the first part of the twentieth century, the Catholic Church continued its role as a leading force in the organization of *Québécois* society. Moreover, during the interwar period, voices emanating from the École des hautes études commerciales

(School of Advanced Business Studies) and from Father Lionel Groulx and his followers spoke out against the dominance of foreign capital in reviews such as *Action française* and *Action nationale*. The militants believed that only an economically viable and dynamic Quebec could assure any measure of French-Canadian influence anywhere.[5]

From 1939 to 1956 Quebec underwent a period of economic expansion and population growth. The post-World War II baby boom and triple-digit manufacturing growth were remarkable, although many public-sector employees could not keep up with rising prices. As more women entered the job market, migration increased to urban centers like Quebec and Montreal. Patterns of religious practice began to shift after the war as well, with fewer *Québécois* practicing actively. The perspective of the Catholic Church, which had defined Quebec as Catholic, French-speaking, and rural, was no longer widely accepted. Provincial government was called upon to play a more important role in resolving social problems.[6] Meanwhile, during the late nineteenth and early twentieth centuries, other provinces had been coming into confederation, all of them with English-speaking majorities. Although some provinces like New Brunswick and Manitoba had strong French-speaking minorities, the importance that French-speaking Quebecers gave to provincial government was understandable. The stage was thus set for the debate on Quebec's uniqueness within the confederation.

The Quiet Revolution

In spite of considerable economic growth within Canada as a whole, by 1960 it was noticeable that French speakers were at the bottom of the economic ladder. Their incomes were 35 percent of English-speaking Quebecers, who represented only 7 percent of the workforce but 80 percent of management.[7] Many *Québécois* perceived economic domination by American, British, or English-Canadian interests as a form of colonial exploitation. In 1961 only 8 percent of businesses were held by French speakers, while 45 percent were owned by foreigners and 47 percent were owned by English-speaking Canadians.[8]

Much of the Quiet Revolution (*la Révolution tranquille*) coincides with the premiership of Jean Lesage, whose *Parti Libéral* (Liberal Party) governed Quebec from 1960 to 1966. Quebecers had begun to express demands for modernization that had been bottled up for years. Even as a *Québécois* federalist, Lesage began to move control in areas of education, health, and social policy away from the Catholic Church and into the hands of the Quebec government. The government set up new health insurance plans, educational scholarships, and support for universities and raised the compensation for civil servants.

The Quiet Revolution brought with it a new consciousness of a national identity, in which the term *Québécois* began to replace French Canadian and the expression *État du Québec* (state of Quebec) replaced *province de Québec* (province of Quebec). The Quebec parliament became the Assemblée nationale (National Assembly).[9] Typical of the period, historian Maurice Séguin (a disciple of Father Lionel Groulx, the *clérico-nationaliste*) in his *L'Idée d'indépendance au Québec* (1968) argued that Quebec was suffering from a past that had been cut off at the roots in 1763 by the Treaty of Paris. Because Quebecers were the victims of the colonial exploitation inherent in Canadian federalism, Quebec would never develop fully as a society if it did not break with its past relationships in order to modernize. Quebec would begin a period of entrepreneurship and technical expertise that would spur growth and economic development necessary for a contemporary framework for *Québécois* traditions. Séguin's teaching and writing were influential in contributing to the new political consciousness that allied itself with existing cultural consciousness and that contributed to the idea of national sovereignty for Quebec.[10]

Violence Erupts: The October Crisis

In July 1967 French president Charles de Gaulle made his famous visit to Quebec. He was welcomed as a liberator and prophet by Quebec nationalists when he cried from a balcony at the city hall of Montreal, "Long live free Quebec!" (*"Vive le Québec libre!"*). Although the nationalists were far from holding a majority in Quebec, René Lévesque, a former member of the Liberal Party, formed the *Parti Québécois* (PQ) in 1968. The goal of the PQ is the peaceful achievement of Quebec's independence from Canada. Lévesque's policy for political independence was joined to a project for economic association with the rest of Canada (*la souveraineté-association*).

During the 1960s the socialist left became more active, and certain unions and student groups became radicalized. One small, secret group, the Front for the Liberation of Quebec (*le Front de libération du Québec*, FLQ), denounced exploitation of workers, the colonialist underpinnings of Canadian federalism, and American capitalist ideology. The FLQ opted for armed liberation of Quebec. Bombs began to go off after 1963, with violence reaching its apogee in 1970. The FLQ was responsible for bank robberies and for thefts of weapons from Canadian armories. It issued a number of manifestos calling for independence and armed insurrection.

On October 5, 1970, members of the FLQ kidnapped British diplomat James Richard Cross. They demanded a $500,000 ransom and the liberation of twelve jailed members of the FLQ. On October 10, 1970, they kidnapped Quebec's minister of labor, Pierre Laporte. After Quebec's premier, Robert Bourassa, requested federal aid, martial law was declared. Canadian army troops were dispatched to Quebec. On October 17, 1970, the murder of Pierre Laporte by the FLQ profoundly shocked Canadians. Some FLQ members were arrested, and some negotiated for safe passage to Cuba in exchange for James Cross's freedom. In spite of the turbulence of this period, by the end of 1970 criminal political acts died out as the vast majority of Quebecers repudiated violence. Nonetheless, many vowed to continue their quest for independence through democratic means.

For many *Québécois*, however, federalism was still the only reasonable arrangement. In 1968 *Québécois* federalist Pierre Elliott Trudeau became Canada's prime minister. In 1971 Trudeau called the Victoria Conference as an attempt to rework the Canadian constitution without consent from Britain. Within any new constitutional arrangement, Trudeau wanted a strong federalism allowing for no particular concessions to Quebec's unique culture. Robert Bourassa, even as a profederalist Liberal premier of Quebec, rejected the Victoria entente because it did not respect Quebec's autonomy. From this point on, confrontations between Quebec and Ottawa increased.

During the October Crisis, the entirely unofficial but highly effective intervention of the PQ and René Lévesque played an important role in defusing the crisis, leading to enhanced prestige for him and his party. In 1976 René Lévesque became the premier of Quebec, promising that *Québécois* would have a voice in any sovereignty decision. The PQ had benefited from Pierre Trudeau's language policy for Canada, in which the country would be officially bilingual. This policy left little incentive for English-speaking Canadians to learn and speak French. Required bilingualism in federal agencies, largely staffed by English speakers, was very unpopular. Within Quebec those French speakers who were forced to speak English interpreted this move as salt rubbed into their wounded cultural pride.

The Constitutional Debate of 1982

In May 1980 the Lévesque government (PQ) in Quebec asked the province's population to vote on a referendum to undertake talks with Ottawa on sovereignty. Trudeau campaigned against separation, preferring to work to correct any historical injustices toward Quebec through constitutional reforms. Sixty percent of Quebec's population voted against sovereignty.

Later, in April 1982, Trudeau moved to institutionalize home rule in Canada by severing constitutional issues from any British legal authority. Whereas the Statute of Westminster of 1931 and the Second World War had assured Canada's independence, its constitution could only be modified by the British Privy Council. The effort to make the Canadian constitution independent was called patriation (*le rapatriement de la Constitution*), resulting in Queen Elizabeth's proclamation of the new Constitution Act (also called the Canada Act) in 1982.

Part of this project entailed forging a new agreement between the provinces and the federal government. Trudeau refused special concessions to any province, including Quebec, which had demanded the right of veto over constitutional change. The new constitution was adopted in 1982, including a Charter of Rights and Freedoms (*la Charte canadienne des droits et libertés*) and a process for amending the constitution. The Charter of Rights and Freedoms guarantees rights including freedom of religious practice, minority language education, and tolerance of cultural diversity. It also contains a clause allowing rights to be overridden by federal or provincial lawmakers and an amendment protocol requiring approval of seven of the provinces and 50 percent of the entire population. Agreement was reached among nine of the Canadian provinces on patriation, but Quebec held out, refusing to join the agreement without the right to veto any federal decision that could work against its interests. Quebec had not seceded from Canada, but neither had it signed the agreement. Thus, its adherence to Canadian federalism was ambiguous. Many Quebecers felt that their identification as a distinct society had been ignored.

The Lake Meech and Charlottetown Accords

In 1987 the premiers of the ten Canadian provinces met at Lake Meech (in the Outaouais region of Quebec) to come to an understanding and to rectify the problems resulting from the 1981–1982 constitutional reforms. Quebec premier Robert Bourassa proposed the establishment of a new federalism that would incorporate conditions enabling Quebec to sign the constitutional law of 1982. These conditions included recognition of Quebec's particular status as a "distinct society," recognition of the duality of French and English, increased jurisdiction for Quebec in matters of immigration, a new formula for federal spending in the province, a guarantee of a number of Supreme Court members from Quebec, and restoration of the right of provinces to veto constitutional changes.[11] These demands were intended to answer the often-asked question in the rest of Canada: What does Quebec want?

Canadian prime minister Brian Mulroney (himself a Quebecer) and the provincial premiers agreed to the Lake Meech Accord on April 30, 1987, in spite of doubts by many, including Native American rights groups. The provincial legislatures had three years in which to approve the agreement. It was ratified by the Assemblée of Quebec in June 1987. As the time limit of June 1990 approached, a wave of Francophobia was palpable in the rest of Canada, engendered in part by Law 178 in Quebec, which confirmed French as the only language to be used for public signage. Many towns in Ontario declared themselves to be solely English-speaking, while in Quebec the greatest number of people on record declared themselves in favor of independence.

Prime Minister Mulroney called the provincial prime ministers together in the spring of 1990. On June 22, 1990, the death knell was sounded for the Lake Meech Accord when the legislatures of Newfoundland and Manitoba refused to ratify the agreement. Robert Bourassa declared, "English Canada must understand in a very clear way that no matter what is said and done Quebec is today and forever a distinct society, free and able to take responsibility for its destiny" ("*Le Canada anglais doit comprendre de façon très claire que quoi qu'on dise et quoi qu'on fasse le Québec est aujourd'hui et pour toujours une société distincte, libre et capable d'assumer son destin*").[12] Many Quebecers who had supported Canadian federalism were deeply affected, having understood that English-speaking Canadians would not recognize Quebec's cultural distinctiveness.

In the aftermath of Lake Meech, Bourassa appointed a commission (*la commission Bélanger-Campeau*) to investigate the direction that Quebec might take. The commission reported growing impatience within Quebec to finalize the constitutional question. Quebecers voiced a desire to vote in another referendum. Opinion polls indicated

Québécois separatist wearing a hat adorned with the Quebec and French flags and the picture of Quebec premier Jacques Parizeau. (© Earl and Nazima Kowall/Corbis)

that the province would be unified on the independence question. Ottawa now tried to engage Quebec in further negotiations as Prime Minister Mulroney proposed a new agreement known as the Charlottetown Accord. Accepted in 1992 by the ten provinces, Canada's native populations, and the federal government, it recognized Quebec's distinctiveness and its French-speaking culture as well as Amerindian rights. Social and economic unity would be reinforced, as would regional development, and the accord proposed a new formula for amending the constitution. Quebec was guaranteed a minimum of one-quarter of the seats in the House of Commons and three of the nine judges on the Supreme Court. Ottawa put the Charlottetown Accord to a vote in a national referendum. On October 26, 1992, Canadian voters opposed Charlottetown by a margin of 54 percent against, 45.5 percent in favor. Among English-speaking Canadians, 83 percent did not want Quebec to be able to exercise veto power over constitutional change. Within Quebec, 56.6 percent voted in opposition. Five of the other nine provinces also voted against it, particularly in Canada's west.[13] As a consequence, Quebec was not separated from Canada, but neither was it fully reintegrated into the Canadian federation. Quebec has not signed on to this day.

Since Charlottetown

In 1995 another independence referendum took place in Quebec. After Lake Meech and Charlottetown, many were convinced that a favorable change in the relationship between Quebec and the rest of Canada would be impossible. The 1995 referendum requested a mandate from Quebecers to discuss separation by offering a new economic and political partnership with the rest of Canada. This referendum lost by a narrow margin of 49.4 percent in favor, 50.6 percent against. Quebec had remained within the Canadian federation by a narrow margin of some 55,000 votes out of more than 4.6 million votes cast. For the first time, however, a clear majority of Quebec French speakers voted for sovereignty.

From 1994 to 2003 Quebec was governed by the *Parti Québécois* under three premiers, Jacques Parizeau, Lucien Bouchard, and Bernard Landry. Faced with elections in April 2003, Premier Landry recognized that most Quebecers were not interested in putting themselves through a third referendum on sovereignty. Nonetheless, at the outset of the campaign he had assured voters that within a thousand days of reelection Quebec would become a sovereign state. He did not, however, explain how this would come about, nor did he promise another referendum. He recognized that the national issue would not necessarily be at the forefront, but that it would be constantly simmering in the background. He called Quebec a nation and wondered why it was still a province of another nation. He promised that former premier and PQ founder René Lévesque, who had died in 1987, would be proven right, that Quebec would become a full-fledged country, and that the goal of the PQ remained Quebec's sovereignty before the next Summit of the Americas, scheduled to take place in 2005.

Landry may have to wait that long, because on April 15, 2003, the *Parti Québécois* was swept from office in favor of the *Parti Libéral* headed by Jean Charest. Since the failure of the Lake Meech Accord Quebec's politics had been responsive to voters who had grown up during the Quiet Revolution and who were sensitive to issues of cultural and economic discrimination. Now a new wind seemed to be blowing. Cultural tensions had abated in the intervening years. The demographics of low birthrate in Quebec, coupled with immigrants who were not attuned to sovereignty arguments, as well as other pressing matters like health care and redistribution of federal monies to the provinces, seemed to have convinced voters to move on to other issues for the time being.

Language and Identity

French is spoken by 6 million of the 7 million *Québécois* who proudly consider themselves to be part of a worldwide French-speaking community of 200 million. Within Canada French speakers represent 24 percent of the Canadian population and 85 percent of Quebec's population. Moreover, the French language is the vehicle of Quebec's history, tradition, and cultural identity. Without it French-speaking Quebecers would cease to exist as a distinct entity.

During the 1960s French-speaking cultural consciousness in Quebec was reaching a crescendo. The title of Pierre Vallières's book, *Nègres blancs d'Amérique* (1969), and the political slogan "Masters in Our Own House" ("*Maîtres chez nous*") summed up the way many *Québécois* felt about their situation. In 1963 Canadian prime minister Lester Pearson formed a commission (*la Commission Laurendeau-Dunton*) to investigate the state of Canada's bilingualism and biculturalism. It accomplished its work between 1965 and 1969, and its conclusions affirmed what many had already known: French-speaking Quebecers were economically disadvantaged; many areas of employment in the federal government were reserved for English speakers, and French-speaking minorities elsewhere in Canada were not treated equally.

The following government, under Prime Minister Trudeau, espoused a policy of Canadian bilingualism as a solution to the problems articulated by the Laurendeau-Dunton Commission (known widely as the commission Bi-Bi for *bilinguisme/biculturalisme*). This policy satisfied no one. English-speaking Canadians did not understand the need to learn French, while French-speaking minorities in the rest of Canada were treated less well than the English-speaking minority in Quebec. *Québécois* did not want to be required to learn English at a moment when Quebec nationalists were in favor of making French the official language. If the rules of the game had been modified, no popular attitudes had been changed.

Within Quebec, the provincial government of Jean-Jacques Bertrand passed Law 63 in 1969, guaranteeing parents free choice in the language of instruction for their children at school. During the 1960s immigration to Quebec had increased. What worried many was the choice of English instruction by parents whose native language was neither English nor French (*les allophones*). In the Montreal area, for example, even where bilingual education was available, up to 75 percent of the material was taught in English.[14] Law 63 satisfied few.

In 1974 the provincial government of Robert Bourassa, following the recommendations of another commission (the Gendron Commission), declared in its Law 22 that French would be the only official language of the province, that it would be the language of schooling, and that children who wanted to attend English schools would have to prove that they were truly English speakers. Standing for biculturalism and bilingualism, Bourassa's pro-federalist Liberal Party did, however, recognize the bilingual nature of Canada as a whole in its Law 22. This stance was perceived as contradictory by many.[15] Quebec nationalists felt that the law did not go far enough in protecting French, while English-speaking Quebecers felt that they would eventually be shunted aside if immigrants could not choose a language freely for their children at school.[16]

Language and identity matters were inseparable for the separatist Parti Québécois, which came to power in Quebec in 1976. Under its leader René Lévesque, a Charter of the French Language (*la Charte de la langue française*) became the preamble to Law 101 in 1977. The first line of the Charter reads: "As the distinctive language of a Francophone people in the majority, the French language permits the *Québécois* people to express its identity" ("*Langue distinctive d'un peuple majoritairement Francophone, la langue française permet au peuple Québécois d'exprimer son identité*").[17] French became the official language of Quebec. All public matters in the province were to be conducted in French. New immigrants to the province would be enrolled in French schools, while English-language schooling was restricted. Further applications and modifications of Law 101 were spelled out in Law 178 in 1988 and Law 86 in 1993. Signage was regulated to permit English in the interior of workplaces, but French remained on the outside.

Law 101 has been challenged in the courts many times since its passage. Some provisions were invalidated as infringing upon Canadian federal law. Law 101 also prompted not a few English speakers to leave Quebec for Ontario, but political scientist Léon Dion summed up the attitude of many *Québécois* French speakers when he said, "The French language was above all the integrating principle of Quebec's society. To renounce this principle would be to undermine the very civil underpinnings of this society" (*"La langue française était avant tout le principe intégrateur de la société québécoise. Renoncer à ce principe, ce serait saper les fondements mêmes de cette société sous sa forme séculaire"*).[18]

Currently, a lot of passions concerning language and culture have died down. While many English speakers did leave Quebec, those who remained generally have been willing to learn French and to conduct their affairs in it. Bilingualism is returning to the agenda in Quebec as French speakers feel protected from assimilation by Quebec's language laws. Feeling more secure about the culture has meant that more Quebecers are comfortable learning and speaking English. The number of bilingual marriages is increasing, and there are other signs of lessening language tensions, although fears of American cultural dominance plays as a theme in Quebec as it does elsewhere in the world. While sovereignty and cultural issues simmer just below the surface for many, these problems may be generational, with younger French-speaking *Québécois* now facing a more global environment with added confidence. Nonetheless, language and culture matter in Quebec. It is normal for a federalist premier like Jean Charest to pay homage to Quebec's French-speaking heritage and its membership in the worldwide *Francophonie* confederation: "As for Quebec, it will take part in all battles to preserve its right to promote its culture and it will always refuse to bargain away its identity." (*"Le Quebec quant à lui sera de toutes les batailles pour conserver son droit de promouvoir sa culture et refusera toujours de brader son identite."*[19])

Discussion

Even though the question of Quebec separatism may be quiescent for the moment, it has the potential to be an ongoing problem for Canada.

The *Québécois* and their culture are adequately protected
by the Canadian Confederation.

Agree

The *Québécois* and their culture are adequately protected by
Canadian laws and principles. There is no reason to break up the
Canadian federation. Canadian federalism isn't perfect, but it has
provided more stability than would Quebec's separation. The federal system is not totally rigid and has given proof of its flexibility
to make accommodations to Quebec's needs. One example is the
evolution of immigration policy. Through agreements signed with
Ottawa, Quebec is now able to choose among immigrants and to
design and implement its orientation and language programs.
Other examples include Quebec's withdrawal from health, education, and welfare programs formerly run by the Church or the federal government that are now run by the provincial government.
Except for a very brief period of violence by radicals, this dialogue
has been carried out democratically, thus proving the adaptability
of the federal system to the particular needs of its adherents.
Finally, many Quebecers have become prime ministers of Canada,
indicating that political avenues are open to Quebec's representation
in federal governance.

Disagree

English-speaking Canadians just do not understand. The Canadian
Confederation came into being in 1867 based upon the premise that
the two dominant groups would share powers within the federated
state. But in 1982 and 1987 the contract of 1867 was changed. The
new Canadian constitution gave primacy to the rights of individual
citizens over those of groups, thereby undercutting the laws promulgated in Quebec to protect French speakers as a group. Opposition in
English-speaking Canada to amending the constitution stymied
efforts to rectify the situation. As recently as 1995, a poll showed that
two-thirds of English-speaking Canadians did not believe *Québécois* to
be a distinct people within Canada.[20] French-speaking *Québécois* justi-
fiably feel that their English-speaking compatriots will never
truly acknowledge their existence as a separate society and that they
are being invited either to conform to the majority view or to
leave. Those *Québécois* who have made it to the position of prime
minister of Canada are federalists and do not speak for the aspirations
of Quebec nationalism.

132

Separation from the rest of Canada would be tantamount
to economic suicide for Quebec.

Agree

Separation from the rest of Canada could be tantamount to
economic suicide for Quebec. Federalism is the best system under
which to ensure Quebec's long-term prosperity. In a worst-case
scenario, there could be problems for Quebec in the free movement of goods and services, support for agriculture and other programs, the division of assets and share of the national debt, and the
negative reaction of international financial markets. Until Quebec's
prospects were sure, investment in the former province would be
slow in coming. To ensure international economic viability, an
independent Quebec would have to adhere to the requirements of
treaties like NAFTA and the World Trade Organization (WTO),
which would create strain at least in the short run, particularly
when it is assumed that revenues would decrease and social welfare
demands would increase. A lot of business now carried out between
Quebec and the rest of Canada could shift to other provinces and
to the United States. On the other hand, Canada could remain a
viable economic entity without Quebec, since Ontario would produce more than 50 percent of manufactured products and exports
alone. The western provinces would produce 38 percent of the
GDP in the rest of Canada.[21] The relative importance of the western provinces would increase without Quebec, thus providing an
offset to secession.

Disagree

Economic integration must be distinguished from homogeneity.
Quebec can remain economically viable and culturally distinctive in the
long run. The recent history of Quebec shows that two-thirds of the
population is employed by sectors of the economy controlled by
French-speaking Quebecers, compared to only one-half in 1960.[22] An
independent Quebec would still be linked to the Canadian dollar and
would seek free exchange of goods and services with the rest of Canada
without customs or trade barriers. An independent Quebec would
keep all of the taxes it generates and would not have to subsidize the
less wealthy provinces through federal transfer, thus seeing to its own
social welfare concerns. Quebec was an original backer of the North
American Free Trade Agreement (NAFTA). In fact, without Quebec
there would not have been enough support in the rest of Canada to
support it or other U.S.-Canadian free trade agreements. Trade

between the United States and Quebec has always been strong and will increase with a sovereign Quebec. Already, total trade between the two is equal to the total trade between the United States and Brazil, Argentina, and Chile combined.[23] Quebec is the eighth largest trading partner of the United States. Quebec is well endowed in resources like minerals, lumber, agricultural products, and hydroelectric power, products in demand in world markets. As a sovereign country, Quebec's GDP would rank just behind that of Austria, Sweden, and Switzerland. All of this would make for an economically viable autonomous state.

A sovereign Quebec would lead to political instability.

Agree

A sovereign Quebec could create instability and political disruption in North America. If Quebec were to secede, Canada would lose over 7 million of its citizens, leaving it with 75 percent of its population. While the Canadian federation would maintain control over 85 percent of its territory, the secession of Quebec would physically separate the Atlantic provinces from the rest of the country. Fragmentation could occur. About one-tenth of Canada would be noncontiguous, creating a feeling of isolation in Atlantic Canada.[24] In addition, without Quebec in the federation, an imbalance would be created, with Ontario becoming preponderant. It would hold almost 50 percent of the population and create over 50 percent of manufacturing and services. It would generate the bulk of federal revenue. Its new clout could create resentment. Poorer provinces fear that rich provinces like Ontario and Alberta might not want to continue to subsidize them if provinces can chart their own course. The net result could be a partitioned Canada resembling India and Pakistan or the former Soviet Union, no longer a strong partner in North America or in the Western alliance.

Disagree

Fears of instability are exaggerated. A sovereign Quebec would not create havoc. Many Quebecers want to make a new relationship with the rest of Canada work, and they will be strengthened in this desire by their newly found confidence as an independent state. Political negotiations with the rest of Canada are assured. Quebec would grant dual citizenship to all Canadians who desired to remain in a sovereign Quebec in order to contribute to its growth and welfare. Their political rights would be assured. Quebec will endorse self-governance for its Native nations. The rest of the world should not fear a sovereign Quebec. It will not be a rogue state, but rather one that seeks normal relationships with other sovereign states. It possesses many assets for national self-determination, such as cultural distinctiveness, well-established and particular legal and governmental systems, and economic viability.[25] Finally, it is not inconceivable that an independent Quebec might seek a new regional relationship with the United States, particularly in the area of defense, thus adding to the stability of the North Atlantic alliance.

Questions and Activities

1. The motto of Quebec is, "*Je me souviens*" (I remember), as seen on the license plates of cars. What does this motto signify? One interesting interpretation is that the motto is said to be an abbreviated portion of the expression, "*Je me souviens que né sous le lys, je crois sous la rose*" (I remember that born under the lily I grow under the rose). If you have access to Lexis-Nexis, check the articles by Stephen Godfrey, "The Pandora's Box Known as '*Je me souviens*'" in the Toronto *Globe and Mail,* January 24, 1991; and Gaston Deschênes, "La Devise du Québec selon le *Globe and Mail,*" *Le Devoir* 2 March 1991; Antoine Robitaille, "Je me souviens," *Québec, espace et sentiment,* Paris: Autrement, 2001; or <agora.qc.ca/ reftext.nsf/Documents/Quebec__Etat—LaDevise_JE_ME_ SOUVIENS_parGaston_Deschenes>. Report your findings about Quebec's motto to the class. Be sure to contextualize what it is that *Québécois* are remembering.

2. Quebec's artists, writers, and filmmakers have made names for themselves on the international scene. Who are the leading figures in these fields? What are some of their important works? What are their themes? (For a start, see Tétu de Lapsade in the Resource Guide.) Pick a major *Québécois* contributor to the arts, and prepare a report or poster that informs the class about this person's contributions to *Québécois* culture.

3. As members of the French-speaking world community, the *Québécois* are very proud of their language. What are its characteristics? Does it differ from French spoken in France? In other regions of the world? Carry out research to determine those aspects of French that are particular to Quebec, and report to the class. You might consult the chapter on language in Tétu de Labsade (see Resource Guide). See also "Le français au Québec," *Langue française* 31 (septembre 1976). Also, check on *joual,* a dialect form of Canadian French. Some examples are found in Hélène Ossipov,

"French Variation and the Teaching of Quebec Literature," *The French Review* 67, no. 6 (1994), esp. 946–52.

4. Traditions serve to unify groups and to link generations in every established culture. What are some important traditions in Quebec? Traditions are often expressed in a culture's products. Investigate the importance of *Carnaval* (see <http://www.carnaval.qu.ca>), the *cabane à sucre* (sugar shack) or foods eaten at special times (see <http://www.theworldwidegourmet.com/holidays/christmas/quebec.htm>). Make some of these dishes. Everyday favorites in Quebec include *la poutine, la soupe aux pois, la tourtière* and *les cretons.*

5. The national holiday in Quebec is June 24, *la Saint-Jean-Baptiste.* What is the origin and contemporary significance of this holiday? See its Web site at <http://www.cfn.org> as well as the reflective article by Martine Delvaux, " 'Et si on se lançait des fleurs': La Fête nationale du Québec et la question d'identité," *Contemporary French Civilization* 27 (Winter/Spring 2003): 20–36.

6. According to the Institut de la statistique du Québec (Statistical Institute of Quebec) the top ten family names in Quebec are Tremblay, Gagnon, Roy, Côté, Bouchard, Gauthier, Morin, Lavoie, Fortin, and Gagné. For the full list, see <http://www.stat.gouv.qc.ca/donstat/societe/demographie/struc_poplt/noms_famille_alpha.htm>. Are there students in your school with any of these surnames? If so, ask them about their family background, family traditions relating to Canada, emigration history, and the like. If possible, invite a parent or grandparent in the family to talk to your class.

7. Are there any Canadians living in your area? In small teams, contact them to sound out their opinions on Canadian constitutional and cultural problems. You might try asking the question, "What does Quebec want?" Find out whether your informants think that the problem is insoluble or if there has been progress. Try to get a representative sample of English-speaking and French-speaking informants. Report your findings back to the class. There are a number of Canadian clubs and registries in the United States. Call the nearest Canadian consulate to find out their locations. You may also find this Web site helpful: <http://www.angelfire.com/il3/CanadianGoose/canadian_clubs_across_the_countr.html>. Quebec maintains a number of Government Houses Cultural Services around the United States where you might make inquiries. See <http://www.mri.gouv.qc.ca/usa/en/new_york/qui_sommes_nous/index.asp>. There are branches in Atlanta, Boston,

Chicago, Los Angeles, Miami, and New York. You'll find their addresses in issues of *The French Review*.

8. Form a debate in your class. Resolved: Quebec should leave the Canadian federation as a sovereign nation.

9. Who are the Amerindians and Inuit people who inhabit Quebec? What is their status? How do they feel about Quebec separatism? See, for example, Alain Beaulieu, *Les autochtones du Québec: des premières alliances aux revendications contemporaines* (Québec: Musée de la civilisation, 2000); Michael Ignatieff, *Blood and Belonging: Journeys into the New Nationalism* (New York: Farrar, Strauss & Giroux, 1994). The site of Canada's National Inuit Organization is <http://www.tapirisat.ca>.

10. The people of the Commonwealth of Puerto Rico have the rights and obligations of U.S. citizens with some important exceptions. Many people have wondered if there is a way that Puerto Ricans can preserve their Latin American culture and language while remaining a part of the United States? What should the association be? Continued commonwealth status? Statehood? Outright independence? When asked in this manner, the parallel with Quebec is striking. Carry out research to answer these questions, or form a debate on the issue with members of the team taking one of the positions. Are there Puerto Rican students in your school? Don't forget to interview them and their families. Some sites of interest are <http://welcome.topuertorico.org/government.shtml> and those of the major Puerto Rican political parties, the Popular Democratic Party (for enhanced commonwealth status), the New Progressive Party (for statehood), and the Puerto Rican Independence Party (for independence). For a good student article, see Joshua R. Fotheringham, "What Should be Done with Puerto Rico?" *Hinkley Journal of Politics* 2 (Spring 2000): 25–32, found online at <http://www.lib.utah.edu/epubs/hinckley/v2/fotheringham.pdf>, or John D. Ingram, "Puerto Rican Independence: Whose Choice?" in the MSU *Law Review* 85 (2001), online at <http://www.law.msu.edu/lawrev/2001-1/ Ingram.pdf>.

11. As populations change, so do their attitudes and their political agendas. What will the U.S. population look like in 2050? Could you be living in a United States that has significant ethnic and cultural groups whose numbers give them increased political clout? What might they want? Would their needs and demands be disruptive, or would they promote positive change? Carry out an inquiry to find out the trends for U.S. population growth and change. What might the political and cultural consequences be? Can the

Canadian situation serve us as a guide? One place to start online is <http://cber.cba.ua.edu/rbriefs/uspoppro.html>.

12. The language debates in Canada lead us to think about the United States, where there has been a steady flow of opinion as to the desirability of making English the official language. Do bilingual programs in the schools help or hinder the assimilation of persons who do not speak English? Should non-English speakers in the United States have special accommodation as a way to include them in American life? If English were the official language, would this policy unify the country and prevent ethnic and cultural problems? Check these sites to see arguments in favor of English-only: <http://www.englishfirst.org/>; <http://www.us-english.org/>. This site presents arguments against the English-only position: http://ourworld.compuserve.com/homepages/JWCRAWFORD/ engonly.htm, or see James Crawford, *Hold Your Tongue: Bilingualism and the Politics of English Only* (Boston: Addison-Wesley, 1992). This site presents the results of a study on the long-term effects of bilingual education: <http://www.cal.org/crede/pubs/ ResBrief10.htm>.

Vocabulary/Vocabulaire

Nouns/Substantifs

advocates	partisans (m.)
agreement	un accord
biculturalism	le biculturalisme
bilingualism	le bilinguisme
charter	la charte
citizenship	la citoyenneté
destiny	le destin
distinctiveness	caractère particulier, distinctif (m.)
dominance	la dominance, l'hégémonie (f.)
ethnicity	l'ethnicité (f.)
failure	un échec
federalism	le fédéralisme
opinion poll	un sondage
political left	la gauche

138

political party	un parti (politique)
political right	la droite
politics	la politique
primacy	la primatie
quest	la recherche
referendum	un référendum
sovereignty	la souveraineté
trade	le commerce
uniqueness	le caractère unique
votes	voix (f. pl.)

Verbs/Verbes

administer	administrer
amend (a bill, law)	amender un projet de loi
colonize	coloniser
fail	échouer
pacify	apaiser
ratify	ratifier
repudiate	rejeter

Adjectives/Adjectifs

English-speaking	anglophone
federalist	fédéraliste
French-speaking	francophone
self-governing	autonome
separatist	séparatiste
sovereign	souverain

Expressions/Expressions

accept an agreement	accepter, adhérer à un accord
accomodate the demands	répondre aux exigences (de)
anti-French feelings	la francophobie

central authority	l'administration centrale (f.)
cultural consciousness	la conscience culturelle
distinct society	une société distincte
economically disadvantaged	économiquement désavantagés
economic reality	la réalité économique (politique, sociale, etc.)
expression of identity	expression d'une identité
government backing independence	gouvernement indépendantiste
in accordance with	conformément à
local authorities	pouvoirs locaux (m. pl.)
long-run	à longue terme
national reconciliation	la réconciliation nationale
natural resources	les resources naturelles
right of self-determination	le droit de disposer de soi-même
self-determination	l'auto-détermination (f.)
self-governement	l'autonomie (f.)
sever all connections	rompre tous liens
sovereign rights	droits de souveraineté (m. pl.)
What does Quebec want?	Que veut le Québec?

Notes

1. Jean Hamlin and Jean Provencher, *Brève histoire du Québec* (Montréal: Les Editions du Boréal, 1977), 47.

2. An extract of the insurgents' declaration may be found in Yves Bourdon and Jean Lamarre, *Histoire du Québec* (Laval, Québec: Beauchemin, 1998), 58.

3. Ibid., 68.

4. Ibid., 86.

5. Ibid., 153.

6. Hamlin and Provencher, *Brève histoire,* 98–102.

7. Ibid., 110.

8. Bourdon and Lamarre, *Histoire,* 214.

9. Ibid., 211.

10. Ibid., 227.

11. Hamelin and Provencher, *Brève histoire,* 125.

12. Quoted in Hamelin and Provencher, *Brève histoire,* 127.

13. Ben Webb, "Québec: not quite a nation once again," *New Statesman and Society* 8 (1995): 8.

14. Françoise Tétu de Labsade, *Le Québec, un pays, une culture,* 2nd ed. (Montréal : Les Editions du Boréal, 2001), 127.

15. Ibid., 127.

16. Bourdon and Lamarre, *Histoire,* 255.

17. The charter may be found at the site of the Office Québécoise de la langue française at <http://www.olf.gouv.qc.ca/>.

18. *Le Devoir* 27 May 1988, quoted in Tétu de Labsade, *Le Québec,* 130.

19. "Allocution du premier ministre du Québec à l'occasion de la journée internationale de la francophonie, Montréal, le 17 mars 2004." <http:www.premier.gouv.qc.ca>

20. Jacques Parizeau, *Pour un Québec souverain* (Montréal: VLB Editeur, 1997), 69–70.

21. Robert A. Young, *The Secession of Quebec and the Future of Canada* (Montréal and Kingston: McGill-Queen's University Press, 1995), 11.

22. Daniel Johnson, "The Case for a United Canada," *Foreign Policy* 99 (Summer 1995): 79.

23. Parizeau, *Pour un Québec souverain,* 44.

24. Ibid., 9–10.

25. Parizeau, *Pour un Québec souverain,* 75.

Bibliography

Bourdon, Yves, and Jean Lamarre. *Histoire du Québec.* Laval, Québec: Beauchemin, 1998.

Hamlin, Jean, and Jean Provencher. *Brève histoire du Québec.* Montréal: Les Éditions du Boréal, 1977.

Johnson, Daniel. "The Case for a United Canada." *Foreign Policy* 99 (Summer 1995): 78–88. (Read with Parizeau, below.)

Parizeau, Jacques. *Pour un Québec souverain.* Montréal: VLB Éditeur, 1997.

———. "The Case for a Sovereign Québec." *Foreign Policy* 99 (Summer 1995): 69–77.

Tétu de Labsade, Françoise. *Le Québec, un pays, une culture.* 2nd ed. Montréal: Les Éditions du Boréal, 2001.

Webb, Ben. "Québec: not quite a nation once again." *New Statesman and Society* 8 (November 10, 1995): 8.

———— "Vive le Québec libre?" *New Statesman and Society* 8 (April 7, 1995): 12–13.

Young, Robert A. *The Secession of Quebec and the Future of Canada.* Montréal and Kingston: McGill-Queen's University Press, 1995.

Resource Guide

Further Reading

Auger, Julie. "Le Français au Québec à l'aube du vingt et unième siècle." *The French Review* 77, no. 1 (2003): 86–100. (NB: *The French Review* will publish a special issue on Quebec in 2005.)

Balthazar, Louis. "The Faces of Quebec Nationalism," *Contemporary French Civilisation* 17, no. 2 (1993): 268–291.

Blackwell, John D., and Laurie C. C. Stanley-Blackwell. "Canadian Studies: A Guide to the Sources." <http://www.iccs-ciec.ca/blackwell.html>.

Boucher, Marc T. "A Quebec Perspective." *Orbis* 41 (Summer 1997): 445–60. (Read with Segal, below.)

———— "A Rejoinder." *Orbis* 41 (Summer 1997): 473–77. (Read with Segal, below.)

Brown, Craig. *The Illustrated History of Canada.* 4th ed. Toronto: Key Porter Books, 2003.

"Canadian Studies: A Core Collection." *Choice: Current Reviews for Academic Libraries* 35 (September 1997): 71–84.

Doran, Charles F. "Will Canada Unravel? " *Foreign Affairs* 75 (September/October 1996): 97–109.

Frenette, Yves. *Brève histoire des Canadiens français.* Montréal: Les Éditions du Boréal, 1997.

Gagnon, Alain-G. *Québec: État et société.* 2 vols. Québec: Éditions Québec Amérique, 1995.

Gagnon, Alain-G., and Mary Beth Montcalm. *Québec: Beyond the Quiet Revolution.* Scarborough, Ontario: Nelson Canada, 1990.

Morton, Desmond. *A Short History of Canada,* 5th ed. Toronto: McClelland and Stewart, 2001.

Riendeau, Roger. *A Brief History of Canada.* New York: Facts on File, 1999.

Segal, Hugh. "A Federalist Perspective." *Orbis* 41 (Summer 1997): 461–71.

Journals

American Review of Canadian Studies (ARCS), published by the Association for Canadian Studies in the United States. Quarterly since 1985, semiannually since 1973.

International Journal of Canadian Studies, published by the International Council for Canadian Studies. 1990–. Semiannual.

Quebec Studies, published by the American Council for Quebec Studies, 1983–. Semiannual.

Newspaper and Journal Articles

Lexis-Nexis <http://web.lexis-nexis.com/universe/> is an excellent source for online searching of newspaper articles, both in English and in French. A good source for journal articles as well as books is the OCLC First Search database. Check with your school librarian as to availability in your school or public library or at a nearby college or university.

Web Sites

Constitutional issues:

<http://www.youthlinks.org/index.do>

Leading newspaper in Quebec is *Le Devoir* of Montreal. The site allows for a limited number of free searches in their archives since 1992. Found at: <http://www.ledevoir.com>.

Farley, John E., "Separatist Trends in the United States and Canada." <http://www.siue.edu/~jfarley/separat.html>.

Images Canada—a searchable database of 75,000 images in Canadian libraries and archives:

<http://www.imagescanada.ca>

Text of the *Charte de la langue française* (Charter of the French Language) and other interesting items from the Office québécois de la langue française:

<http://www.olf.gouv.qc.ca/>

Quebec as a distinct society:

O'Neal, Brian. "Distinct Society: Origins, Interpretations, Implications." Library of Parliament, 1995.

<http://www.parl.gc.ca/information/library/PRBpubs/bp408-e .htm.>.   Available in English or French.

General overview of the search for *Québécois* identity: "To Be Who We Are: Quebec's Quest."

<http://www.frenchteachers.org/>. From there navigate to Title VI grant projects located at the sidebar.

CHAPTER 7

The Ghost of France
in the Construction
of Postcolonial Identities

Most of the French-speaking (Francophone) African countries are celebrating with pomp and circumstance their forty-plus years of political independence. One would expect that the celebration of these crucial maturation years would translate into the complete independence of these nations by the severance of all unequal ties with their former colonial power. But by all accounts, France continues to play a dominant role in French-speaking Africa, a role that is perhaps even more pronounced today than it has ever been, including during the heyday of colonialism.

What accounts for the continued overbearing presence of France in its former colonies in Africa? Why does France continue to haunt the society of its former colonial empire like a ghost? Why did independence not translate into a radical departure for either partner? The answer is seen in two issues that best illustrate France's continued construction of postcolonial identities in French-speaking Africa: civil and ethnic conflicts, and language policy. But before we examine those issues, a short geopolitical history of French-speaking Africa will be helpful.

Background

The area known as Francophone Africa is made up of fourteen West and Central African states formerly part of France's colonial empire, as well as three Central African states formerly under Belgian rule that have retained French as their official or national language.[1] The bulk of Francophone Africa was brought into existence in its present form as a result of French conquest, European hegemonic practice, and colonial rule. The colonial conquest of Africa reached its height when, in 1884–1885, to avoid quarreling over "their African slice of cake," European empire-building powers such as Britain, France, and Germany convened at a conference in Berlin (then capital of a German empire governed by Chancellor Otto von Bismarck) and agreed to partition the African continent among themselves without fighting each other. Most of the political boundaries of today's independent African states were carved out and fixed on the map at the Berlin conference. At the peak of France's colonial glory, its vast African empire stretched from Senegal on the western Atlantic coast to Madagascar in the Indian Ocean.

In sub-Saharan Africa (excluding North Africa and colonies in the Indian Ocean), the French territories were divided into two blocs of colonies: *l'Afrique Occidentale Française* (A.O.F., French West Africa) in the west, consisting first of seven colonies, then eight when the colony of Le Haut-Senegal Niger was split into two (Sudan and Upper Volta) in 1919; and the territories of *l'Afrique Equatoriale Française* (A.E.F., French Equatorial Africa), once administered as one colony, then divided into four separate colonies.[2] With the exception of Togo in West Africa and Cameroon in Central Africa, two colonies that were granted to France by the League of Nations after World War I in 1923, these two blocs of colonies were administered as federal units with capital headquarters in Dakar, Senegal, for the A.O.F. and Brazzaville, Congo, for the A.E.F.

Although the French minister of the colonies in Paris (*Ministre des colonies*) was legally responsible for their administration, the central figure of the French colonial administration was *le gouverneur général*, the governor of each federal unit. He was the chief executive of a pyramidal colonial administrative system known in the French colonies as direct rule, a centralized administration that co-opted or coerced local rulers into the French administrative machinery. This practice deliberately created an African elite that would accept French standards and then become "associated" with French rulers

in the work of governing the colonies.[3] In short, in this highly centralized administrative system, *les gouverneurs généraux* and their
colonial governments directly ruled the colonies under their control
"through their own white officials and African servants."[4] Although
the official goal of French administrative policy was eventually to
assimilate all Africans by making them equal citizens of the French
empire, the overall colonial system was essentially a despotic and seg-
regated one, in which the African masses were almost without exception relegated to the status of the *indigénat* (a legal status that made
the African a subject and not a citizen with rights).

This oppressive and exploitative colonial rule, which lasted for
more than seventy years, was bound to be challenged both internally
and externally by new historical realities. The best opportunity to
undermine the colonial system came after World War II. Indeed,
"nowhere before World War II did the idea of actual political independence from colonial rule gather much momentum."[5] In addition
to weakening the colonial powers, the war helped raise the political
consciousness of the African elite. Africans had contributed to the
war effort as soldiers, porters, or servants. In the French colonies,
more than 211,000 soldiers of the colonial armies were known as les
Tirailleurs Sénégalais, even though they were drawn from all corners
of French West Africa and French Equatorial Africa. During the
Second World War, *les Tirailleurs Sénégalais* joined Charles de Gaulle
and his Free French movement in the fight against Nazi Germany.
After the war, they became, along with the French-educated African
elite, agents for decolonization of the empire.

As World War II drew closer to its end, General de Gaulle called
for a conference in Africa attended by all the *gouverneurs des colonies*
and ranking administrators of the colonial administration in Brazzaville, the capital of the colony of the Congo, in order to respond to
the growing demands and pressures from Africans. His goal was to
preserve the French colonial empire. At the conference, de Gaulle
made it very clear that France's "civilizing mission" was incompatible
with any idea of full independence without French blessing.[6] Africans
were to be advanced progressively toward full emancipation through
a framework that would be dominated by France.[7]

Given the French view that control of its African possessions was
essential for the postwar rebuilding of its ruined economy and the
maintenance of its superpower status, France resisted the nationalist
pressure for independence. Instead, it chose a gradual path to

decolonization in order to retain full control of the process. This gradual process, which began with the Brazzaville Conference of early 1944 and continued through the constitution-making of the French Fourth and Fifth Republics in 1946 and 1958, sought to reform the colonial system (rather than to destroy it) in order to best preserve it.[8]

This policy would lead to the creation of a French Union between France and its overseas territories as written into Article 41 of the new French constitution of 1946. According to the preamble of the constitution, only France, faithful to its traditional mission, has the discretionary power to lead the peoples under its sovereignty to complete independence. With the collapse of the French Fourth Republic, the new constitution of 1958 created the Franco-African Community (*la communauté franco-africaine*) in which, under French sovereignty, the colonies would be granted greater autonomy. But other decolonizing pressures—such as the instability and eventual collapse of the Fourth Republic, the French defeat in Indochina in 1954, the start of the Algerian liberation war the same year, the independence of the British colony of the Gold Coast (today's Ghana) in 1957, and the refusal by leaders such as Sékou Touré of the colony of Guinea to join the Franco-African Community—forced de Gaulle, by then president of France, to negotiate a peaceful transition toward full independence. In 1960 the two federations of the A.O.F. and A.E.F., which were already functioning as separate autonomous colonies thanks to the *Loi Cadre*, a 1956 French administrative reform act, became independent sovereign nation-states.

Today, after almost half a century of independence, most analysts of the region would agree that French policy, regardless of particular political ideology, has viewed Francophone Africa as a French private preserve (*une chasse gardée*) because "historical links and geographical proximity justified placing Francophone Africa within France's sphere of influence."[9] This claim is formalized through such institutions as *la Francophonie*, a greater French-speaking community seeking first and foremost to consolidate and to promote the spread of the most notable aspects of French culture. These efforts include the French language and intellectual tradition. Many former African colonies are also tied to a Franc Zone, a supranational financial system in existence since 1948. France has served as the Central Bank to provide a common currency in which the *Communauté Financière Africaine* (CFA) franc was linked to the French franc and guaranteed by the French treasury.[10] The French treasury has maintained its responsibility for guaranteeing the convertibility of CFA francs into euros. Finally, France and its former colonies maintain mutual defense agreements. In short, more than forty years after the political divorce of independence in 1960, France and its former African colonies are still linked not only by wide economic and political ties (formalized through the policy of *la Coopération Franco-Africaine*), but also by a deep and emotional bond symbolized by *la Francophonie*.

What is the mutual advantage of preserving the special relationship between these unequal partners? The ghost of France in Francophone Africa is illustrated by France's self-imposed involvement in the political crisis in the Ivory Coast (*Côte d'Ivoire*), and by the language policy of most of these countries in the postcolonial period.

The Ghost of France in African Politics

The Case of the Crisis in the Ivory Coast

Since September 2002 the Ivory Coast, a country formerly known for its stability in an unstable region, has been plunged into a serious political crisis that started with a violent military coup attempt and then degenerated into a civil war. This violence is the tragic culminating point of a decade-long period of instability that started in the aftermath of the death of Félix Houphouët Boigny, the country's founding father and first president.

During the night of September 18–19, 2002, an armed group composed of disgruntled soldiers who were soon to be dismissed from the military and former soldiers in exile in neighboring countries (mainly Burkina Faso) attacked major military and civilian institutions of the country. They killed several thousand civilians and created the largest refugee population in the country's history. After several hours of intense battles on all fronts between republican loyalists and rebels, Abidjan, the economic capital of the country, was liberated. But the northern region and the city of Bouaké (in the center) fell to the rebels.

Alleging the need to spare foreigners from the violence, the French government, through its local military base in Abidjan, created a demarcation line from east to west across the country, dividing it into two separate zones: a northern region controlled by the rebels, and a southern region controlled by government loyalists. The president of Ivory Coast, Laurent Koudou Gbagbo, called for an emergency

A newly arrived member of the 1st Company of the 2nd Regiment of French Foreign Legion paratroopers stands at a checkpoint on the Sassandra river near Guessabo, Ivory Coast, Wednesday, December 18, 2002. (AP/World Wide Photos)

meeting of the ECOWAS, a regional West African organization, to deal with the crisis. The ECOWAS condemned the coup attempt and called for a negotiated settlement of the crisis between rebel forces and the government. It put President Gnassingbe Eyadema of Togo, dean of the African presidents' corps, in charge of negotiating a settlement between the rebels and the government. Two months of negotiations produced no substantive results.

The inability of the ECOWAS to find an African solution to the crisis prompted a call by French foreign minister Dominique de Villepin in December 2002 for a conference, characterized as a last resort by the Ivorian press.[11] The conference took place outside of Paris and was attended by all the French-selected political players of this deadly political drama, but it did not include an official representative of the government of Ivory Coast, although France had previously recognized it as the legitimate, democratically elected government of the country. The Paris conference produced a peace agreement (baptized Linas-Marcoussis) among all the political forces of the country, including all the rebel factions and all the political parties. To enforce this French-brokered peace agreement, the French government applied for and received from the United Nations authorization to form a special transnational force that would decertify (that is, remove the sovereignty of) the Ivorian state in case of noncompliance.

As of today, the deal has yet to bring about the promised peace. But regardless of the final outcome of the Ivorian crisis, two observations can be made. First, France was eager to interject itself in what it has described as a civil, domestic conflict logically under the sovereign jurisdiction of the independent nation-state of the Ivory Coast. Some have even suggested that France played a role in the failure of the ECOWAS efforts so that it could have control over the outcome of the conflict. Second, the political class (leaders of political parties as well as the administrative and civil elite) of the Ivory Coast was too willing to submit itself to French dictates in the resolution of the conflict by undermining all local African peace missions. For what reasons? Why were they beholden to France?

Explaining the Ivorian Crisis

The most widely held explanation of the Ivorian crisis is linked to theories concerning civil conflicts in Africa (and elsewhere): "the clash of civilizations," "the battle between cultures," or "ancient ethnic and tribal hatreds." The argument generally suggests that civil wars are the spectacular expression of ancient hatreds or cultural conflicts between primordial tribal, ethnic, religious, linguistic, and racial communities because culture is the driving force behind human behavior. One scholar maintains that the fundamental source of conflict in the post–Cold War world will not be primarily ideological or primarily economic, but will be the clash of civilizations.[12] In this view, the great divisions among humankind and the dominant source of conflict will be the plurality of cultures between and within the nation-states. The rise of ethnic and religious fundamentalism in all parts of the world has been described as a function of ancient hatreds.[13]

This argument was used mainly by the influential French media and by French politicians to explain the Ivorian crisis to the world. The problem was traced back to an extreme exclusionary ideology called *ivoirité*, an ancient hatred that supposedly pits a Muslim north against a Christian and Animist south. *L'ivoirité*, as framed in the French media, is said to be an anti-immigration, nationalist ideology that glorifies Ivorian values at the expense of immigrant communities that tend to originate from northern neighboring Islamic countries such as Burkina Faso, Mali, Niger, and Senegal. In its worst form, *ivoirité* is said to deny citizenship even to descendants of these northern Muslim communities who lived in the Ivory Coast before independence in 1960.

One argument in favor of *ivoirité* suggests that, to understand the roots of the political crisis in the Ivory Coast, one must examine the effect of historical and ethnographic forces on politics because the ethnic factor remains a divisive and disturbing theme in the country's internal political struggles. Since independence in 1960, Ivorians have not changed their perspective: "Foremost in their psyches is their identity as members of a regional extended family and corporate kin groups competing with others for their share of scarce economic resources and political clout."[14]

But how much truth is there in this cultural theory? And in the case of the Ivory Coast, can the latest crisis be characterized as no more than a deadly competition between primordial ethnic groups? In other words, is the Ivorian crisis caused or fueled by the ideology of *ivoirité*? Can the drawing of the Ivorian fault line between a so-called Muslim north and a Christian and Animist south resist any critical challenge?

The claim in favor of the classification of Africans in cultural groups called tribes or ethnic groups or nations, and the dire prediction of a violent clash between these civilizations or cultures, cannot survive much historical examination and critical scrutiny. First, it is virtually impossible to set the boundaries of the competing primordial ethnic groups in the Ivory Coast (or elsewhere). In the Ivory Coast, the notion of the Great North, a homogenous ethnographic political enclave composed of Muslims only, is a myth that masks the actual ethnic and cultural complexity of these regions.[15]

The ethnic and cultural diversity of the Ivory Coast's inhabitants is reflected in their religious and linguistic practices. In other words, the idea that there are regions composed of direct descendants of ancient families, neatly divided between the north and the south, each of them sharing a deep commitment to common values and inherited identities, is a myth. There is as much cultural diversity within each region as there is between them. Indeed, the ethnic inventory of the Ivory Coast is so diverse that anthropologists and ethnographers have identified and broken it down into sixty different groups. Moreover, all major religions in the country (indigenous, Islam, and Christianity) are practiced, although in unequal proportion, in all the regions of the country.

The assertion that there is an enduring and inevitable tribal clash fueled by the ideology of *ivoirité* proves untrue. Primordial ethnic groups (in the Ivory Coast and elsewhere) have gotten along more often than they have gone for each other's throats.[16] To date, apart from a few isolated incidents during the chaotic transitional period in the aftermath of the 2000 presidential and legislative elections, there have been no reports of systematic destruction of religious symbols in the country.

In fact, the history and daily lives of "tribal" and ethnic groups in the Ivory Coast (and in most of the African continent) are characterized by cooperation, borrowing, intermarriage, tolerance, and peaceful resolution of normal social conflicts. There is not a village or a hamlet in even the most remote corners of the country, especially in the richer agricultural south, where one cannot find a migrant farmer or trader from the north or from the neighboring countries of Mali, Niger, and Burkina Faso who does not get along perfectly well with members of local communities. These "immigrants," some of whom have lived in these local communities since before the country's independence in 1960, practice their religion freely, attend to their business, till their land, and raise and care for their families the best way they can, completely free of any fear, except fear of the hardship of rural life in an underdeveloped country and fear of the constraints imposed by dictatorship, fears that are experienced by all, including local communities. The same can be said of urban and semi-urban neighborhoods, except that here the immigrants come from much more diverse foreign origins and in greater numbers than in rural areas.

In their article entitled "Modern Hate," Rudolph and Rudolph conclude that so-called ancient hatreds are made as much as they are inherited and that to call them ancient is to pretend that they are primordial forces, outside of history and human agency.[17] The same conclusion can be reached about many ethnic or tribal conflicts in Africa because they are generated by the same historical processes and produced by the same human agency. The only difference is that the Ivorian crisis is mainly the creation of an external agent (France) that has the motivation and power to structure the pattern of political group formation in its former colonies in Africa. Indeed, the pattern of political cleavage observed in the Ivorian crisis may be best explained by a focus on the clout exercised by France in the political process of the Ivory Coast. France, through its powerful media and thanks to its influential political and financial networks, has strategically manipulated normal regional, language, religious, and ethnic differences into polarizing ones in order to preserve its privileged position in West Africa.

The Cultural Realm

The ghost of France in the sharpening or polarization of group differences is also manifest in the language policy of its former colonies. This cultural realm is where the presence of France in the construction of the postcolonial identities of Africans is deeply felt. Since early colonial times, France organized schools not only to train auxiliaries for its colonial administration and commerce, but also to spread the French language and culture in its colonies. Members of the future elite were brought together from throughout the colonies and trained at French-subsidized parochial schools as well as in some specialized public schools that trained government employees for teaching, general administration, health care, and technical services.[18] The most outstanding students such as Camara Laye, author and main character of the autobiographical novel *L'Enfant noir* (The Dark Child, 1953), were sent to France to further their education. Although most Francophone countries now have established their own national universities, more than 100,000 African students continued to attend French universities throughout the 1980s.[19] As a result of successful socialization through the colonial and post-colonial French-derived educational system, a great majority of the Francophone African elite then and now has a common cultural referent: *la Francophonie*.

Cameroonian writer and social critic Mongo Beti declared Paris the capital of Francophone Africa: "*Afrique Francophone, capitale, Paris!*"[20] Indeed, from the yearly Franco-African summits for heads of state to the solemn gatherings of the Francophone Summit (*Sommet francophone*), Francophone political actors and intellectuals are linked to Paris by a broad common cultural referent and by a shared exposure to Paris-based media such as the shortwave broadcasts of Radio France International (RFI) and the print media such as *Jeune Afrique*.[21] French films, newspapers, books, and special television programs through the satellite facilities of Canal France International have a wide audience among the African elite.[22] But by far the most enduring legacy of the French-derived educational system is the survival of French as the national language in many countries. Although mother-tongue instruction has been introduced successfully in some countries, especially in primary education, most students in

Francophone Africa continue to be influenced by the French language through their schooling.

The issue of why the French language persists in its former colonies in Africa has been extensively debated. Shortly after independence, all of the countries consecrated French as their official language, sometimes going so far as to enshrine this provision in their new constitutions. It was argued that, because of the arbitrary nature of their political boundaries, which resulted from the logic of colonial design, Africa's new states were a concoction of diverse and sometimes opposing ethnic groups speaking their own languages. This linguistic heterogeneity was perceived as a mortal threat to the task of nation-building, that is, the promotion of national unity, the fostering of national loyalty, and the granting to every citizen a sense of belonging in the nation-state.[23] Furthermore, because the French language was already enjoying international prestige, the use of this instrument of global communication would prevent the marginalization of the new nation-states. Membership in *la Francophonie* was therefore perceived as a matter of vital national interest because it was a precondition for the very existence (internal cohesion and external recognition) of these new countries. Although these arguments may appear to be compelling, the fact remains that, if language is, as is commonly believed by many commentators, the key to decolonizing the mind, how meaningful is Africa's statutory independence if these countries' cultural, political, and social productions are expressed in the French language?[24]

Some critics take the position that, "so long as Africans continue to use French or any other European language in politics, literature, law, and everyday life, they will be chained to the colonial system and follow its patterns."[25] For other commentators, the quarrel is with the uncritical acceptance of *la Francophonie* by the African elite not as a mere instrument of communication, but as the ultimate, dominant cultural referent for millions of their fellow countrymen, the majority of whom are functionally illiterate in French. Put differently, the European languages operate in these countries as a basis for the framing or construction of new national or ethnic identities. Yet in countries such as Cameroon that have several dozen local languages, one of the most polarizing cleavages is between English speakers and French speakers. Moreover, it may be said that these countries are referred to as French-speaking African countries, or Francophone Africa, not because they were colonized by France or because French is their dominant language, but because French is imposed by the intellectual elite and political actors.

La Françafrique: A Polygamous Love Affair

We might ask why the African French-speaking elite cannot imagine alternative linguistic and cultural possibilities outside *la Francophonie*? The internal logic of France's colonialism in Africa and even the post-colonial policy of *la Coopération Franco-Africaine*, a series of cooperative and partnership agreements between France and its former African colonies, have created, maintained, preserved, and even strengthened France's privileged yet unequal relationships with the former colonies. France's stake in the preservation of its privileged position in Francophone Africa by the strategic manipulation of political conflicts and Francophone Africa's unwillingness or inability to end its linguistic and cultural subordination to France have been characterized as a relationship between master and slave, center and periphery, colonizer and colonized, and father and child. All these characterizations presuppose the possibility of at least a gradual separation, if not a violent revolution, to end the hierarchical relationship once and for all.

It would seem, however, that the real reason for the enduring unbalanced relationship is that France is engaged in a polygamous matrimonial bond with its former colonies. And like all polygamous relationships, it is not only virtually impossible to break, but it survives even formal divorce (independence). This is so because the two unequal partners have a stake in the preservation of the relationship, however pathological and dysfunctional it might be. For the many wives (African countries), pride and self-worth come from the filiation with a powerful husband (France) and his homestead. This explains why the Ivorian political class was too willing to undermine local African efforts at settling the conflict, in order to give the honor to France. As a loyal polygamous wife, the Ivorian political class, called the Marcoussis bloc (*le bloc Marcoussiste*) in the Ivorian press because of its passionate support for the French-brokered Marcoussis peace agreement, had to refuse the hand of regional African suitors such as ECOWAS and other African leaders. Any flirting with a rival local suitor would have constituted a social transgression of the marital bond, punishable by the husband in terms of political, economic and even military sanctions. For the husband, power (France's claim to superpower status) comes from the multiplicity of wives, a sure sign of social, political, and economic status. Thus, "France's involvement in the sub-Saharan region of Africa has resulted, above all, from a desire to maintain and increase its power and prestige in Europe and in the world."[26] For that reason, even though the Françafrican divorce was settled more than forty years ago, and though France may have died in the hearts of its former African colonies, its ghost will still haunt the lives of its Francophone African wives for a long time.

Discussion

The best method to achieve decolonization and liberation is violent upheaval.

Agree

Frantz Fanon, in his essay *The Wretched of the Earth* (1961, *Les Damnés de la terre*), argues that colonization is essentially a violent order and that the settler or colonial master knows only one reality: brute force. Therefore, no decolonization through peaceful negotiations can efface the marks of violence; only violence itself can destroy them. In addition, when decolonization is achieved through peaceful negotiations, it is perceived as a gift from the former colonizer, a gift worthy of grateful praise and adoration from the colonized native. This gift of independence perpetuates both colonial complexes: the complex of superiority in the mind of the settler and the complex of inferiority in the mind of the colonized native. Finally, negotiated settlements are always perceived as compromises between the colonial master and the local emerging bourgeoisie meant to preserve the colonial order. Violence has the virtue of uniting the population because all segments of the new nation have participated and sacrificed equally in the armed struggle for liberation, and will therefore take a collective and personal stake in preserving the freedom of the new nation. In short, those in favor of the argument for violence make the case that a violent decolonization, where the blood of both the native peoples and the colonizing settlers flows, leads to the genuine eradication of colonial superstructures.

Disagree

Violence begets violence. In colonial countries where decolonization was achieved by armed struggle, the blood of the people continues to flow even after years of independence. Algeria is a perfect example. (See Chapter 3, on the Aussaresses trial.) More importantly, the achievement of independence through a violent armed struggle may not bring about the expected unity of the peoples of the new nations nor the promised destruction of the colonial superstructures.

Countries such as Algeria and others are not only still divided along religious, class, and ethnic fault lines that threaten their internal peace, but they are also dependent on their former colonial masters such as France.

The status of the French language should be maintained in Francophone Africa.

Agree

African countries are characterized by their linguistic heterogeneity due to the artificiality of their state borders. Thus, the French language is the best neutral means to foster a common national bond among these otherwise diverse linguistic and ethnic groups. The promotion of one local language over the others as the national language will spark ethnic conflicts. Furthermore, these local African languages are minor tongues not developed enough for modern communication in a globalized world. On the other hand, French is not only a global language that affords a wider audience to its users, but it is also capable of translating the abstract concepts of the modern world. Finally, as argued by Léopold Sédar Senghor, poet and first president of Senegal, French must be maintained as the language of modern communication in Francophone Africa because "it is the language of the gods" ("*il [le français] est la langue des dieux*").[27]

Disagree

A language is not a neutral symbolic means of communication. It is a carrier of culture and civilization. To maintain French in Africa at the expense of local languages is to condemn these local African languages to a permanent second-class status, if not to certain death. Moreover, the use of a colonial language can lead only to the perpetuation of colonial cultural structures. True independence can only be achieved through the decolonization of the mind, with language as the key. Thus, the aspiration for independence from France compels African countries not only to promote local languages, but also to abolish European languages entirely. Finally, in spite of the colonial and postcolonial imposition of French, it remains a marginal language, having penetrated only the surface of the African social fabric. The most optimistic estimations set at 35 percent those who are functionally literate in French in most

Francophone African countries. The majority of African people communicate either within their own linguistic groups or through other local languages. French remains an elite language that condemns the majority of people who do not speak it to the status of second-class citizens.

Questions and Activities

1. Today, there are fourteen Francophone African countries. Some of them have changed their names over the years. Provide a list of the fourteen Francophone African countries and their capital cities. Check an up-to-date atlas, and make a map or poster for your classroom.

2. What is the importance of the Conference of Berlin (1884–1885) in the history of Africa? The following Web sites will help you understand the issues: <http://geography.about.com/library/weekly/aa021601a.htm>; <http://www.saburchill.com/history/chapters/empires/0054.html>; and <http://library.thinkquest.org/C004488/edu-BCbg.html>. You may also want to check Basil Davidson, *Modern Africa: A Social and Political History,* listed in the Resource Guide. Form a small group to explain to your class what happened at Berlin.

3. In 1885, Jules Ferry, French statesman and important political figure in the Third Republic, said during a parliamentary debate on colonialism, "Gentlemen . . . we have to declare openly that superior races have a duty with regard to inferior races . . . they have the duty to civilize inferior races" (*"Messieurs . . . il faut dire ouvertement que les races supérieures ont un droit vis-à-vis des races inférieures . . . elles ont le devoir de civiliser les races inférieures,"* quoted in Raoul Girardet, *Le Nationalisme français 1871-1914,* 2nd ed., Paris: Armand Colin, 1966, 104). Explain the implications of this perspective with regard to France's "civilizing mission" in Africa or elsewhere in its former empire.

4. Explain the difference between the French colonial administrative policy of direct rule and the British colonial administrative system of indirect rule. Are the two colonial systems substantially different? One resource to check is Joseph Ki-Zerbo, *Histoire de l'Afrique Noire,* listed in the Bibliography.

5. Who is referred to by the term *Tirailleurs Sénégalais?* Learn more about *les Tirailleurs Sénégalais,* and provide to the class a sense of their contribution not only to the liberation of France during both

world wars, but also to the liberation of their own countries. A good place to start is Myron Echenberg, *Colonial Conscripts: The Tirailleurs Sénégalais in French West Africa, 1857–1960*, Social History of Africa Series (Portsmouth, NH: Heinemann, 1991). You might also consult the Web site at <http://www.worldwar1.com/france/tseng.htm>. For views of uniforms and insignia of the *Tirailleurs*, see <http://tdm.vo.qc.ca/uniforme/un010.htm> and <http://mapage.noos.fr/4edmm/histo%20senegalais.htm>. You may also want to study in class Léopold Sédar Senghor's poem *Aux tirailleurs sénégalais morts pour la France*, available at <http://www.perso.wanadoo.fr/legs/poesie/senghor3.htm>.

6. Research the literary movement known as *la Négritude*. Who were the African and Caribbean authors associated with it? What sorts of works did they write? Some sources to get you started are Lilyan Kesteloot, *Black Writers in French: A Literary History of Negritude*, trans. Ellen Conroy Kennedy (Washington, DC: Howard Univesity Press, 1991); Belinda Jack, *Negritude and Literary Criticism: The History and Theory of "Negro-African" Literature in French*, Contributions in Afro-American and African Studies (Westport, CT: Greenwood Publishing Group, 1996); Edward A. Jones, *Voices of Negritude: The Expression of Black Experience in the Poetry of Senghor, Césaire & Damas* (Valley Forge, PA: Judson Press, 1971); and Léopold Sédar Senghor, *Le Dialogue des cultures* (Paris: Seuil, 1993). Two helpful Web sites are <http://www.geocities.com/africanwriters/origins.html> and <http:// www.afrol.com/archive/francoph_lit.htm>.

7. What is the relationship of the American Harlem Renaissance movement of the 1920s to the *Négritude* literary movement? Research the Harlem Renaissance, consulting some of the following sources: Geneviève Fabre and Michel Feith. eds., *Temples for Tomorrow: Looking Back at the Harlem Renaissance* (Bloomington: Indiana University Press, 2000); Trudier Harris, ed., "Afro-American Writers from the Harlem Renaissance to 1940," *Dictionary of Literary Biography*, 51 (Detroit, MI: Gale, 1987); and Victor A. Kramer and Robert A. Russ, eds., *The Harlem Renaissance Re-examined* (Troy, NY: Whitson Publishing, 1997). Try this Web site for a portrait of Harlem between 1900 and 1940: <http://www.si.umich.edu/CHICO/Harlem/>. This site contains biographies and bibliographies of leading poets of the Harlem Renaissance: <http://www.poets.org/exh/Exhibit.cfm?prmID=7>. Choose a poem from the Négritude movement and the Harlem Renaissance movement that the class can analyze and compare.

8. As a class project, research the former French colony of Indochina and its struggle for independence beginning in 1945. Include a short biography of Ho Chi Minh, the father of Vietnamese independence. Explain the significance of the year 1954 and the subsequent circumstances of the partition of the country. Finally, how did French decolonization in Indochina lead to American involvement in Vietnam? Helpful sources include Stanley Karnow, *Vietnam, A History*, 2nd ed. (New York: Penguin, 1997); Nicola J. Cooper, *France in Indochina: Colonial Encounters* (Oxford: Berg, 2001); Martin Shipway, *The Road to War: France and Vietnam, 1944–1947* (Providence: Berghahn Books, 1996); Jacques Dalloz, *La Guerre d'Indochine, 1945-1954* (Paris: Editions du Seuil, 1987); and Ellen J. Hamme, *The Struggle for Indochina* (Palo Alto: Stanford University Press, 1966). An older but still valuable contribution is Bernard B. Fall, *Street without Joy*, rev. ed. (Mechanicsburg, PA: Stackpole Books, 1994). For a fictional account of the beginnings of America's involvement in Vietnam, read the acclaimed novel by Graham Greene, *The Quiet American*, rev. ed. (New York: Penguin Books, 1991). Note also the film by the same name (Videocassette. Dir. Phillip Noyce, Perf. Michael Caine. Buena Vista Home Video, 2003; and on DVD, Miramax Home Entertainment, 2003). Finally, you may wish to see Pierre Schoendoerffer's 1965 Indochina film, *The 317th Platoon* (Videocassette, Interama, 1990), or the popular 1992 film *Indochine* (Dir. Régis Wargnier. Perf. Catherine Deneuve, Videocassette, Columbia/Tristar Studios, 2000).

9. Research and explain what *la Coopération* is as part of France's foreign policy in its former colonies and territories all over the world. How is *la Coopération* related to the concept of *la francophonie*? (See <http://www.france.diplomatie.fr/cooperation/dgcid/>, the Web site of the French *Ministère des Affaires étrangères*.) You may also want to check the Web site of CODOFIL, an organization that promotes the use of French in Louisiana, at <http://www.codofil.org/francais/>. In what ways is *la Coopération* similar or dissimilar to the U.S. Peace Corps? (See, for example: <http://www.peacecorps.gov/>.)

10. If it can be said that France exercises a hegemonic (controlling) influence in Africa, can it also be said that the United States exercises dominance in the world? If you think this is the case, give some examples of U.S. policies and actions that could be qualified as imperialistic. Would you agree that the Monroe Doctrine is an invitation to such policies? Form a debate within the class: Resolved: the United States is one of the world's leading hegemonic powers.

Some sources to consider might be David Slater and Peter J. Taylor, *The American Century: Consensus and Coercion in the Projection of American Power* (Oxford: Blackwell, 1999); Noam Chomsky, *Hegemony or Survival: America's Quest for Global Dominance* (New York: Metropolitan Books, 2004). Contrast this with Michael Mandelbaum, *Ideas That Conquered the World: Peace, Democracy and Free Markets in the Twenty-First Century* (New York: Public Affairs, 2002); Robert Kagan, *Of Paradise and Power: America and Europe in the New World Order* (New York: Knopf, 2003); Charles A. Kupchan, *The End of the American Era: U.S. Foreign Policy and the Geopolitics of the Twenty-First Century* (New York: Knopf, 2002). See also *America in the World*, listed in the Resource Guide.

11. Consider the cases of the former Yugoslavia, of Rwanda, and of Afghanistan. Can the conflicts in these countries be considered clashes of civilization? As part of a class project (or in collaboration with a world history class), form three teams to investigate each of these areas and the problems caused by ethnic, religious, or cultural differences. You may want to consider several chapters from Samuel Huntington's book, noted in the Bibliography. See also Norman Cigar, *Indictment at the Hague: The Milosovic Regime and Crimes of the Balkan War* (New York: New York University Press, 2002); Mahmood Mamdani, *When Victims become Killers: Colonialism, Nativism and the Genocide in Rwanda* (Princeton University Press, 2002); Ahmed Rashid, *Taliban: Militant Islam, Oil and Fundamentalism in Central Asia* (New Haven: Yale University Press, 2000). As part of your research, consider what the role of the United States should be in genocidal conflicts elsewhere in the world. You may want to consider Samantha Powers, *A Problem from Hell: America and the Age of Genocide* (New York: Basic Books, 2002). Consider also Chris Hedges, *War Is a Force That Gives Us Meaning* (New York: Public Affairs, 2002).

Vocabulary/Vocabulaire

Nouns/Substantifs

army	l'armée (f.)
author	l'auteur (m.)
border	la frontière
capital city	la capitale
circumstance	la circonstance

civilizing mission	la mission civilisatrice
colonization	la colonisation
colonizer	le colonisateur
conflict	le conflit
decolonization	la décolonisation
force	la force
foreign policy	la politique étrangère
globalization	la globalisation, la mondialisation
history	l'histoire (f.)
independence	l'indépendance (f.)
inferiority	l'infériorité (f.)
issue	l'enjeu (m.)
key	la clé
liberation	la libération
majority	la plupart, la majorité
master	le maître
means	le moyen
mind	l'esprit (m.)
movement	le mouvement
native	l'indigène (m.)
negotiation	la négociation
partition	le partage, la partition
people (nation)	le peuple
politician	le politicien
race	la race
relationship	le rapport
significance, meaning	la signification
social fabric	le tissu social
struggle	la lutte
superiority	la supériorité
system	le système
violence	la violence
war	la guerre
work (literary)	l'oeuvre (f.)

Verbs/Verbes

abolish	abolir
colonize	coloniser
condemn	condamner
control	contrôler
decolonize	décoloniser
dominate	dominer
liberate	libérer
maintain	maintenir
negotiate	négocier
struggle	lutter
translate	traduire

Adjectives/Adjectifs

armed	armé, -e
colonial	colonial, -e
French-speaking	francophone
inferior	inférieur, -e
literary	littéraire
racist	raciste
superior	supérieur, -e
symbolic	symbolique

The authors wish to thank Dr. Marc Papé for his contribution to the body of this chapter.

Notes

1. David E. Gardinier, "The Historical Origins of Francophone Africa," in *Political Reform in Francophone Africa,* eds. John F. Clark and David E. Gardinier (Boulder, CO: Westview Press, 1997), 9.

2. Joseph Ki-Zerbo, *Histoire de l'Afrique Noire* (Paris: Hatier, 1978), 436.

3. April A. Gordon, and Donald L. Gordon, *Understanding Contemporary Africa* (Boulder, CO: Lynne Rienner, 1996), 47.

4. Basil Davidson, *Modern Africa: A Social and Political History* (London: Longman, 1983), 5.

5. Bohannan and Curtin, quoted in Gordon and Gordon, *Understanding Contemporary Africa,* 49.

6. Ki-Zerbo, *Histoire,* 499–500.

7. Gardinier, "Historical Origins," 12.

8. Ibid.

9. Peter Schraeder, "Cold War to Cold Peace: Explaining U.S.-French Competition in Francophone Africa," *Political Science Quarterly* 115, no. 3 (2003): 398.

10. Ibid.

11. *L'Inter On-line,* 15 Jan. 2003, <http://www.abidjan.net./a/?n=36565>.

12. Samuel Huntington, *The Clash of Civilizations and the Remaking of World Order* (New York: Simon and Schuster, 1996).

13. Karen Mingst and Jack Snyder, *Essential Readings in World Politics* (New York: W.W. Norton, 2001), 359.

14. Jeanne Maddox Toungara, "Ethnicity and Political Crisis in Côte d'Ivoire," *Journal of Democracy* 12, no. 3 (July 2001), <http://muse.jhu.edu/journals/journal_of_democracy/v012/12.3toungara.html>.

15. Ibid.

16. Rudolph and Rudolph, quoted in Mingst and Snyder, *Essential Readings,* 359.

17. Ibid., 359–61.

18. Gardinier, "Historical Origins," 11.

19. Ibid., 14.

20. Mongo Beti, *La France contre l'Afrique: Retour au Cameroun* (Paris: La Découverte, 1993), 135.

21. Jennifer A. Widner, *Economic Change and Political Liberalization in Sub-Saharan Africa* (Baltimore: The Johns Hopkins University Press, 1994), 50.

22. Gardinier, "Historical Origins," 14.

23. Crawford Young, "Democracy and the Ethnic Question in Africa," *Africa Insight* 27, no. 1 (1997): 7.

24. French philosopher Jean-Paul Sartre was among the first to note the dilemma of the African writer in expressing cultural independence (*négritude*) in a foreign language, French. "Now that which dangerously threatens to curb the effort of the Negro to reject our tutelage is that the apostles of the new negritude are constrained to edit their gospel in French. To incite the oppressed to unite they must have recourse to the words of the oppressor." *Black Orpheus* (1948), trans. S.W. Allen (Paris: Présence Africaine, 1963), 22. (*"Or ce qui risque de freiner dangereusement l'effort des noirs pour rejeter notre tutelle, c'est que les annonciateurs de la négritude sont contraints de rédiger en français leur évangile; pour inciter les opprimés à s'unir ils doivent avoir recours aux mots de l'oppresseur." Orphée Noir* [1948], Preface to *Anthologie de la nouvelle poésie nègre et malgache de langue française* by Léopold Sédar Senghor [Paris: Presses Universitaires de France, 1969], xviii.)

25. Christopher Miller, *Theories of Africans* (Chicago: University of Chicago Press, 1990), 182.

26. Gardinier, "Historical Origins," 10.

27. Senghor, *Éthiopiques* [1956] quoted in Jean-Louis Joubert, *Anthologie de la Littérature Francophone* (Paris: Nathan, 1992), 188.

Bibliography

Beti, Mongo. *La France contre l'Afrique: Retour au Cameroun*. Paris: La Découverte, 1993.

Clark, John F., and David E. Gardinier. *Political Reform in Francophone Africa*. Boulder, CO: Westview Press, 1997.

Davidson, Basil. *Modern Africa: A Social and Political History*. London: Longman, 1983.

Fanon, Frantz. *The Wretched of the Earth*. Preface by Jean-Paul Sartre. Translated by Constance Farrington. New York: Grove Press, 1963.

Fearon, James D., and David Laitin. "Ethnicity, Insurgency, and Civil War." *American Political Science Review* 97, no. 1 (2003): 75–90.

Gordon, April A., and Donald L. Gordon. *Understanding Contemporary Africa*. Boulder, CO: Lynne Rienner, 1996.

Huntington, Samuel. *The Clash of Civilizations and the Remaking of World Order*. New York: Simon and Schuster, 1996.

Joubert, Jean-Louis. *Anthologie de la Littérature Francophone*. Paris: Nathan, 1992.

Ki-Zerbo, Joseph. *Histoire de l'Afrique Noire*. Paris: Hatier, 1978.

Laitin, David D. "Hegemony and Religious Conflict: British Imperial Control and Political Cleavages in Yorubaland." *Bringing the State Back In*. Edited by Peter Evans et al. Cambridge: Cambridge University Press, 1985.

Laye, Camara. *L'Enfant noir*. Paris: Hatier, 1998. *The Dark Child*. Translated by James Kirkup. New York: Hill & Wang, 1994. A classic coming of age autobiography of communal life in colonial Guinea.

Mingst, Karen, and Jack Snyder. *Essential Readings in World Politics* (New York: W. W. Norton, 2001).

Sartre, Jean-Paul. *Black Orpheus*. Translated by S. W. Allen. Paris: Présence Africaine, 1976.

Schraeder, Peter. "Cold War to Cold Peace: Explaining U.S.-French Competition in Francophone Africa." *Political Science Quarterly* 115, no. 3 (2003): 395–419.

Toungara, Jeanne Maddox. "Ethnicity and Political Crisis in Côte d'Ivoire." *Journal of Democracy* 12, no. 3 (2001): 63–72. <http://muse.jhu.edu/journals/journal_of_democracy/v012/12.3toungara.html>.

Young, Crawford. "Democracy and the Ethnic Question in Africa." *Africa Insight* 27, no. 1 (1997): 4–14.

Widner, Jennifer A. *Economic Change and Political Liberalization in Sub-Saharan Africa*. Baltimore: The Johns Hopkins University Press, 1994.

Resource Guide

Further Reading

Adiaffi, Jean-Marie. *La carte d'identité*. Abidjan: CEDA, 1980. One of this novel's themes is the maintenance of French in the African educational system.

America in the World. The Hedgehog Review: Critical Reflections on Contemporary Culture 5, no. 1 (Spring 2003). The entire issue of this journal, published by the Institute for Advanced Studies in Culture at the University of Virginia, is of value. See in particular the articles by Samuel Huntington, Lionel Jospin, Robert Kaplan, and Carl Bowman.

Bâ, Mariama. *Une si longue lettre*. Dakar: Les Nouvelles Éditions Africaines, 1980. *So Long a Letter*. Translated by Modupé Bodé-Thomas. Oxford: Heinemann, 1989. A prize-winning short novel concerning life in postcolonial Senegal and the condition of women.

Boahen, A. Adu. *African Perspectives on Colonialism*. Johns Hopkins Symposia in Comparative History 15. Baltimore: Johns Hopkins University Press, 1989.

Gurr, Ted Robert. *Minorities at Risk: A Global View of Ethnopolitical Conflicts*. Washington, DC: United States Institute of Peace Press, 1993.

Kaplan, Robert D. *The Coming Anarchy: Shattering the Dreams of the Post Cold War*. New York: Random House, 2000.

———. *Black Writers in French: A Literary History of Negritude*. Washington, DC: Howard University Press, 1991.

Kesteloot, Lilyan. *Anthologie Négro-Africaine*. Vanves, France: EICEF, 1992.

Kom, Ambroise. *La Malédiction Francophone: Défis Culturels et Condition Post-Coloniale en Afrique*. Yaoundé: Clé, 2000.

Kourouma, Ahmadou. *The Suns of Independence*. Montréal: Les Presses de l'Université de Montréal, 1968.

Kulick, Katherine. *Voix Francophones: Discussions sur le monde contemporain*. Boston: Heinle & Heinle Publishers, 1994.

M'Bokolo, Elikia. *Afrique Noire et Civilisations*. Paris: Hatier, 1992.

Miller, Christopher. *Theories of Africans*. Chicago: University of Chicago Press, 1990.

Packer, George. "Gangsta War." *New Yorker*, November 3, 2003, 68–77.

Politique Africaine 89 (mars 2003). Entire issue is devoted to *"La Côte d'Ivoire en guerre"* (the Ivory Coast at war).

Taras, Raymond C., and Ganguly, Rajat. *Understanding Ethnic Conflict.* New York: Addison-Wesley Educational Publishers, 2002.

Films/Videos

All films listed below have English subtitles.

Aimé Cesaire: Une Voix Pour l'Histoire. Dir. Euzhan Palcy. Saligna and So On. Videocassette. California Newsreel, 1994. A long, three-part documentary on the life and poetry of Césaire, the *martiniquais* statesman and poet who was one of the fathers of the *Négritude* movement.

Black and White in Color (*La Victoire en chantant*). Dir. Jean-Jacques Annaud. Perf. Jean Carmet, Jacques Dufilho. Allied Artists, 1977. Videocassette. Lorimar Home Video, 1987. Often hilarious parody of colonial decadence and exploitation during the First World War in French Equatorial Africa.

Chocolat. Dir. Claire Denis. Perf. Isaach de Bankolé, Aimée Dahlens. Verbotene Sehnsucht, 1988. Videocassette. Orion Classics, 1989. The story of a young Frenchwoman who returns to Cameroon, where she had spent her childhood in a colonial outpost.

Frantz Fanon: Black Skin, White Mask. Dir. Isaac Julien. Perf. Colin Salmon. Arts Council of England. Videocassette. California Newsreel, 1996. Biographical treatment of the *martiniquais* psychiatrist who became a leading theorist of anticolonialism.

La Rue Cases-Nègres (*Black Shack Alley*). Dir. Euzhan Palcy. Perf. Darling Legitimus, Garry Cadenat. SUMAFA Productions, 1983. Videocassette. New Yorker Video, 1995. Well-loved adaptation of Joseph Zobel's 1953 autobiographical novel about growing up black and poor in neocolonial Martinique in 1930.

Le Grand Blanc de Lambarene. Dir. Bassek ba Kobhio. Perf. André Wilms, Marisa Berenson. Cameroon/France. Videocassette. California Newsreel, 1995. The film interprets Nobel Peace Prize winner Albert Schweitzer through the eyes of the colonized.

Lumumba: La Mort du Prophète. Dir. Raoul Peck. Perf. Eriq Ebouaney, Alex Descas. France/Germany/ Switzerland. Videocassette. California Newsreel, 1992. Acclaimed documentary about Patrice Lumumba, first president of the former Belgian Congo (now Zaïre, or Republic of Congo), the role of the Western media in portraying him, and the fate that awaited him.

Pièces d'Identités. Dir. Mweze Ngangura. Perf. Gérard Essomba Many, Dominique Mesa. Congo/Belgium. Videocassette. California Newsreel, 1998. Prize-winning film dealing with the heritage of colonialism and the African diaspora in Europe.

Newspaper and Journal Articles

If your library or a nearby college or university library subscribes to Lexis-Nexis or ProQuest, you will find these to be valuable sources for searching newspaper and journal articles in English or French.

Web Sites

K-12 Electronic Guide for African Resources on the Internet:
> <http://www.sas.upenn.edu/African_Studies/K-12/menu_EduLANG.html>

Articles tracking the latest developments in Ivory Coast, as well as a photo essay on political issues:
> <http://allafrica.com/cotedivoire/>

Daily news about Ivory Coast:
> <http://www.abidjan.net/>

Links to national institutions, political parties, and other information sources concerning Ivory Coast:
> <http://www.gksoft.com/govt/en/ci.html>

Côte d'Ivoire-Libertés, a site for dialogue and exchange about the future of the nation:
> <http://www.cotedivoire-libertes.org/>

Fraternité Matin, an online newspaper covering all aspects of life in Ivory Coast, including culture, society, politics, and sports:
> <http://www.fratmat.co.ci/>

Competing view of the political situation in Ivory Coast can be found on the Web site of the *Mouvement Patriotique de Côte d'Ivoire* (MPCI), which also includes links to other news sources around the world:
> <http://www.mpci–online.fr.st/>

Africa Web Links: An annotated resource list:
> <http://www.sas.upenn.edu/African_Studies/Home_Page/WWW_Links.html>

PART III

Equality

CHAPTER 8

The Parity Law of 2000: *Aux Armes, Citoyennes!*

La parité (parity), meaning equal representation for women in political life, has been relatively slow to arrive in France in spite of the nation's historic commitment to equality. Article 6 of the Declaration of the Rights of Man and of the Citizen (*Déclaration des droits de l'homme et du citoyen*, 1789) states that "all citizens, being equal, are eligible for all public functions, positions and employment, according to their ability and without any distinction other than that of their skills and talents" ("*Tous les citoyens étant égaux sont admissibles à toutes dignités, places et emplois publics, selon leur capacité et sans autre distinction que celle de leurs vertus et de leurs talents*"). Two years later, the early feminist writer Olympe de Gouges published her own version of Article 6 in her *Déclaration des droits de la femme et de la citoyenne* (1791), in which she corrected the original to read "*toutes les citoyennes et tous les citoyens.*" De Gouges seemed to understand very well that the masculine form of the word *citoyen* would not necessarily apply universally to all French citizens, and that women might well be excluded from equality of opportunity in public life. She was guillotined in 1793.

Some two hundred years later, French women came to embrace de Gouges's perspective on the integration of women in French political life. In 1999, as a result of many years of lobbying by feminists and others concerned with women's rights, the French legislature, meeting at Versailles, amended two articles in the constitution of the Fifth Republic, and then enacted in June 2000 a parity law—the first of its kind in the world—that would ensure that men and women have equal representation in elective office and in the public sphere.

Background

French Women and Politics

The history of the evolution of women's presence—or absence—in elective office in France should probably take into account certain monarchical traditions that separate France from many other European countries. In the British, Dutch, and Danish monarchies, for example, women may succeed to the throne and rule as monarchs, rather than as wives of monarchs with no political power. Salic law, adopted by the French monarchy in the fourteenth century, denied the crown to female offspring.[1] (*Salic* is the adjective referring to the Salian Franks, who ruled France during the fifth century.) When King Louis X died in the early part of the fourteenth century, leaving only a six-year-old daughter, and when King Philippe V died a few years later, leaving no male heirs, adult male relatives were crowned instead of the female children who were in line to succeed their fathers. As a result, women were systematically excluded from royal power, though many functioned as regents when their children were not old enough to rule. This situation lasted for well over five hundred years.

The French Revolution did not bring political power to women, since it accorded limited suffrage only to men. The revolution of 1848, though it extended suffrage further, still did not seek to include women. During the years of the Third Republic, the deputies debated the vote for women and proposed first to give it only to war widows, and then only to women older than twenty-five years of age, and finally only in local elections.[2] Frenchwomen did not receive full suffrage until the liberation of the nation at the end of World War II, after the French Senate had refused several times to ratify the National Assembly's legislation in this regard. Some scholars have theorized that Frenchwomen had to wait for the vote more than twenty years longer than their Anglo-Saxon counterparts because the centrist and leftist governments in power after World War I were afraid that women, given their long association with domestic and family concerns and their close ties with the

Catholic Church in France, might vote too conservatively and thus return the right to power.

Since World War II, Frenchwomen have not generally improved their presence on the political scene.[3] Some critics ascribe their exclusion from power to electoral traditions that favor incumbents, some of whom have been in office for several terms, and to the practice, only recently limited, of allowing politicians to hold a number of offices at the same time (*le cumul des mandats*). The consequence of that practice was to control the number of new faces that might enter politics. French politicians also quite often circulate among various posts, staying active in political life for decades.[4] The effect of these practices has been until very recently to make it seem as if public life in France were somehow a closed men's club, a fratriarchy, as one critic terms it,[5] where women are neither invited nor tolerated. This exclusion had already been predicted during the late nineteenth century by the suffragette Hubertine Auclert, who maintained that the right to vote would not necessarily guarantee equality between men and women, and that the law "should impose equality in representation."[6] In addition, French legislative and municipal elections, for example, function through majority rule rather than proportional representation, which is the case for elections to the European Parliament. As a result, smaller parties and nontraditional candidates are unlikely to gain representation.

If the experience of women in French political life is compared to that of women in the countries of northern Europe, the disparity becomes even more noticeable. Women in Scandinavian countries, for example, hold in most cases at least one-third of the seats in parliament, compared to the French *Assemblée Nationale*, where at the end of the twentieth century women held less than 6 percent of the seats, though they represented 53 percent of the electorate. Only Greece was below France in this regard.[7] On a local level, Frenchwomen fare even worse. Of the thirty-five cities with more than 100,000 inhabitants, only one has a female mayor. In the remainder of the 36,000 communes in France, women represent less than 8 percent of mayors.

How is it possible, in a nation that proclaimed the universal values of *liberté*, *égalité*, and *fraternité*, that women have been so systematically marginalized from public life? The word *fraternity* perhaps contains a clue, insofar as it seems already to assume that women will be absent from definitions of citizenship.[8] Some have argued that seventeenth- and eighteenth-century scientific theory judged the nature of women to be entirely different from that of men. According to one scholar, liberal democratic theory, elaborated during the era just before the French Revolution, "divides human activity into the public and private realms, and assigns politics to the public and women to the private."[9] Women's exclusion from the public sphere in France in turn became the basis of their inferior status through the next centuries, and still plays a role in sex discrimination.

The confining of women to domestic life meant as well that they would play no role at all in the important decisions in the life of the country. The domestic work they performed was thus devalued; their status was reduced to that of inferiority to their husbands and fathers. In fact, the *Code Civil*—the set of laws that governs French society enacted at the beginning of the nineteenth century under Napoleon—enshrined this inferiority in law. Women maintained the same status as minors and were kept completely under the tutelage of their husbands. A wife needed her husband's authorization to spend her salary check as she wished, and until the mid-1960s she needed his permission to work.[10] More importantly, perhaps, until the end of the 1960s women typically did not choose to enter the university. They preferred shorter courses of study, since their aspirations were not necessarily to embark upon careers.

It is true as well that the French feminist movement only recently began to claim for women their place in the halls of political power. In the 1970s and 1980s, when French feminism was most active, the struggle focused primarily on questions of equality of opportunity in the workplace, on domestic inqualities,[11] and on the individual rights of women in areas such as reproduction and abortion.[12] For example, abortion was legalized in 1975, the same year women won the right to divorce by mutual consent. Many radical feminists believed at the time that any participation in the political process amounted to a compromise with patriarchal power, which they saw as completely oppressive. It was not until the 1990s, and to some extent with the example of their sisters elected to the European Parliament in Strasbourg from other countries in the European Union, that Frenchwomen turned their attention to their lack of participation in electoral life.

Achieving Parity

The early movement toward parity took the form of a demand for quotas that favored a certain percentage of women. In 1982 it was proposed that electoral lists in municipal elections be composed of no more than 75 percent of candidates of the same sex—presumably male.[13] The *Conseil Constitutionnel* ruled that such a law would have the effect of dividing French citizens into categories—something the constitution of the Fifth Republic does not tolerate.[14] It understands a citizen to be someone either male or female, so that the proposed law would effectively undermine the "unity and indivisibility of the French people."[15] Put slightly differently, the constitution does not recognize the gender of French citizens, and thus the notion of a quota to achieve affirmative action for women was automatically rejected. Some feminists were not in favor of the proposition either, finding it humiliating that women, who compose more than 50 percent of the electorate, might settle for only 25 percent representation.[16] In addition, many felt that instituting a quota would have the effect of creating a ceiling, rather than a base for expansion.[17] This decision by the *Conseil Constitutionnel* made it preferable that the constitution be amended in order to provide for parity.

About ten years after the decision, a book relaunched the parity debate. *Au pouvoir citoyennes: liberté, égalité, parité* (1992, *Women in Power: Liberty, Equality, Parity*), written by Françoise Gaspard, Claude Servan-Schreiber, and Anne Le Gall, proposed that parity be written into the law in such a way as to avoid the notion of quotas. The authors suggested that any elected bodies in France, whether local or national, be composed of as many men as women. Those in favor of this proposal cited the charter recently drawn up by representatives to the summit on women in power held in Athens in 1992, claiming that true democracy required parity in "the representation and administration of nations."[18] Shortly afterward, a group of 289 women and 288 men published the *Manifeste des 577 pour une démocratie paritaire* in the November 10, 1993 issue of *Le Monde*. This document called for a law that would ensure that all elected assemblies in France be composed of as many men as women. The number 577 was chosen for its symbolic value; it represented the number of deputies in the National Assembly. Three years later, another manifesto, this time signed by ten important female political figures, was published in *L'Express*, again calling for equal representation of women in elected positions. At the same time, female ministers in several different governments in Europe signed a charter calling for women to participate in European politics and institutions.[19]

By the mid-nineties, the parity movement was in full swing; the French electorate was well over 80 percent in favor of parity; and several laws proposing a change in the constitution of the Fifth Republic had been put forward. In addition, several leftist party lists (especially the Green Party, *les Verts*) for representatives to the European Parliament had expressly chosen to achieve parity. Finally, Jacques Chirac, elected to his first term as president in 1995, created a group known as the *Observatoire de la parité* (Equal Opportunity Observatory) and charged with the mission of "producing analyses and making proposals concerning the situation of women" (*"produire des analyses et faire des propositions concernant la situation des femmes"*).[20] Chirac's center-right government did not go far enough to meet the wishes of those who were militating for parity, but when the left returned to power in the National Assembly, the new prime minister, Lionel Jospin, announced his intention to modify the constitution. His government proposed adding a new element to Article 3 stating the following: "The law favors equal access of men and women to elective office and public functions" (*"La loi favorise l'égal accès des femmes et des hommes aux mandats et fonctions"*). During the debate that followed this proposal, the French legislature also adopted an amendment that modified Article 4 of the constitution requiring political parties to put into practice the principle stated in Article 3.[21]

In 1999 the government proposed a law that would require that party electoral lists for towns of more than 3,500 inhabitants as well as for regional, senatorial, and European elections be composed of 50 percent women. Political parties would be fined if their lists for legislative (National Assembly) elections were not made up of an equal number of male and female candidates. With respect to gender balance, then, France had gone much farther than other countries in Europe, for which the quota for female candidates remained at 33 percent.[22] After a year of negotiation, the law was accepted as constitutional by the *Conseil constitutionnel*, and in June 2000 was ratified by the National Assembly.

Gisèle Halimi, the Socialist deputy who proposed the original 1982 amendment to the municipal electoral law that the *Conseil constitutionnel* had annulled, reminds us that the amendments to the constitution voted by the deputies do not mention the word *parity*. She suspects that the lawmakers were reluctant to challenge outright the concept of universalism on which French citizenship is founded. Halimi notes as well that the use of the verb *favoriser* rather than a stronger one, such as *établir* or *assurer*, makes it possible for any strong measures taken to ensure true parity to be challenged again by the *Conseil constitutionnel*.[23]

The ten women members of the original *Observatoire de la Parité* representing political, social, educational, business and press organizations, 1997. (© Micheline Pelletier/Corbis Sygma)

In the elections for the European Parliament in 1999, Frenchwomen achieved an important victory. They won thirty-five seats out of eighty-seven, or about 40 percent of the total. In the municipal elections of 2001, women candidates fared even better; almost 48 percent of the members of local councils are now women (in towns of more than 3,500 inhabitants). On the legislative side, however, things have not gone as well. In the last elections for the National Assembly in June 2002, women raised their presence from 11 percent in 1997 to just 12 percent of the deputies.

The newly elected women in local councils tend to be younger than the men and to come from the middle and upper classes. The large majority are highly educated. They are less likely to have children and less likely to be married. In this respect, the parity law has not addressed other inequalities, such as social class, level of education, and other markers of the elite in France.[24] In contemporary France, women form almost one-half of the workforce, and they now outnumber men in postsecondary education. These two factors, along with a decline in the practice of religion, can explain to a large extent not only women's growing interest in politics, but also their tendency to vote left of center.[25]

Parity and Affirmative Action: Is There a Difference?

Those who are in favor of parity are quick to distinguish it from affirmative action as it is practiced in both the United States and some Scandinavian countries. While affirmative action and parity both depend on the premise that women are oppressed, those who support affirmative action maintain that it is meant to redress the historical imbalance of power between two groups. Affirmative action depends on the concept of a cultural construction of gender, rather than any real biological difference between men and women. Since society is responsible for creating inequality between men and women, society must reverse this situation by enacting laws that reject a difference between the sexes.[26] On the other hand, some of those who favor parity in France argue instead that there *is* a difference between men and women, and that this difference must be inscribed in the constitution in order that women not be subsumed as a category of men.[27]

Creating quotas to redress historical grievances is not the same thing as parity, which demands fifty-fifty representation, or what its supporters term "*une sur deux.*" Because parity does not depend on quotas, there would seem to be no implicit discrimination involved. Many of those opposed to parity on the basis that it could be considered as the enactment of a quota cite affirmative action in the United States as a poor model for France. These critics are thoroughly opposed to any kind of identity politics that create fragmentation in society and bring about the constant threat of particular groups claiming special privileges.

Affirmative action tries to correct the results of differential treatment between men and women (or between whites and minorities) by attempting to remedy what appears to be a statistical imbalance that results from discrimination. Although there exists in France a law regarding professional equality intended to combat sex discrimination in the workplace (the *Loi Roudy* of 1983, named for the former minister of women's rights, Yvette Roudy), affirmative action has never been enacted on a national or local scale. The many municipal, state, workplace, and school affirmative action committees and officers that we are familiar with in the United

States do not exist in France, even though France has signed the United Nations Convention on Women that urges countries to take measures against inequality. In addition, in 1996 the European Union adopted a recommendation that member countries institute strategies to guarantee "the promotion of a balanced participation of men and women in the decision-making process, and the development of appropriate measures" to ensure the enactment of these strategies.[28] France's parity law of 2000 is a first step in addressing the issue of inequality.

Discussion

Parity is needed for a true democracy.

Agree

Parity for women will enhance the functioning of democracy. Equality is the very basis of democratic theory, as it is the foundation of the feminist critique of masculine domination. While other homogeneous groups, such as ethnic minorities, blacks, Jews, and homosexuals, have experienced oppression at different moments in history, the marginalization of women has been a constant throughout history; and even within oppressed groups, women are frequently treated as inferior.[29]

History shows that regimes that oppress women (Vichy France and Nazi Germany during the Second World War; more recently the Taliban in Afghanistan)—enacting laws such as death sentences for abortion or adultery, consigning women to the home, and giving preference to religious law over civil law—are inevitably totalitarian in nature.[30] Extending parity to women is thus a step toward greater respect for democratic structures.

There is currently a gap between citizenship and representation, in the sense that while the French republic proclaims equality, in reality there are different definitions of the concept for men and for women. The social division of work and the relegation of women to the domestic or private sphere have caused women to be underrepresented in politics as well as in the decision-making process as it affects economic and social conditions.

European countries generally, including France, have for the last thirty years created structures to achieve change from the top down. That is, they have instituted government ministers or secretaries for the family, for youth, and for women. Yet in spite of this

181

"state feminism," as one critic terms it, equality has yet to be achieved in a number of areas, including education, salaries, and women's rights (including abortion, contraception, sexual harassment, and violence against women).[31] Legislatures with balanced male–female representation can be expected to be more attuned to the problems of women and minorities than all-male or primarily male assemblies.

The notion that supporting parity will open the door to all minority claims for representation doesn't seem logical where women are concerned, since women do not represent a community in the same way minorities do. The sharing of public power by women can, on the other hand, encourage diversity and pluralism in representation, thus ensuring that all voices will be heard.

Disagree

Parity is not suited to the concept of republican citizenship. The idea that the citizen is either male or female is a dangerous one because it encourages the division of the citizenry into groups or communities. The French republic is founded on the notion of a unitary relationship between the citizen and the state. That is, there are no exclusive categories of individuals (such as sex, religion, or ethnicity), but rather simply individuals. The notion of parity, depending as it does on the idea of categories, would open the door for any number of other groups, minorities, or communities to claim lack of proportional representation.

Elected representatives serve citizens, not members of a particular sex, religion, or race. As one analyst has remarked, "a person is elected not to represent individual particularities, but all the citizens in their neutrality, which is the basis of their rights and their freedom."[32] The demand for parity assumes that elected women are meant only to represent female citizens, and elected men will only represent male citizens. This suggests that the notion of gender is more important than the condition of citizenship.[33]

Furthermore, the parity law is itself incompatible with the notion of real equality in a democracy because, rather than confronting or acting on the obstacles that stand in the way of women achieving equal access to public life (educational limitations, family obligations), it simply creates or substitutes a false equality. In this respect, the parity law does not address the question of class or economic difference. That is, not all women experience discrimination to the same degree.

Legislation is necessary to ensure equality of representation.

Agree

Equality of representation of men and women in a democracy must acknowledge the question of difference between the sexes. Why is this so? The notion that in a universalist nation like France there is no difference between men and women has for centuries been responsible for the exclusion of women, by equating the feminine sex with the masculine.[34] The claim that universalism includes women (and all minorities) is abstract and doesn't take into account the reality that the citizen is always implicitly white and male—in spite of the fact that Frenchwomen outnumber Frenchmen. From this perspective, equality of rights does not necessarily guarantee equality of opportunity. That is why either a law or an amendment to the French constitution was necessary.

The idea of universalism has always masked discrimination, since the history of France shows that elected assemblies have been homogeneous with regard to sex, color, and social class. Parity assumes that women are "neither a minority nor a social category." They constitute, rather, one-half of the population and can be found in "all social categories."[35] In addition, the *Code Civil* already recognizes a difference between men and women. The constitution of the Fifth Republic, dating from 1958, explicitly guarantees equal rights for women.

The argument that women who run for office under a parity system might be less qualified does not make sense, since female candidates would be chosen from among active party members, just as male candidates are now.[36] In this respect, they would have the same political commitment as men. Presidential elections in France have shown that qualified women frequently run independently for office when they are not constrained by party politics.

The notion that voters will be forced to cast their votes for female candidates against their will ignores the fact that for decades women have virtually had no choice other than male candidates. However, those who support parity have proposed a system by which new districts will be created in the National Assembly in order to run a male and a female candidate in each one. This solution responds to critics who argue that their free choice is being affected.

Disagree

It is not the case that French universalism (here, the notion that the French state does not recognize the gender of citizens) is responsible for discrimination against women, but rather that the principles of universalism have never been respected. The argument that universalism is a mask for excluding one-half of the human race thus seems to turn facts on their heads. In addition, if women were excluded from French political life because of their difference, isn't it now paradoxical to wish to include them by asserting their difference?[37]

While it is true that women are underrepresented in political and public life generally, this is due to their lack of participation in organizations that affect politics. The preamble to the French constitution already states that "the law guarantees, in all areas, equality of men and women." Parity may have the effect of denying freedom to voters by forcing them to vote for female candidates.

Women can only achieve parity through the personal qualifications and competence that will get them elected. Instituting parity will probably mean that women will be selected to run for public office because of their sex, rather than their talents or abilities. In fact, legislating difference might mean that traditional or stereotypical views of women as more practical, more sensitive, or less individualistic than men would once more be legitimized. If women have struggled for decades to overcome the idea that biology is destiny, why support legislation that might give new credence to those who maintain that women have a special nature? Doesn't the parity law therefore deprive women of their freedom by asserting that they can become only what their gender dictates? Doesn't it suggest that women are incapable of achieving equality based on their merits? Doesn't the parity law support the image of women as victims?

Questions and Activities

1. Much of the debate about parity in France turned on the problem of identities or categories. That is, recognizing women as a category could lead to acknowledgment of the demands of other minority categories, such as those based on race or ethnicity. This system of identity politics is something that French universalism does not tol-

erate. Debate in class whether it is possible to see the category of gender as somehow different from other kinds of identities.

2. In a similar vein, one important argument against parity was suggested by a certain faction on the left that believed that women should retain their identification with oppressed minorities rather than establish gender as a category transcending all others. Organize a debate in which you discuss whether women as a category share many of the social and economic concerns of minorities.

3. Compare the issue of parity with the question of *discrimination positive* (affirmative action) at Sciences Po (Chapter 9). Are these two concepts related? Do they differ in significant ways? Write a short report.

4. The 2002 presidential elections in France were noteworthy for the large number of candidates (sixteen) in the first round. Working in groups, research the women candidates who ran, and report on the platforms and parties they represented. See, for example, Corinne Lepage, <http://www.adminet.com/poli/lepage/>; Christiane Taubira, <http://www.assemblee-nat.fr/12/tribun/fiches_id/ 2791.asp>; Arlette Laguiller, <http://www.lutte-ouvriere .org/elc2002/pre/>; and Christine Boutin, <http://www .assemblee-nat.fr/12/tribun/fiches_id/632.asp>.

5. The Green Party (*Les Verts*) has been in the forefront of women's rights since the 1980s. Look up *Les Verts* online at <http:// www.les-verts.org/> and report back to the class on the main objectives of the party with regard to women's issues.

6. Those in favor of parity in France base their arguments largely on the notion that entire categories of citizens (women, minorities) are excluded by an abstract notion of universalism, one that in fact posits a white, male citizen. Has this also been the case in the United States? Justify your perspective.

7. Many of those who support the parity law in France make a distinction between sex and gender. How would you define this difference?

8. Those who argue for parity support the notion that a greater representation of women in the French parliament would have an effect on the way politics is conducted. What influences can one imagine women might have on the decision-making process? In what ways might parity bring about social change? You may want to debate in class the entire question of whether women have special qualities that make their approach to politics different from that of men.

9. Research the Equal Rights Amendment (ERA) to the Constitution of the United States, first proposed in 1921. See, for example, <http://www.now.org/issues/economic/eratext.html>. What

were the reasons for proposing this amendment? Why did it fail? What cultural reasons might explain the failure of the ERA in the United States, but the passage of a parity law in France? Debate the need for the ERA in class.

Vocabulary/Vocabulaire

Nouns/Substantifs

abortion	l'avortement (m.)
access	l'accès (m.)
amendment	l'amendement (m.)
candidate	le candidat, la candidate
category	la catégorie
change	le changement
citizen	le citoyen, la citoyenne
citizenship	la citoyenneté
commitment	l'engagement (m.)
competence	la compétence
death sentence	la peine de mort
debate	le débat
democracy	la démocratie
equality	l'égalité (f.)
gap	le fossé
gender	le genre
government	le gouvernement
individual	l'individu (m.)
legislature	l'assemblée nationale (f.)
minister	le (la) ministre
parity	la parité
political party	le parti politique
political platform	la plate-forme électorale
politics	la politique
power	le pouvoir
presidential elections	les présidentielles (f.)
quality	la qualité
regime	le régime

salary	le salaire
secretary	le (la) secrétaire
sex	le sexe
sexual harassment	le harcèlement sexuel
sphere	la sphère
stereotype	le stéréotype
theory	la théorie

Verbs/Verbes

act	agir
confront	affronter
decide	prendre une décision
deserve	mériter
elect	élire
function	fonctionner
guarantee	garantir
share	partager
run (for office)	être candidat (e)
vote	voter

Adjectives/Adjectifs

elected	élu, -e
feminine	féminin, -e
feminist	féministe
homogeneous	homogène
individual	individuel, individuelle
masculine	masculin, -e
totalitarian	totalitaire

Notes

1. In fact, the origins of the Hundred Years' War in the fourteenth century can be traced to a dispute between France and England about Edward III's right to the French throne through his mother's line. See Geneviève Fraisse in Elaine Viennot, ed., *La démocratie "à la française,"* (Paris: Publications de l'Université de Paris VII, 1996), or Janine Mossuz-Lavau, "La Parité

hommes/femmes en politique," available at http://www.info-france-usa.org /fr/aaz/par_hf.asp, January 2001, p. 1.

2. Françoise Gaspard, "La Parité se heurte-t-elle à des contraintes juridiques?" in *La Parité. Enjeux et mise en œuvre*, ed. Jacqueline Martin (Toulouse: Presses Universitaires du Mirail, 1998), 215.

3. During the Fourth Republic (1946–1958), however, a healthy Communist Party wielded significant electoral clout and was responsible for bringing more women into the political process. See Dorothy McBride Stetson, "Democracy and the Representation of Women: France in Comparative Context," *Contemporary French Civilization* 25, no. 2 (2001), 182.

4. Jack Lang, for example, a member of the Socialist Party, has served as municipal council member, regional council member, representative in the *Assemblée Nationale*, minister of culture, minister of education, and European deputy, all in the space of only twenty years, and frequently holding overlapping positions.

5. Françoise Gaspard, "La Parité, principe ou stratégie?" *Le Monde diplomatique*, novembre 1998, 27.

6. Quoted in ibid., 26.

7. It is the case, however, that the European Union, though pronouncing itself in favor of equal rights for all citizens (in the 1992 Treaty of Maastricht), is nevertheless very unequal in the representation of women in administrative positions. See Eliane Vogel-Polsky, "Faire de l'Union un levier pour l'égalité des sexes," *Le Monde diplomatique*, juillet 1996, 7.

8. See Stetson, "Democracy," on this point, 188.

9. Ibid., 185.

10. Laurence Wylie and Jean-Claude Brière, *Les Français*, 3rd ed. (Upper Saddle River, NJ: Prentice-Hall, 2001), 129.

11. Through the end of the twentieth century, women in France continued to bear the heaviest burden of domestic tasks. In households with children, women (though working outside the home) continued to be the primary caregivers. See "Famille: les 'nouveaux pères' ont disparu," *Le Monde* 27 mai 2000, 1.

12. Janine Mossuz-Lavau, "La Parité hommes/femmes en politique," and Gaspard, "La Parité, principe ou stratégie," 26.

13. In municipal elections, candidates form a list (usually party-based), and electors vote for the entire list rather than for single candidates.

14. The nine members of the *Conseil Constitutionnel* are charged with overseeing presidential and other elections and referenda, and ruling on the constitutionality of proposed laws.

15. Gisèle Halimi, "Parité, je n'écris pas ton nom . . . ," *Le Monde diplomatique*, septembre 1999, 7.

16. Gisèle Halimi, "Etablir l'égalité politique: un référendum pour les femmes," *Le Monde diplomatique*, octobre 1994, 32ff, and Mossuz-Lavau, "La Parité hommes/femmes," 2.

17. Gaspard, "La Parité, principe ou stratégie?," 26.

18. Mossuz-Lavau, "La Parité hommes/femmes," 2.

19. In 1995 Prime Minister Alain Juppé named twelve women to ministerial and secretarial posts in his government, and later fired eight of them. The media referred to them satirically as miniskirts (*les jupettes*). The manifesto in *L'Express* was probably written in response to what was perceived as the tokenization of women in politics. See Sandrine Dauphin and Jocelyne Praud, "Introduction: Debating and Implementing Gender Parity in French Politics," *Modern and Contemporary France* 10, no. 1 (2002), 8.

20. Mossuz-Lavau, "La Parité hommes/femmes," 3.

21. Ibid.

22. Ibid.

23. Halimi, "Parité," 7.

24. Mariette Sineau, "Débuts laborieux pour la parité," *Le Monde diplomatique*, mars 2002, 23.

25. Janine Mossuz-Lavau, *Femmes/hommes: pour la parité* (Paris: Presses de Sciences Po, 1998), 17–21.

26. Christine Delphy, "Comment en finir avec l'exclusion des femmes," *Le Monde diplomatique*, mars 1997, 6.

27. Ibid. See also Joan Scott, *Gender and the Politics of History* (New York: Columbia University Press, 1998), on the paradox that has always faced French feminists. On the one hand, they must argue against difference in order to be considered as individuals; on the other, they must argue for difference in order to be heard.

28. Quoted in Eliane Viennot, "Pour la parité," *Le Monde diplomatique*, mars 1997, 6.

29. Vogel-Polsky, "Faire de l'Union," 6.

30. "Etablir l'égalité politique: un référendum pour les femmes," *Le Monde diplomatique*, octobre 1994, 32ff.

31. Vogel-Polsky, "Faire de l'Union," 6.

32. Georges Obidzinski, "Un référendum pour les femmes," *Le Monde diplomatique*, novembre 1994, 2.

33. Ibid.

34. Halimi, "Etablir l'égalité politique," 32ff.

35. Viennot, "Pour la parité," 6.

36. Mossuz-Lavau, "La Parité hommes/femmes," 4.

37. See <http://www.mix-cite.org/expose/index.php3?RefArticle=148> for an excellent discussion of this paradox (p. 6).

Bibliography

Dauphin, Sandrine, and Jocelyne Praud. "Introduction: Debating and Implementing Gender Parity in French Politics." *Modern and Contemporary France* 10, no. 1 (2002): 5–11.

Delphy, Christine. "Comment en finir avec l'exclusion des femmes." *Le Monde diplomatique* mars 1997: 6–7.

"Famille: les 'nouveaux pères' ont disparu." *Le Monde* 27 mai 2000: 1.

Gaspard, Françoise. "La Parité, principe ou stratégie?" *Le Monde diplomatique* novembre 1998: 26–27.

———. "La Parité se heurte-t-elle à des contraintes juridiques?" In *La Parité. Enjeux et mise en oeuvre*. Edited by Jacqueline Martin. Toulouse: Presses Universitaires du Mirail, 1998.

———, Claude Servan-Schreiber, and Anne le Gall. *Au pouvoir citoyennes: liberté, égalité, parité*. Paris: Seuil, 1992.

Halimi, Gisèle. "Etablir l'égalité politique: un référendum pour les femmes." *Le Monde diplomatique* octobre 1994: 32ff.

———. "Parité, je n'écris pas ton nom . . ." *Le Monde diplomatique* septembre 1999: 7.

Mossuz-Lavau, Janine. *Femmes/Hommes: pour la parité*. Paris: Presses de Sciences Po, 1998.

———. "La Parité hommes/femmes en politique." <http://www.info-france-usa.org/fr/aaz/par_hf.asp> (rubrique bienvenue en france), January 2001.

Obidzinski, Georges. "Un référendum pour les femmes." *Le Monde diplomatique* novembre 1994: 2.

Sineau, Mariette. "Débuts laborieux pour la parité." *Le Monde diplomatique* mars 2002: 23.

Stetson, Dorothy McBride. "Democracy and the Representation of Women: France in Comparative Context." *Contemporary French Civilization* 25, no. 2 (2001): 175–92.

Viennot, Eliane, ed. *La démocratie 'à la française' ou les femmes indésirables.* Paris: Publications de l'Université de Paris VII, 1996.

———. "Pour la parité." *Le Monde diplomatique* mars 1997: 6–7.

Vogel-Polsky, Eliane. "Faire de l'Union un levier pour l'égalité des sexes." *Le Monde diplomatique* juillet 1996: 6–7.

Wylie, Laurence, and Jean-Claude Brière. *Les Français*. 3rd ed. Upper Saddle River, NJ: Prentice-Hall, 2001.

Resource Guide

Further Reading

Allwood, G., and K. Wadia. *Women and Politics in France 1958–2000*. New York: Routledge, 2000.

Badinter, Elisabeth. "La Parité est-elle une régression?" *L'Evénement du jeudi* 4 février 1999: 86–89.

Bard, Christine. *Les Filles de Marianne, histoires des féminismes, 1914–1940*. Paris: Fayard, 1999.

Bataille, Philippe, and Françoise Gaspard. *Comment les femmes changent la politique*. Paris: Editions la Découverte, 1999.

Beaugé, Florence. "La démocratie inachevée." *Le Monde diplomatique* mars 1997: 6.

Duchen, Claire. *Women's Rights and Women's Lives in France: 1944–1968*. New York: Routledge, 1994.

Martin, Jacqueline, ed. *La Parité. Enjeux et mise en oeuvre*. Toulouse: Presses Universitaires du Mirail, 1998.

Picq, Françoise. "Parité, la nouvelle 'exception française.'" *Modern and Contemporary France* 10, no. 1 (2002): 13–23.

Schor, Naomi. "The Crisis of French Universalism." *Yale French Studies* 100 (2001): 43–64.

Scott, Joan W. *Gender and the Politics of History*. New York: Columbia University Press, 1988.

Sensier, Sophie. "Spécificité française: la démocratie sans les femmes." *Le Monde diplomatique* mars 2002: 23.

Sineau, Mariette. "The Two Faces of Parity." *Le Monde diplomatique* décembre 1997, back page.

Tahon, Marie-Blanche. "La parité en débat au-delà de Versailles." *Modern and Contemporary France* 10, no. 1 (2002): 25–40.

Journals

Contemporary French Civilization 25, no. 2 (2001): special issue on parity.

Modern and Contemporary France 10, no. 1 (2002): special issue on parity.

Newspaper and Journal Articles

Lexis-Nexis <http://www.lexis-nexis.com/universe/> is an excellent source for online searching of newspaper articles, both in English and in French. A good source for journal articles as well as books is the OCLC First Search database. Check with your school librarian as to availability in your school or public library or at a nearby college or university. A CD-ROM of *Le Monde diplomatique,* containing articles on French culture and society from that journal through 2000, is available for purchase.

Web Sites

<http://www.observatoire-parite.gouv.fr/>
<http://www.social.gouv.fr/femmes/index.htm>
<http://www.insee.fr/fr/ffc/docs_ffc/femmes_et_hommes.htm>
Complete bibliography on the issue of parity:
<http://www.ac–bordeaux.fr/Etablissement/Sud/Medoc/ses/1999/parit_OO.htm>

CHAPTER 9

———•———

Affirmative Action at Sciences Po: Leveling the Playing Field

In October 2001 the Institut d'Etudes Politiques (known familiarly as Sciences Po) in Paris granted admission for the first time to a group of seventeen high school students who had not taken the usual route to this prestigious educational institution, one of France's *grandes écoles*. They had not passed the difficult entrance exam; rather, they entered Sciences Po with only their *baccalauréat* and a recommendation from their teachers in seven disadvantaged high schools in suburban Paris and the region of Nancy in northeastern France. Although the group was small, representing only about 5 percent of the incoming class, the decision to recruit these students in a nontraditional way opened the door to a continuing debate in France about the necessity and desirability of what the French call *discrimination positive*, or affirmative action.

To understand why admitting this small number of students would create nationwide discussion and parliamentary debate, we have to understand a number of things about how the French post-secondary educational system is structured, how it functions, whom it serves and prepares, and why the concept of affirmative action seems so distant from the founding principles of French education. Is it the case that, as one critic has noted, "equality is inscribed in the French mentality, but the egalitarian principles of the republic have not achieved hoped-for results" ("*En France, l'égalité est inscrite dans les mentalités, mais les principes égalitaires de la République n'ont pas donné les résultats escomptés*")?[1]

Background

Secondary and Postsecondary Education in France

The French school system is both public and private, though the Ministry of Education manages both sectors, paying salaries to teachers in both and ensuring that standards are maintained. About 15 percent of elementary students in France attend private schools (usually Catholic), as do about 20 percent of high school students. Students in both public and private high schools pass the *baccalauréat* exam at the end of their last year (*terminale*). They will have prepared a program of courses leading to three kinds of *baccalauréat* exams: general, technical, or professional. The general *baccalauréat* itself has three options: courses in the humanities and literature (Bac L), social sciences and economics (Bac ES), or the sciences (Bac S). The general *baccalauréat* is considered more difficult and more prestigious than the other two types.

In 1985 the government of President François Mitterrand announced a fifteen-year goal of 80 percent in the numbers of students passing the *baccalauréat*, a number that had previously hovered around 65 percent. That goal has been realized, opening up in turn the possibility of higher education for the vast majority of French children. About 70 percent nationally complete their education to the age of eighteen or nineteen, obtaining the *baccalauréat* diploma or a technical diploma (*brevet de technicien supérieur*) in vocational or technical subjects. Simultaneously, the number of French teenagers leaving school without any diploma has fallen to about 10 percent. More than 50 percent of teenagers go on to study for diplomas in higher education, a number that is seven times that of the previous generation. Clearly, French children of the third millennium are much better educated—certainly they stay in school longer—than their parents.

French universities accept all students who have completed their secondary education and have successfully passed the *baccalauréat* exam. Students may then choose from a wide variety of undergraduate and graduate diplomas and programs that last from two to eight years, opting to attend the university or to take further courses (*prépa*, short for *préparatoire*) that would prepare them for another postsecondary educational establishment, such as a *grande école*. The *grandes écoles* are far more selective and competitive than either the universities or the other technical schools (*Instituts universitaires de Technologie*, or IUTs; *Instituts universitaires de formation de maîtres*, or teacher education institutions). The elite *grandes écoles* prepare students for degrees in engineering (the Polytechnique, nicknamed X), teaching (the Ecole Normale Supérieure), administration and management (Ecole Normale d'Administration), and other scientific careers. These schools require five years of postsecondary coursework for entrance; candidates either have an advanced university degree or take a competitive entrance exam (*concours d'entrée*).

The French educational system is structured as a meritocracy; that is, at a series of different levels, success on exams will allow students to move onward and upward. Given these facts, then, and the very encouraging situation in what appears to be the democratization of the French education system, it is perhaps hard to understand why it might still be necessary to adopt *discrimination positive* to ensure that certain categories of students have access to the *grandes écoles*.

Higher Education and Social Privilege

Pierre Bourdieu and Jean-Claude Passeron's sociological studies of inequalities in the French school system show very clearly how social classes are reproduced through the examinations and *concours* that mark the progress of the French child through the grades from elementary school to university.[2] They argue that the use of such exams to differentiate among students "transforms privilege into merit," since social origin ensures that the middle- and upper-class child will automatically do better.[3] Why is this so? As Bourdieu and Passeron explain, the reasons are complex and involve both the family and the educational milieus.

Children of the middle and upper classes already have the cultural capital that comes from families in which certain ways of speaking and reasoning as well as habits of reading, visiting museums, listening to classical music, and other attitudes toward extracurricular culture are inculcated from an early age. This cultural capital is always recognized by teachers, who tend to reward certain kinds of writing and speaking styles and to denigrate others that do not connote particular kinds of intellectual aptitudes or signal membership in the intellectual elite.[4] As a result, children who do not share these sorts of social privileges usually come to believe that they will fail academically because they do not have the talent and the ability that they need to succeed. In the best of cases, they will tend to prepare diplomas that are less prestigious, such as those awarded by universities or IUTs.

School is therefore not necessarily a guarantee of social promotion for the working classes or for those who are socially disadvantaged (for example, by not living in a large city near theaters and museums), but rather a place in which the current social inequities and class divisions are reproduced. It is no wonder, then, that students who do not form part of the social elite are rarely to be found in the halls of the *grandes écoles*.

It is for these reasons that France's attempt to democratize access to higher education—dating primarily from the beginning of the 1980s—has yet to prove entirely successful. While it is true that young people today are far more likely to be educated (*scolarisé*), statistics show that not everyone has the same equality of opportunity. For example, children of working-class parents are seven times less likely than middle-class children to enroll in the university. Similarly, while middle-class children spend over seven and one-half years in higher education, working-class children spend less than half that time.[5] Moreover, contemporary sociologists argue that the middle class has benefited the most from the attempt to bring a true meritocracy to the French educational system, and that, as a result, the influx of masses of students has created an even more marked hierarchy among postsecondary institutions. In addition, the university has lately been losing its reputation for excellence, and a university diploma no longer guarantees financial and social success.[6] The *grandes écoles* continue, however, to maintain their elitist and exclusive status.

The Goals of the Grandes Ecoles

The first *grandes écoles* were founded by the monarchy in the middle of the eighteenth century to train both civilian and military engineers. These schools existed parallel to the university, which generally had no interest in providing preprofessional training. The first of these was the Ecole des Ponts et des Chaussées (a civil engineering school); some years later, during the revolutionary period, the Conservatoire National des Arts et Métiers (an applied arts school) and the Ecole Polytechnique (originally a military engineering school) joined their predecessors.

In the following century, the arrival of the Industrial Revolution in France created further need for technically educated students, as well as for managers of developing businesses. At the present time, graduates of the *grandes écoles* fill the majority of important government positions and serve as chief executives in major French companies. Many of these are engineering graduates from some of the schools mentioned above; others completed their studies at the Ecole Nationale d'Administration (ENA), a top-flight training institution for technocrats.[7] The *grandes écoles* are clearly meant to train France's managerial and technical elite; these schools maintain close ties with industry and government.

Sciences Po is no exception to the elitist profile sketched here. In comparison with the university, children of salaried employees are six times less represented, while children of workers are twelve times less likely to enroll. Over 80 percent of the students at Sciences Po are from the middle and upper classes; almost three-quarters of these are the children of teachers, managers, or executives.[8] The children of the working class make up less than 2 percent of the student body. Interestingly, Sciences Po has had to give scholarships to many of its students in recent years; almost one-quarter of the students receive scholarship aid in addition to the state tuition scholarships they already hold. This suggests that the children of teachers, in particular, fall into a group that could be considered needy.

For most students, admission to Sciences Po is usually based on a *concours d'entrée* (competitive entrance examination) which is different from a normal test. In a *concours*, there is no passing or failing grade. The number of candidates who succeed depends upon the number of places available, so that if there are twenty spots, the candidates who receive the top twenty grades will be accepted.[9] The seventeen students who were admitted under special circumstances to Sciences Po in the fall of 2001, though they did not take the *concours*, were nevertheless subjected to a very rigorous selection process and to very intensive preparation, culminating in an oral interview with a jury of professors from the school intended primarily to judge their motivation and potential for entrance to a *grande école*.

The students were all from high schools in what are known as *zones sensibles* (sensitive areas) or *zones d'éducation prioritaire* (ZEP priority education zones). These are areas (usually in the suburbs of large cities) with high immigrant and working-class populations.[10]

Eighty-five percent of the students were children of workers and salaried employees, and a third held dual citizenship (primarily from former French colonies).[11] For most students in these high schools, a *grande école* would be virtually inaccessible. Is this simply the nature of their high schools, or are there other forces at work to discourage ZEP students from seeking admission to elite postsecondary educational establishments?

In the foreground of the attempt to democratize higher education in France, a report authored by Jacques Attali in 1998 entitled *Pour un modèle européen d'enseignement supérieur* was one of the motors of the reform at Sciences Po. Attali's report indicated that it was virtually impossible for a child who attended elementary school in a ZEP to aspire to a *grande école*. Not only does the system function in order to maintain an elite, but the disadvantaged students themselves are psychologically and intellectually unprepared to attempt to enter a *grande école*.[12] In addition to the fact that they often come from broken families and live in poverty, they have internalized an attitude that excludes them.

As Bourdieu and Passeron predicted, students at high schools in *zones sensibles* are not oriented toward the *grandes écoles* because they do not have the cultural capital that would allow them either to succeed on the entrance exam or to do well in their courses. The *concours* for Sciences Po, for example, is a two-part exam. On the first part, candidates are expected to demonstrate wide knowledge of general culture (without any specific curricular preparation); on the second, they must show an excellent command of a second language. The cultural bias inherent in the first part of the exam is evident. In addition, students from disadvantaged schools virtually never have the opportunity to spend time in a foreign country in order to improve their language skills (*un séjour linguistique*).

Moreover, coursework at a *grande école* normally lasts between three and five years. Families of modest means cannot afford the luxury of such a lengthy time commitment. For this reason, students from working-class families are often oriented toward either short-term or technical diplomas in IUTs. These kinds of degrees can lead more quickly to jobs that demand specific skills.

The Sciences Po Experiment

Needless to say, the decision to accept students who had not taken the entrance exams did not meet with everyone's approval. Many students already at Sciences Po were resentful, worrying that their

Richard Descoings, director of the Institut d'Etudes Politiques (Sciences Po), stands outside the entrance of the school in Paris, March 15, 2001. (AP/Wide World Photos)

diplomas might be devalued because of the presence of others who had not met the same admissions criteria. A few students even referred to the newcomers uncharitably as boat people, alluding to the refugees who escaped from Southeast Asia after the fall of Saigon and who sought political asylum in the West.[13] Some of the newcomers were criticized for their refusal to observe the unofficial dress code at the school, and others were disparaged for using the familiar pronoun *tu* when addressing their professors. It became clear that the class gulf identified by Bourdieu and Passeron was present.

Less than two months after the Sciences Po plan was announced by its director, Richard Descoings, *Uni*, a right-wing student union, filed suit in the administrative court in Paris questioning the reform and requesting that it be suspended before the beginning of the following school year. The students in *Uni* cited the reform as being contrary to the principle of equality that prevails among high school *baccalauréat* recipients elsewhere in France.[14] The suit was ultimately rejected, and the candidates entered Sciences Po as planned. In November 2003, the administrative appeals court in Paris ruled that, in principle, the program of *discrimination positive* at Sciences Po is lawful.

In the future, Sciences Po plans to admit as many as sixty students per year by this nontraditional route (about 15 percent of the student body). In addition, merit scholarships, created by the former minister of education Claude Allègre in 1998, currently allow about five hundred students from disadvantaged backgrounds to prepare the entrance exams for the *grandes écoles* nationwide. Both students who are deemed admissible and their teachers will benefit from special preparation for Sciences Po. The teachers will familiarize themselves with the kind of written work expected of Sciences Po students and will have access to audiovisual materials to help students improve their oral expression. In their last year of high school (*terminale*), the future Sciences Po candidates will prepare and present a research project. Finally, once accepted at Sciences Po, these students will receive merit scholarship aid and funds for tutoring and housing.[15] Just before the school year begins, they will take intensive foreign language courses and receive further instruction in methodology and research. Clearly, the present policy of the French government, whether on the right or on the left, is intended to remedy a situation that seems to exclude students of modest means.

Change is often difficult to achieve in the French education system, which remains very centralized and thus resistant to innovation. The French generally agree that the egalitarian ideals of the system are not always achieved. They therefore understand the need to create ways of achieving social mobility among immigrant and second-generation immigrant children so that the future governing and managing elites can be more multiculturally and socially diverse. As for the pioneering students at Sciences Po, they showed themselves capable of doing as well as their more privileged peers: only two of the seventeen did not pass the year's work, which compares favorably with the normal 10 percent failure rate at the school.

Discussion

Testing is needed to ensure admission based on merit.

Agree

A lack of uniformity in admissions standards in the *grandes écoles* creates unfairness in the system. There are many students at Sciences

Po who arrive through the traditional route; that is, they work very hard for many months preparing for the entrance exams. Their families are not particularly wealthy or privileged, and they have no special help. Is it fair to admit others who might be slightly less advantaged? And what of those high schools that don't sign an agreement with Sciences Po, so that their students are excluded from the possibility of entering by nontraditional means? Is it fair to identify only certain ZEP high schools as eligible and ignore others, such as rural schools? Doesn't this create a system whereby the identity of the high school is more important than the notion of an exam itself?

A Sciences Po diploma has a certain meaning and a worth that stem in part from the difficulty of the entrance exams. Allowing students to bypass these exams means that the diploma loses its value. If the *grandes écoles* choose to revise their entrance criteria, they will become exactly like the universities, which admit everyone with a *baccalauréat*.

Finally, the *concours* provides an egalitarian method of judging candidates because it is an anonymous written examination. It is not the exam itself that is undemocratic, but the ways in which certain students are prepared to take it, while others are excluded from that opportunity as early as elementary school. In other words, the problem is one of equality of opportunity.

In preparation for this exam, it is theoretically already possible to recruit likely students in their sophomore year in high school (*seconde*), and to give them the necessary academic preparation for the entrance exams. Students who show potential could be identified early and could be tutored or prepared for the Sciences Po *concours*. Those who have chosen to attend the university could also be tutored, after they achieve a two-year diploma, in preparation for this exam. This is therefore a problem of counseling, not one of elitism. Rather than adopt a policy that creates a parallel route to the *grandes écoles*, it is better to fix the system that already exists and that is egalitarian in principle.

Disagree

If the education system in France is truly to be egalitarian, it must go beyond unquestioning allegiance to the shape of the present *concours* and accept that there are other ways of evaluating potential students. The method proposed by Sciences Po can even be considered more rigorous than an exam; students do, after all, complete an extensive research project and undergo an interview. In any case, at the present moment, there are already differences in the way candidates are evaluated, since ZEP students are not the only ones who are excused from the *concours d'entrée*.

Social inequalities are always reproduced in the school system, so it is hard to imagine a general *concours d'entrée* that could be completely fair. One could, however, test students on other, more specific forms of acquired scientific knowledge that those with technical or professional diplomas are better prepared to demonstrate.[16] This change would be predicated on opening Sciences Po admissions to students with degrees that usually exclude them from the *grandes écoles*, such as technical or shorter-cycle university diplomas.

However, as long as disadvantaged children continue to be oriented toward the less selective diplomas, there will never be a critical mass of these students in the elite schools. As the French system functions now, students are eliminated at every level, as those who demonstrate merit advance toward the most selective degrees. Ironically, the *baccalauréat* has begun to lose its value as the pass rates have increased, so that those French students who previously aspired to this diploma as a guarantee of social mobility now realize that it is only one step along a longer road. This is why it is important to create more varied methods of evaluation.

Affirmative action is the best way to achieve the democratization of higher education.

Agree

The best way to democratize the *grandes écoles* is to adopt a policy of *discrimination positive*. Affirmative action makes sense in a context where there has been a persistent lack of socioeconomic diversity in the nation's elite schools. In addition, admitting students from different backgrounds may well ensure multicultural diversity in the *grandes écoles*, which are otherwise socially and racially homogeneous. Studies in the United States have shown that the presence of minority students in the classroom can have a positive effect on student attitudes. More importantly for France, admission of students from widely diverse socioeconomic backgrounds may bring about a similarly diverse future generation of the nation's managing and technical elites.

For affirmative action to be more effective, however, it would be necessary to expand the number of ZEP schools that are included in the Sciences Po plan, and also to address the question of schools in rural France, where students are often just as socially and culturally disadvantaged as those in the *banlieues* (suburbs).[17] In addition, selection processes and coaching of students identified as good candidates for postsecondary education must begin even earlier than in high school.

Disagree

Selecting a few token representatives from disadvantaged schools (often immigrants or students of color) as a way of compensating for past imbalance can do a disservice to these students. They may feel that they are not the equal of their classmates because they benefited from special treatment, and remain stigmatized for the rest of their professional lives because their socioeconomic background may suggest that they were accepted at Sciences Po without passing the entrance exams. Such a situation actually encourages, rather than discourages, racial discrimination. It also preserves inequality in that the basic makeup of the school doesn't change; the only difference is that a small minority of students are from disadvantaged backgrounds. (The French refer to this kind of tokenism in schools as *étudiants alibis*, alibi students.) There is research in the United States that indicates that students do not necessarily rate a diverse campus more favorably than one with less diversity. Moreover, this research suggests that race relations are worse on campuses with high diversity levels and that there is "dissatisfaction with the quality of education."[18] Finally, while the attempt to democratize higher education is praiseworthy, by creating two kinds of students (those who take the admissions exam and those who don't), one creates two parallel systems with different criteria. In a democracy, this doesn't make sense. What would be more rational is a more generalized policy for addressing the issues of exclusion raised not only by the *concours d'entrée* to Sciences Po, but also by other diplomas (medicine and pharmacy, for example) and other elite schools (such as the Polytechnique).

Questions and Activities

1. Research the *baccalauréat* exam online, consulting <http://www.siec.education.fr/examens/bcg/Description.htm> or <http://www.annabac.com/>, particularly for an indication of the kinds of essay questions that are asked. What is its purpose? What subjects are included in each of the different types of *baccalauréat*? How is it graded? Is this type of exam possible in the United

States? Why or why not? Report your findings for these and other aspects of the exam to the class.

2. French sociologists have pointed out that if a school system is based on the idea that all of its pupils are equal, then it "cannot recognize any inequalities other than those arising from individual gifts."[19] Discuss this idea with reference to both France and the United States.

3. Although they do not specifically target immigrant children, ZEP schools nevertheless enroll primarily minority students and were created in areas where it is generally agreed that teaching conditions are not ideal. The ZEP policy provides for more teachers and thus smaller class sizes, as well as for larger budgets. Many French people objected to this unequal treatment for certain schools in a system that is based on egalitarian principles, even though the measure creating ZEP schools was intended to remedy a situation in which it was clear that students were not getting the same quality of education. What plans have been advanced in the United States to deal with similar situations? (Smaller class sizes, charter schools, and vouchers are a few.) Study each of these remedies. Do they work? Are they fair?

4. Can you think of analogous exams in the United States that might be criticized for the same reasons as the entrance exams for Sciences Po? Are there alternatives to these exams? You may want to look up the debate over College Board SAT exams in the United States. See, for example, Jacques Steinberg, "Challenge Revives SAT Test Debate," New York Times, November 19, 2001, sec. A, 14. See also <http://www.pbs.org/newshour/bb/education/jan-june01/ sat_03-30.html>, a Web site that gives the text of a debate held on March 30, 2001, on the On-line NewsHour on PBS. Finally, see <http://www.fairtest.org/examarts/fall99 /Strivers_Debate_ Highlights_SAT_Flaws.html> for information on the debate and links to other sites concerned with this issue.

5. Imagine that you are called upon to help the French minister of education draw up a plan to democratize the French secondary and postsecondary education system. What suggestions would you make? What techniques seem to you to be the fairest and the most practical in terms of allowing all students equal opportunity for the most prestigious diplomas?

6. Research the case of Regents of the University of California v. Bakke, which was argued before the United States Supreme Court in 1978 (<http://www.civnet.org/resources/teach/basic/ part6/41.htm>). In what ways does this case recall the issues in the decision taken at Sciences Po? In what ways does it differ?

7. More recently, the University of Michigan's Law School and its College of Literature, Science and the Arts were sued by three unsuccessful candidates for admission, who challenged the school's policy of making race a factor in admissions decisions. The University of Michigan acknowledged that it maintains such a policy in order to achieve diversity among the student body. Research this case online at <http://www.npr.org/news/specials/michigan/stories.html>; study the Supreme Court decision that was rendered in 2003 (<http://www.npr.org/news/specials/michigan/>); and then compare the issues involved with the events at Sciences Po. Is diversity a primary concern at this *grande école*, or are there other, more important issues?

8. Texas, Florida, and California have adopted alternative plans for achieving diversity in their state universities. Texas, for example, grants admission to the top 10 percent of the graduating classes in high schools across the state. In what ways does this race-neutral system favor minority students? In what ways might it continue to disadvantage them? Would such a plan work in France? Why or why not?

Vocabulary/Vocabulaire

Nouns/Substantifs

affirmative action	la discrimination positive
alternative	l'alternative (f.), le choix
baccalaureate exam	le baccalauréat (le bac)
case	le cas
course (preparatory)	le cours (préparatoire)
course of study	la discipline
diploma	le diplôme
educational system	le système d'éducation
elite	l'élite (m.)
entrance exam	le concours
examination	l'examen (m.)
goal	le but
imbalance	le déséquilibre
inequality	l'inégalité (f.)
junior year	la première
merit	le mérite

measure	la mesure
meritocracy	la méritocratie
opportunity	l'opportunité (f.), l'occasion (f.)
percentage	le pourcentage
reform	la réforme
senior year	la terminale
sophomore year	la seconde
university	l'université (f.), la faculté
value	la valeur

Verbs/Verbes

democratize	démocratiser
eliminate	éliminer
evaluate	évaluer
exclude	exclure
fail (an exam)	rater (un examen)
matriculate	s'inscrire (à)
pass (an exam)	réussir, être reçu, -e
recruit	recruter
take (an exam)	passer
teach	enseigner

Adjectives/Adjectifs

admitted	admise, -e
disadvantaged	désavantagé, -e
egalitarian	égalitaire
elementary, primary	primaire
prestigious	prestigieux, prestigieuse
privileged	privilégié, -e
secondary	secondaire
traditional	traditionnel, traditionnelle
written	écrit, -e

Notes

1. Ezra Suleiman, interviewed by Baudouin Bollaert in *Le Figaro*, March 26, 2001.

2. See Pierre Bourdieu and Jean-Claude Passeron, *Les Héritiers* (Paris: Editions de Minuit, 1964), and *La Reproduction* (Paris: Editions de Minuit, 1971). Translations of these difficult texts are available. See, for example, Bourdieu and Passeron, *The Inheritors*, trans. Richard Nice (Chicago: University of Chicago Press, 1979).

3. Bourdieu and Passeron, *The Inheritors*, 68.

4. Ibid., 19–20.

5. Stephanie Le Bars, "L'Education nationale tente depuis vingt ans de corriger les inégalités scolaires et de promouvoir la méritocratie," *Le Monde*, 27 février 2001.

6. Ibid.

7. See <http://www.paristech.org/anglais/ge.html>.

8. Nathalie Guibert, "Sciences-Po s'ouvre aux élèves défavorisés en les dispensant de concours," *Le Monde*, 27 février 2001.

9. It should be noted that not every candidate takes a *concours d'entrée*. Foreign students are admitted on the strength of their academic records. French students in doctoral programs are not required to take the exam.

10. Alain Savary, the socialist minister of education, created these schools in 1981 to address difficulties encountered by immigrants and children of immigrants, largely in the *banlieues* (See Antoine Prost, "Immigration, Particularism, and Republican Education," *French Politics and Society* 16, no. 1 (1998), 16–17. Arguably, they already represent a form of affirmative action, since they receive special treatment.

11. See "Education: Sciences Po élargit son recrutement dans les ZEP," *Les Echos*, 1er octobre 2002.

12. Sandrine Blanchard, "Les grandes écoles accueillent avec scepticisme l'ouverture de Sciences-Po aux lycées défavorisés," *Le Monde*, 27 mars 2001.

13. M.-C. Tabet, "Education: Le directeur de l'école, Richard Descoings, a annoncé hier la création d'une 'troisième voie,'" *Le Figaro*, 27 février 2001.

14. See "Sciences Po: L'Uni veut faire annuler la réforme," *Le Figaro*, 4 avril 2001.

15. Guibert, "Sciences-Po."

16. Hervé Baro, Antoine Colombani, Perrine Corcuff, and Georges Lahitte Dupon, "Démocratisation de Sciences-Po: attention aux fausses solutions," *Le Monde*, 4 avril 2001.

17. There are currently forty-four ZEP high schools in France. Sciences Po recently expanded its recruitment efforts to thirteen of these schools.

18. Stanley Rothman, "Is Diversity Overrated?" *New York Times*, March 29, 2001, sec. A, 25.

19. Bourdieu and Passeron, *The Inheritors*, 67.

Bibliography

Baro, Hervé, Antoine Colombani, Perrine Corcuff, and Georges Lahitte Dupon. "Démocratisation de Sciences-Po: attention aux fausses solutions." *Le Monde* 4 avril 2001.

Blanchard, Sandrine. "Les grandes écoles accueillent avec scepticisme l'ouverture de Sciences-Po aux lycées défavorisés." *Le Monde* 27 mars 2001.

Bollaert, Baudouin. "Enseignement: Faut-il faciliter l'entrée aux grandes écoles au nom de la mixité sociale?" *Le Figaro* 26 mars 2001.

Bourdieu, Pierre, and Jean-Claude Passeron. *The Inheritors.* Translated by Richard Nice. Chicago: University of Chicago Press, 1979.

"Education: Sciences Po élargit son recrutement dans les ZEP." *Les Echos* 1er octobre 2002.

Guibert, Nathalie. "Sciences-Po s'ouvre aux élèves défavorisés en les dispensant de concours." *Le Monde* 27 février 2001.

Le Bars, Stephanie. "L'Education nationale tente depuis vingt ans de corriger les inégalités scolaires et de promouvoir la méritocratie." *Le Monde* 27 février 2001.

Prost, Antoine. "Immigration, Particularism, and Republican Education." *French Politics and Society* 16, no. 1 (1998): 13–22.

Rothman, Stanley. "Is Diversity Overrated?" *New York Times,* March 29, 2001: A25.

"Sciences Po: L'Uni veut faire annuler la réforme." *Le Figaro* 4 avril 2001.

Tabet, M.-C. "Education: Le directeur de l'école, Richard Descoings, a annoncé hier la création d'une 'troisième voie.'" *Le Figaro* 27 février 2001.

Resource Guide

Further Reading

Bourdieu, Pierre. *The State Nobility.* Translated by Lauretta C. Clough. Stanford, CA: Stanford University Press, 1996.

———, and Jean-Claude Passeron. *Reproduction in Education, Society and Culture.* Translated by Richard Nice. Beverly Hills, CA: Sage Publications, 1977.

Compagnon, Béatrice, and Anne Thévenin. *L'Ecole et la société française.* Paris: Complexe, 1995.

Kedadouche, Zaïr. "Sciences-Politiquement correct." *Libération* 8 mars 2001: 6.

Mitchell, Lucy. "French Education: Equal or Elitist?" In *Contemporary French Cultural Studies.* Edited by William Kidd and Siân Reynolds, 51–65. New York: Oxford University Press, 2000.

Plenel, Edwy. *La République inachevée. L'Etat et l'Ecole en France.* Paris: Stock, 1997.

Weidmann-Koop, Marie-Christine. "Démocratisation de l'enseignement en France: illusion ou réalité." In *France at the Dawn of the Twenty-first Century.* Edited by Marie-Christine Weidmann-Koop, 97–114. Birmingham, AL: Summa Publications, 2000.

Newspaper Articles

Lexis-Nexis (<http://web.lexis-nexis.com/universe>) can be searched for newspaper articles relating to the issue of *discrimination positive* and Sciences Po. Many have been published since 2001 in *Le Monde* and other French newspapers such as *Le Figaro* (conservative) and *Libération* (liberal). For comparison purposes, the *New York Times* can be searched for articles concerning affirmative action and the University of Michigan case in 2003.

Web Sites

French Ministry of Education, for an overall government view of how the system functions: <http://www.education.gouv.fr/index.php>

Other information concerning the French educational system: <http://www.discoverfrance.net/France/Education/DF_education3.shtml>

General information concerning the *grandes écoles*: <http://www.paristech.org/anglais/ge.html>

Institut d'Etudes Politiques can be accessed at <http://www.sciences-po.fr/>. Study the press documents and communiqués under the rubric *Convention d'éducation prioritaire* for further information and frequently asked questions concerning the affirmative action plan at Sciences Po.

PART IV

Globalization

CHAPTER 10

French Cinema and the Cultural Exception: Holding Off Hollywood

Are movies just entertainment? Or can they be considered primarily a means of artistic expression? This question has been at the heart of a free trade controversy that has for several years pitted French and European cinema against Hollywood movies in a number of world economic forums. Jacques Delors, president of the European Commission in 1993, famously told reporters covering the free trade talks at the Uruguay Round negotiations of the General Agreement on Tariffs and Trade (GATT) that "the audiovisual sector is not merely merchandise" ("*l'audiovisuel n'est pas une marchandise comme les autres*"). This simple statement summed up the French position on the matter, which would later be articulated as a firm request to exclude works of audiovisual expression from negotiations on free trade, and which would come to be called the cultural exception (*l'exception culturelle*).

To what extent can it be argued that the French perspective on cinema, television, and music is an attempt to preserve French and European cultures from the dangers of Americanization and globalization? To what extent is this attempt bound up with notions of French and European identities? A look at the events that took place during the GATT negotiations of 1993, as well as a historical overview of the relationship between the French and American cinema industries, will help us better understand why the two countries have been at odds for so long about how to define the products of cultural expression.

Background

The GATT Talks and the Framing of the Cultural Exception

In 1944 an international monetary conference was held at Bretton Woods, New Hampshire, for the purpose of developing plans for rebuilding the world economy after the devastation of World War II. In the course of this meeting, the original participating nations formed the GATT, a forum intended to coordinate world trade and to regulate the exchange of goods. Membership in the GATT finally numbered more than 120 nations, representing all stages of development and industrialization. The role of the GATT was primarily to negotiate in trade conflicts between the member nations and to decide how to reduce tariffs and other barriers to free trade.

During the so-called Uruguay Round of the GATT negotiations, which took place from 1986 to 1993, discussions focused on such areas as agriculture and textiles and on trade in services and intellectual property. As the United Nations Educational, Scientific and Cultural Organization (UNESCO) reported, some countries "expressed concern that enforcement of the GATT principles on goods and services as well as on copyright protected products would undermine their cultural specificity (and unique status)" to the detriment of their commercial value. A number of countries objected to the possibility that their own culture industries (film, television, music) might be at a disadvantage when confronted by what UNESCO termed "greater financial muscle due to their multinational presence and monopoly position."[1] In fact, the cinema in many European countries had been able to prosper thanks to a combination of important restrictions in the form of quotas and other kinds of government support.

In the course of the GATT negotiations during the fall of 1993, the French were largely responsible for getting a majority of participants to agree to exclude film and other audiovisual goods and services from GATT rules. They called this clause the *cultural exception*. This means that nations will be allowed to continue to subsidize their domestic industries and, most importantly, that world film markets will be protected from the financial muscle of the Hollywood blockbuster film, which thrives on free market exchange.

Representatives of the French audiovisual sector based their arguments in favor of the cultural exception on a number of reasons. In the first place, they asserted, the audiovisual sector is an expression of national culture, and as such should not be considered a commercial item. In addition, the health of domestic audiovisual production ensures diversity in forms of cultural expression and avoids what the French termed uniformization or standardization of images and tastes. As UNESCO explains this perspective, "the cultural exception is based on the principle that culture is not like any other merchandise because it goes beyond the commercial: cultural goods and services convey ideas, values and ways of life which reflect the plural identities of a country and the creative diversity of its citizens."[2]

There is a certain irony in the implementation of the cultural exception as a way of defending against an American cultural invasion. In the early 1950s, the United States adhered to the Florence Agreement, an early form of the GATT, which promoted free trade. The agreement contained a reserve clause, actually suggested by the United States, that "allowed countries to avoid importing cultural goods that may prejudice the development of national cultural products."[3] Now, many years later, the French and the Americans found themselves arguing on different sides of the issue, with the United States asserting the commercial value of audiovisual products and the French insisting on their worth as cultural artifacts.

Germinal and *Jurassic Park*

Into this combat arena rode two films that were destined to serve as examples of just how crucial the cultural exception might be to the life of the French film industry and to the continued importance of French cinema on the world scene. In fall 1993 Claude Berri's *Germinal* and Steven Spielberg's *Jurassic Park* opened within a few weeks of each other. *Germinal*, based on the nineteenth-century novel by Emile Zola, told of the sad plight of coal miners in northeastern France. In Berri's words, his film would "depict the misery, the mining towns, the hovels, the gray skies of the north, death, hope, the heart of man."[4] And of course, given its subject matter—the struggles of exploited workers—the film would be sanctioned by the French left, then in power. Ironically, though the film was made in the département du Nord, there were actually no longer any active coal mines in that area; they had long before ceased to be profitable.

Germinal's budget was well over $25 million, a very large sum for the French cinema—indeed, the most expensive film ever made in France until then—and the film enjoyed a variety of government and regional subsidies. Because Berri filmed entirely on location, the economically depressed northern region stood to benefit from the creation of jobs (extras, set construction, hotels, and restaurants), as well as from the prestige of having a feature film linked to the history and heritage of coal mining.[5]

Germinal was truly the cinematic event of the year, a film that carried enormous official prestige and in which a great deal more than money had been invested. On the occasion of its premiere in Lille, the capital of the département du Nord, in late September, President François Mitterrand was on hand, as were many other government figures. In addition to the *TGV* (*train à grande vitesse*, or high-speed train) bringing politicians to Lille, another regional express carried many former miners and their children and grandchildren, who had played the roles of miners and their families during five months of filming. The crowd at the train station gave them a huge ovation. Berri was awarded a gold medal by the coal miners' union. Schoolchildren in Lille went en masse to see *Germinal* during the weeks it played in the city. The film opened nationwide in three hundred theaters and did very respectably in its first three weeks. *Germinal* was ultimately chosen to represent France as its Academy Award nominee for best foreign film.

The film also benefited from favorable press on the left, for the most part. *Germinal* was considered to be a "highly successful popular spectacle" ("*un grand film populaire et spectaculaire réussi*"),[6] a movie whose images and dialogue President Mitterrand praised and that Jacques Siclier, the influential movie critic in *Le Monde,* called "courageous and necessary," praising as well its relationship to present-day issues such as unemployment, hostility to immigrants, and fractures in French society.[7]

While critics in right-leaning newspapers were generally lukewarm to *Germinal,* the left for the most part allied itself with Berri's film in a period of economic crisis, thus making *Germinal's* premiere as much a political event as a cultural one. The film became the subject of a political and social debate, as several leftist newspapers pointed out ironically that the mining industry had recently experienced huge layoffs, so there seemed to be little to celebrate in that regard.

Only a very short time later, Steven Spielberg's dinosaurs came loping over the savannah and tromping through the jungle. When they did, *Jurassic Park* quickly replaced *Germinal* on screens throughout France—and all the more so since it was released in over 10 percent of the theaters in the country, a good deal more than had screened *Germinal*. By the time it reached France three months after its U.S. debut, *Jurassic Park* had already earned ten times its initial cost of $60 million. It could not fail to do similar business in France, where for several months prior to its opening "dinomania" had been carefully orchestrated in both fast-food restaurants (where it was possible to buy "dinomeals" and other souvenirs of the film) and boutiques specializing in clothing with dinosaur motifs. A number of food products (yogurt, cheese, soft drinks) carried the *Jurassic Park* logo. Video games and other derivatives completed the panoply of products generated by the film.[8] This extensive marketing and merchandising campaign, combined with *Jurassic Park*'s extraordinary special effects, made it clear that the film would be as successful in Europe as it had been in the United States.

No wonder, then, that very rapidly *Jurassic Park* was seen in France as the lumbering Tyrannosaurus rex, crushing the French cinema in its monstrous claws. Two critics even suspected that the film itself was just a two-hour commercial spot "intended to promote a jungle of related products."[9] Naturally, *Jurassic Park* played to packed houses in France for weeks, prompting the French minister of culture, Jacques Toubon, to announce his intention to release ninety more copies of *Germinal* to theaters in the provinces. The socialist newspaper *Libération,* though, regretted that *Germinal* had been made into a sort of Jeanne d'Arc of the cinema in order to defend France against the invading dinosaurs, and that what it called a mediocre film would have to bear the burden of France's "cultural patriotism."[10]

This call to cultural arms was made clear on the occasion of the GATT talks in 1993 as French directors and actors devoted a great deal of their time and energy to speaking on behalf of the cultural exception. The director Bernard Tavernier, for example, noted that to accuse France and Europe of being protectionist would be to ignore the fact that in the United States only 2 percent of the films distributed are of foreign origin, while in European theaters well over 50 percent of the films shown are American.[11] It is this imbalance that the cultural exception is intended to redress. The director Jean-Jacques Beineix stated that the French were not opposed to independent

Hollywood cinema (he cited the important contributions of Woody Allen, for example), but mainly to what he called "*hamburgers culturels*," the kind of films that seem to roll off the Hollywood assembly line, each one resembling the last.[12]

Even the American multiplex was seen as a threat to local European cinema and to the magnificent old movie theaters that were important entertainment venues in most European cities. Nowadays, though, it is becoming fairly common to find twenty-screen multiplexes in the new shopping malls that have come to Europe in the past decades and that are often located on the fringes of cities, rather than in city centers. The perception of multiplexes is that they will eventually put the small, local movie houses out of business and will primarily be dedicated to showing imported American films.[13]

Franco–American Cinema Relations

In many ways, the heated debates at the GATT talks in 1993 were simply a remake of other discussions and disputes going back to the 1920s, when the United States and France were the two largest cinema powers in the world. It is useful, then, to put the latest version of the controversy in its historical context in order to better understand the arguments on both sides.

World War I had disrupted film production in Germany and in France, allowing the United States to step into the breach and become the world's leading exporter of movies.[14] Though France and Germany managed to rebuild their industries after the war, America remained dominant. According to one observer, the Hollywood star system and production values rapidly came to define quality films and attract large audiences. In addition, a powerful distribution network ensured that American films benefited from sophisticated marketing in foreign countries that could not hope to compete.[15]

The French took steps to deal with the threat to their film industry by proposing in 1928 a quota system as the only way to regulate Hollywood imports and support their own cinema. Their policy suggested that, "for every seven foreign films imported into France, one French film was to be purchased and exhibited overseas."[16] The justification for this protectionist attitude strongly resembled the argument made many years later for the cultural exception. Edouard Herriot, then minister of education, cited the importance of preserving national customs and traditions that would be compromised if the number of foreign films continued to grow at the expense of

French cinema.[17] American producers resisted the quota, since it meant that the number of films they could export to France would be severely limited. Eventually, after negotiations, it was agreed that the French would not restrict the number of American films they imported, though they did ensure that there were incentives for marketing their own films abroad.[18]

At the end of World War II, a similar controversy arose, but with potentially more serious consequences for the French film industry. Although France had continued to make films during the German occupation, she had not imported any American films since 1940. This meant that Hollywood had four years' worth of films waiting to be distributed in France and other countries that had been under German control. Just after the liberation in 1944, American soldiers brought with them several dozen dubbed films that the Office of War Information gave to French distributors.[19] At war's end, the U.S. film industry was determined to gain a favorable—and even unrestricted—market for its products.[20]

As one scholar relates, the cinema market in France was not in a position to "absorb as many films as before the war" because it lacked enough screens to accommodate both local production and foreign imports.[21] Obviously, the French government was eager to renegotiate trade agreements between the two countries. But there were so many soon-to-be-classics waiting to be shown—*Casablanca*, *Citizen Kane*, and *Gone with the Wind*, to name a few—that French distributors knew their profits depended on their freedom to program American films. In 1946 former French prime minister Léon Blum and U.S. secretary of state James Byrnes concluded what came to be known as the Blum-Byrnes Agreement, affecting commerce between the two countries in a number of areas. The document regulated trade in essential products such as coal and wheat, which France badly needed, and in less essential ones, such as movies. Initially, France was expected to allow competitor nations to show films with no restrictions for thirty-six weeks per year, but in fact distributors ignored the quotas and acceded to the popular will.[22]

At the time, many French critics and filmmakers blamed Blum for what they perceived as selling out French cinema and for caving in to American demands. Yet history shows that the quota established by the Blum-Byrnes Agreement allowed French cinema at least to survive those early years after the war when Hollywood films invaded

French screens and threatened to overrun the entire industry. At the very least, the agreement guaranteed that French films would not disappear altogether from national screens. Nevertheless, the French Communist Party, which was then very powerful (25 percent of the French electorate voted Communist until the early 1950s), consistently opposed American products, beginning with Coca-Cola, which had arrived in France not long after the liberation, and continuing with Hollywood cinema. Maurice Thorez, the general secretary of the French Communist Party, warned that American films "poison the souls" of French young people and cause them to turn their backs on the "moral and intellectual values" nourished by the republic.[23] A committee to defend French cinema was formed, as much to reconstruct the industry as to make sure that American films did not overwhelm the domestic market.

By the time of the GATT negotiations in 1993, forty years later, it had become clear that allowing free trade in films could seriously threaten the survival of national cinemas as they confronted Hollywood blockbusters that seemed to come out with alarming regularity. France thus took the lead in speaking for European countries by demanding that imported audiovisual products be removed from free market exchange, and be subject to quotas and other restrictions. Though these were considered by American representatives at the GATT negotiations to be protectionist policies, the French position would ensure that national cinemas continued to exist. France, for example, currently mandates that 60 percent of the profit from every movie ticket sold will be reinvested in the domestic industry. This means, of course, that American films, because of their popularity, are financing French cinema.

The cinema is not the only outlet for audiovisual products to be subject to restraint of free trade under the terms of the GATT agreements. Television programming of films is controlled by quotas, so that a majority of the programs are of European origin (60 percent in France, of which 40 percent must be French). Broadcasting time on radio for non-French popular music is similarly restricted. In this way, France (and Europe generally) manages to protect its important audiovisual industry. Of course, there are no restrictions on how many CDs of non-French popular music one may buy, so these kinds of quotas do not necessarily change young people's taste.

What is the American view of the cultural exception? Mickey Kantor, the U.S. trade representative at the GATT talks, remarked that since about 5 million Americans work in the entertainment industry, it would seem logical to admit that this sector of the economy is not simply devoted to artistic expression, but also involves jobs and business.[24] Jack Valenti, president of the Motion Picture Association of America and the country's major lobbyist in favor of free trade in the audiovisual sector, maintained that there was no need for a cultural exception, since if French audiences do not want to see American films, they can just stay home or choose another product. If they instead buy tickets for Hollywood productions, this is proof of the quality and popularity of American films.[25]

During the course of the World Trade Organization's talks in Seattle a few years later, the issue was still very much alive. Catherine Trautmann, the new French minister of culture, assured the world that the cultural exception was nonnegotiable. Her discussion of the pressures on the audiovisual sector made it clear that, six years after the GATT talks, the cultural exception was now not just a French concern, but also a European one. Citing the very important contributions of European film directors like Jean-Luc Godard, Pedro Almodovar, and Alain Resnais, Trautmann declared that the cinema risked becoming part of a single culture if the cultural exception did not defend it from the free market. She called for the development of European programs on television (like the Arte channel, which is a French-German coproduction), and for other European initiatives in the audiovisual sector.[26]

The debate continues. As the World Trade Organization began discussing free trade in 2003, there was an attempt to "campaign for preservation of the cultural exception" by suggesting that UNESCO propose a "global convention on cultural diversity."[27] Such a convention would guarantee that cultural products might never be subject to free market exchange. The need for action in this area seems ever more pressing; most recently, Canal Plus, the French cable channel that finances 80 percent of annual French film production, has been having serious financial problems and may have to do some radical cost-cutting that would affect its support of the cinema.

On the occasion of the *Germinal–Jurassic Park* confrontation, President Mitterrand made a statement that still rings true for all Europeans who favor preserving cultural diversity. The point of the cultural exception, he said, is to protect "the identity of our nations, the right of each nation to its own culture, the freedom to create and to choose our images" (*"l'identité de nos pays, le droit de chaque nation à sa propre culture, le droit de créer et de choisir nos propres images.*").[28] Mitterrand was above all concerned that a society might abandon its ways of representing itself and become a slave to images exported by a superpower.

Discussion

Cultural products should be protected.

Agree

Products of cultural expression have a special nature that distinguishes them from other kinds of merchandise. François Mitterrand, on the occasion of the GATT negotiations in 1993, asked whether nations had the right to protect their own means of self-expression. He believed (as do others) that allowing one country's cultural products to supersede all others would lead to standardization or uniformization of films and other intellectual products. He feared that America's virtual monopoly in world cinema would further erode European cultures, a process that has been underway for the last fifty years and is visible all over Europe in fast-food restaurants, American clothing styles, and the omnipresence of English. For these reasons, France and Europe have to take a stand against free market exchange of the products of audiovisual expression.

Disagree

Products of mass culture should not benefit from special protective measures. Jack Valenti believes that the world of television and the cinema is a world of competition, and that it is a "pitiless universe" in which the best-marketed product will be the most profitable.[29] He denies that there is any difference between a commercial product and a cultural product, saying that films, television shows, and CDs are all in the same category: mass-produced merchandise. It is also true that, even within France, French movies are subject to the same kind of fierce competition for audiences. Films typically open in Paris and other large cities, but if they do not attract large audiences, they never find their way to screens in the provinces. This means that, while the cinema may in theory be a product of artistic expression, it is also clearly subject to the laws of the market. The system already encourages making films that appeal widely to all audiences and discourages financing films with unknown actors, or by young directors who do not yet have a reputation.[30]

There should be commercial opportunity in a free market.

Agree

All films of quality have equal chances to succeed in an open market. Jack Valenti argues that the American market is "totally open, absolutely free." This means, of course, that there is "fierce competition" for audiences.[31] In addition, a number of foreign actors now star in American films (Gérard Depardieu, Jean Reno) and there are coproductions filmed abroad, making it impossible to say whether a movie is an American film or a foreign film. If foreign films are not successful in the American market, it is probably because dubbing or subtitling is not a viable option and, even more importantly, because Americans do not readily understand the cultural norms that characterize foreign films. There are reasonable solutions for this situation. One practice has been to rewrite and recast foreign films before they are distributed in the United States. *Three Men and a Baby* (*Trois hommes et un couffin*), *True Lies* (*La Totale*), and *Point of No Return* (*La Femme Nikita*) are examples of French films that were redesigned for American audiences after their scripts were sold to Hollywood.

Finally, if a film is good it will be popular, no matter where it is shown. Rather than assume that Hollywood is stealing French audiences, why not try to compete by making more interesting movies that will appeal to a wider public, as Hollywood films do? This might mean spending more money to create films that exploit special effects, and that are thus more appealing to younger audiences.[32]

Disagree

Minimal distribution of foreign films in the United States guarantees the failure of this cinema. In some European markets, however, the American share is over 70 percent. In this respect, there is no reciprocity. What looks like an open market is in fact closed due to a variety of practices. Foreign films, even those that are filmed in English, do not, as a rule, get wide circulation in the United States. There are exceptions, of course; some films do make it out of what has been called the "art-house ghetto."[33] *Crouching Tiger, Hidden Dragon* and *Amélie* are two recent films that have been marketed successfully beyond major U.S. cities. Some cities with large immigrant populations have always had their own neighborhood theaters in which to view foreign-language films. But by and large, those who live in middle America do not get a chance to decide for themselves if they might like to see a foreign film. The reason for this is that profitability guides all decisions. Distributors and theater owners do not wish to risk showing films that they suspect will not be hits. It is safer, if not a guarantee of diversity, to remain with a product that has a ready-made audience.

In addition, it is inaccurate to say that American movies are more popular than French films because they are better. If French movie critics gave as much space to reviewing domestic films as they do to Hollywood blockbusters, perhaps French audiences might be encouraged to support local productions. Instead, according to some French film directors, French critics seem almost eager to attack their own cinema when it is intended for a mass audience.[34] In any case, European productions typically do not have the financing that is available for American blockbusters. No French film has ever approached even one-quarter of the cost of a film like *Titanic*, for example.

Finally, American films are always marketed very intensely before they open in foreign countries, so that an audience is created even before a film opens. European production companies simply do not have the finances needed to launch such advertising campaigns.

Questions and Activities

1. Write about a French film you have seen in a theater, its themes, and your reaction to it.

2. You have probably seen a number of French films on video or DVD, often as part of your classwork. Which ones did you prefer? For what reasons?

3. Some French films have been relatively popular with American audiences (*Amélie, Au Revoir les enfants, La Femme Nikita, The Return of Martin Guerre*). Think about why they might have achieved both critical acclaim and popularity in this country. Is there something special about their plots and characters, for example, that might transcend cultural boundaries? Explain your perspective.

4. Since the early 1980s, a great many French films have been remade by Hollywood (*Return of Martin Guerre/Sommersby; Trois hommes et un couffin/Three Men and a Baby; La Femme Nikita/Point of No Return; La Cage aux folles/The Birdcage*, for example). View one of these pairs (or another recommended by your teacher). Compare and contrast the themes in the films. What important differences did you notice? To what extent are these differences the result of cultural specificity?

5. Many famous American film directors of the late 1960s and 1970s (Martin Scorsese, Robert Altman, Francis Ford Coppola) were influenced by the films of the French New Wave (*Nouvelle vague*) in the late 1950s. What made this movement different from the cinema style that preceded it? Research New Wave directors online, and report to the class on the most well-known (François Truffaut, Jean-Luc Godard, Alain Resnais). You might start with G. Nowell-Smith, ed., *The Oxford History of World Cinema* (New York: Oxford University Press, 1996). The following texts will be useful: Richard Neupert, *A History of the French New Wave in Cinema* (Wisconsin: University of Wisconsin Press, 2002); Chris Wiegand, *French New Wave* (Oldcastle: Gallery Press, 2002). Many French New Wave films are available on DVD or videocassette. You might watch Truffaut's *Les Quatre Cents Coups* (1959) or *Jules et Jim* (1962); Godard's *A bout de souffle* (1960) or *Weekend* (1967); and Resnais' *Hiroshima mon amour* (1959).

6. If a foreign-language film has never played at your local mall multi-plex, make an appointment to talk with the theater manager, and ask about how the film distribution system works and what pressures there might be to show certain kinds of films. Report back to the class.

7. The French government sponsors theaters known as *Art et essai* (art and experimental films) that program foreign-language and independent films that could not otherwise find distributors because their audiences are bound to be very small. If you have an independent movie theater in your town, talk to the theater manager to find out what kinds of audiences are attracted to independent and foreign films. Report back to the class.

8. Consider the following question: Are uniformization and standardization something to be feared only in the case of audiovisual expression? Think about the worldwide success of the Harry Potter books, for example. Can written works of fiction also have a negative effect on cultural diversity, or is there something special about cinematic images that might make them more persuasive or habit-forming than the written word?

9. André Malraux, the French minister of culture under President Charles de Gaulle in the 1960s, maintained that "*le cinéma est un art et une industrie*" (the cinema is an art *and* an industry), highlighting the fact that movies share qualities of both. Form a debate with other students in the class in which you argue for and against the cinema as sheer entertainment.

10. American cinema has not been the only target of French criticism of the importing of American cultural products. When Disneyland-

Paris was planned (as Euro Disney) in the mid-1980s, almost immediately questions arose about the "Americanness" of the proposed park, and whether an American theme park could be successfully transplanted to Europe. Disney representatives in France had to assure the French that the park would not be the cultural catastrophe (*"Tchernobyl culturel"*) that French theater director Ariane Mnouchkine had predicted it would become. But at the same time, they felt strongly that the park should be a real Disneyland, rather than a Europeanized version of the original. Marketing studies showed that prospective European tourists preferred the authentic Disney experience as they imagined it, complete with Mickey and his friends, Frontierland, and Main Street. One concession to French taste was the conversion of Tomorrowland to Discoveryland, featuring a film based on the work of French science fiction author Jules Verne. English, of course, is everywhere in the park, even though the featured characters are from European fairy tales, such as Cinderella, Snow White, and Sleeping Beauty.[35] When the park finally opened in 1992, many critics wondered whether Euro Disney would become the principal reason tourists would want to visit France. American popular culture is so seductive, they reasoned, that tourists will eventually abandon such traditional attractions as Versailles, the Louvre, and Notre Dame, all of which represent the flowering of French civilization. Disneyland thus threatens Paris's stature as the artistic capital of the world. Debate this topic: All of European culture is being confiscated and deformed, then homogenized into Disney folklore. Myths and legends tell important stories about the civilizations that produce them. If French children are now going to grow up admiring the heroes of the American West, what will become of French folklore? Sources include many articles in *Le Monde* available at Lexis-Nexis using the keywords *EuroDisney* or *Disneyland Paris*. See also Martha Zuber, "Mickey-sur-Marne: une culture conquérante?" in *French Politics and Society* 10, no. 3 (1992): 63–80, and Alice Y. Kaplan, "Diamond Lil at Euro-Disneyland: A Conversation," *Sub-stance* 76/77 (1995): 154–68.

11. Hegemony, or ideological power, has been defined as the process by which dominant classes retain their control in a society. Schools, churches, and the media (worldwide satellite television, for example) are among the institutions that are responsible for producing and reproducing such power. Can American domination in world cinema (a condition that President Mitterrand referred to as being enslaved by exported images) be seen as being closely linked to, or

legitimizing, its power in the geopolitical, economic, and military order? Why or why not? Justify your point of view.

Vocabulary/Vocabulaire

Nouns/Substantifs

audience	le public
cable	le câble
circulation	la distribution
competition	la concurrence
culture	la culture
director	le réalisateur, la réalisatrice
dubbing	le doublage
entertainment	le divertissement
failure	l'échec (m.)
film (art form)	le cinéma
financing	le financement
free trade	le libre-échange
hit	le gros succès
image	l'image (f.)
industry	l'industrie (f.)
market	le marché
merchandise	la marchandise
monopoly	le monopole
movie	le film
movie theater	la salle de cinéma
opening (of a film)	la sortie
original version	la version originale
popularity	la popularité
product	le produit
satellite	le satellite
screen	l'écran (m.)
script	le scénario
sector	le secteur
slavery	l'esclavage (m.)

special effects	les effets spéciaux (m.)
specificity	la spécificité
standardization	la standardisation
subsidy	la subvention
subtitle	le sous-titre
theme	le thème
trade	le commerce
uniformization	l'uniformisation (f.)

Verbs/Verbes

attract	attirer
compete	concourir
confiscate	confisquer
distribute	distribuer
dub	doubler
legitimize	légitimer
make a film	tourner un film
open (a film)	sortir
produce	produire
rewrite	récrire
subtitle	sous-titrer
transform	transformer

Adjectives/Adjectifs

audiovisual	audiovisuel, audiovisuelle
commercial	commercial, -e
domestic	domestique
foreign	étranger, étrangère
free	libre
independent	indépendant, -e
intellectual	intellectuel, intellectuelle

Notes

1. Culture and UNESCO, Culture, Commerce, and Globalisation, UNESCO, 2003, <http://www.unesco.org/culture/industries/trade/html_eng/question16.shtml>.

2. Ibid.

3. Culture and UNESCO, Culture, commerce, and globalisation, UNESCO, 2003, <http://www.unesco.org/culture/industries/trade/html_eng/question19.shtml#19>.

4. Quoted in Isabelle Hourcade, "Sortie mercredi en France du film *Germinal*," Agence France Presse, 26 septembre 1993.

5. S. G., "Nord-Pas-de-Calais: Film de Claude Berri—*Germinal* oppose le Nord-Pas-de-Calais à l'Etat," *Les Echos,* 16 juillet 1993, 9.

6. Annie Coppermann, "Cinema: *Germinal* de Claude Berri—Un grand film populaire et spectaculaire réussi," *Les Echos,* 29 septembre 1993, 42.

7. Jacques Siclier, "*Germinal,* le nouveau film de Claude Berry [sic]. Les mineurs de la colère," *Le Monde,* 30 septembre 1993.

8. See Karen Saranga, "Le grand cirque de *Jurassic Park,*" *L'Express* no. 2205 (14 octobre 1993), 34–36, for a description of the marketing of *Jurassic Park* in France.

9. Henri Béhar and Danièle Heymann, "Cinema: *Jurassic Park* de Steven Spielberg et l'opération de marketing pour la sortie du film 'les profitosaures,'" *Le Monde,* 20 octobre 1993.

10. Quoted in Jean-Luc Bardet, "*Jurassic Park* contre *Germinal,*" *Agence France Presse,* 20 octobre 1993.

11. *France-TV Magazine,* University of Maryland-Baltimore Campus and FR2/Médiane Films, December 1993.

12. Ibid.

13. John Tagliabue, "Now Playing Europe: Invasion of the Multiplex," *New York Times,* January 27, 2000, sec. C.

14. See Kristin Thompson, *Exporting Entertainment* (London: BFI, 1985), pp. 100ff, for a discussion of this point.

15. Ian Jarvie, "Free Trade as Cultural Threat: American Film and TV Exports in the Post-War Period," in *Hollywood and Europe,* ed. Geoffrey Nowell-Smith and Steven Ricci (London: BFI, 1998), 36.

16. Robert Sklar, *Movie-Made America* (New York: Vintage, 1994), 219.

17. Serge Regourd, *L'exception culturelle* (Paris: PUF, 2002), 27.

18. Sklar, *Movie-Made America,* 23.

19. Jean-Pierre Jeancolas, "Free Trade as Cultural Threat," in Nowell-Smith and Ricci, *Hollywood and Europe,* 48.

20. Jarvie, "Free Trade," 39.

21. Jeancolas, "Free Trade," 48.

22. Ibid., 50.

23. Ibid., 51.

24. Frédéric Castel, "Mickey Kantor a vu trois fois *Jurassic Park,* Leon Brittan en a 'entendu parler,'" *Agence France Presse,* 13 octobre 1993.

25. Jacques Buob, "Culture: l'assaut américain," *L'Express* no. 2205 (14 octobre 1993), 33.

26. Catherine Trautmann, "L'exception culturelle n'est pas négociable," *Le Monde,* 11 octobre 1999.

27. Alan Riding, "Filmmakers Seek Protection from U.S. Dominance," *New York Times,* February 5, 2003, sec. E.

28. Buob, "Culture," 31.

29. Ibid., 33.

30. Michèle Soulignac, "Vers un cinéma à deux vitesses?" *Vacarme,* Janvier 2002 <http://vacarme.eu.org/article239.html>.

31. Jarvie, "Free Trade," 40.

32. The top-grossing film in France in 2002 was *Astérix & Obélix Versus Caesar.* However, seven of the next nine top-grossers were American, including *The Matrix* and *Star Wars: Phantom Menace.*

33. Jarvie, "Free Trade," 41.

34. Alan Riding, "French Fume at One Another over U.S. Films' Popularity," *New York Times,* December 13, 1999, sec. E.

35. Interestingly, Disney had originally considered creating a theme park containing replicas of European historical and cultural landmarks, but then decided to return to the tried-and-true format of the American parks: that is, fairy tales and comic book characters.

Bibliography

Bardet, Jean-Luc. *"Jurassic Park* contre *Germinal." Agence France Presse* 20 octobre 1993.

Béhar, Henri, and Danièle Heymann. "Cinéma: *Jurassic Park* de Steven Spielberg et l'opération de marketing pour la sortie du film 'les profitosaures.' " *Le Monde* 20 octobre 1993.

Buob, Jacques. "Culture: l'assaut américain." *L'Express* 2205 (14 octobre 1993): 30–34.

Castel, Frédéric. "Mickey Kantor a vu trois fois *Jurassic Park,* Leon Brittan en a 'entendu parler.' " *Agence France Presse* 13 octobre 1993.

Coppermann, Annie. "Cinéma: *Germinal* de Claude Berri—Un grand film populaire et spectaculaire réussi." *Les Echos* 29 septembre 1993: 42.

Culture and UNESCO. Culture, commerce and globalisation. UNESCO. 2003. <http://portal.unesco.org/culture/en/ev.php@URL_ID= 2461&URL_DO=DO_TOPIC&URL_SECTION=201.html>

———. <http://www.unesco.org/culture/industries/trade/html_eng/ question16.shtml>.

———. <http://www.unesco.org/culture/industries/trade/html_eng/ question19.shtml#19>.

France-TV Magazine. University of Maryland-Baltimore Campus and FR2/Médiane Films. December 1993.

Hourcade, Isabelle. "Sortie mercredi en France du film *Germinal." Agence France Presse* 26 septembre 1993.

Jarvie, Ian. "Free Trade as Cultural Threat: American Film and TV Exports in the Post-War Period." In *Hollywood and Europe*. Edited by Geoffrey Nowell-Smith and Steven Ricci, 34–46. London: BFI, 1998.

Jeancolas, Jean-Pierre. "Free Trade as Cultural Threat." In *Hollywood and Europe*. Edited by Geoffrey Nowell-Smith and Steven Ricci, 47–60. London: BFI, 1998.

Regourd, Serge. *L'exception culturelle*. Paris: PUF, 2002.

Riding, Alan. "Filmmakers Seek Protection from U.S. Dominance." *New York Times*, February 5, 2003, sec. E.

———. "French Fume at One Another over U.S. Films' Popularity." *New York Times*, December 13, 1999, sec. E.

Saranga, Karen. "Le grand cirque de *Jurassic Park*." *L'Express* 2205 (14 octobre 1993): 34–36.

S.G. "Nord-Pas-de-Calais: Film de Claude Berri—*Germinal* oppose le Nord-Pas-de-Calais à l'Etat." *Les Echos* 16 juillet 1993: 9.

Siclier, Jacques. "*Germinal*, le nouveau film de Claude Berry [*sic*]. Les mineurs de la colère." *Le Monde* 30 septembre 1993.

Sklar, Robert. *Movie-Made America*. New York: Vintage, 1994.

Soulignac, Michèle. "Vers un cinéma à deux vitesses?" *Vacarme*. Janvier 2002. <http://vacarme.eu.org/article239.html>.

Tagliabue, John. "Now Playing Europe: Invasion of the Multiplex." *New York Times*, January 27, 2000, sec. C.

Thompson, Kristin. *Exporting Entertainment*. London: BFI, 1985.

Trautmann, Catherine. "L'exception culturelle n'est pas négociable." *Le Monde* 11 octobre 1999.

Resource Guide

Further Reading

Collard, Susan. "French Cultural Policy: The Special Role of the State." In *Contemporary French Cultural Studies*. Edited by William Kidd and Siân Reynolds, 38-50. New York: Oxford University Press, 2000.

Forrest, Jennifer, and Leonard R. Koos. *Dead Ringers: The Remake in Theory and Practice*. Albany: State University of New York Press, 2002.

Harris, Sue. "Cinema in a Nation of Filmgoers." In *Contemporary French Cultural Studies*. Edited by William Kidd and Siân Reynolds, 208–19. New York: Oxford University Press, 2000.

Kuisel, Richard. *Seducing the French*. Berkeley: University of California Press, 1996.

Levin, Colette. "Hollywood Remakes of French Films: Cultural and Cinematic Transformation." In *France at the Dawn of the Twentieth*

Century. Edited by Marie-Christine Weidmann-Koop, 255–64. Birmingham, AL: Summa Publications, 2000.

Marks, John, and Enda McCaffrey. *French Cultural Debates.* Monash Romance Studies 2001. Delaware: University of Delaware Press, 2001.

Mazdon, Lucy. *Encore Hollywood: Remaking French Cinema.* London: British Film Institute, 2000.

Nowell-Smith, Geoffrey, and Steven Ricci, eds. *Hollywood and Europe.* London: BFI, 1998.

O'Shaughnessy, Martin. "Republic of Cinema or Fragmented Sphere: The Debate between Film-Makers and Critics." In *French Cultural Debates.* Edited by John Marks and Enda McCaffrey, 65–79. Monash Romance Studies 2001. Delaware: University of Delaware Press, 2001.

Rigaud, Jacques. *L'exception culturelle.* Paris: Grasset, 1996.

Ulff-Moller, Jens. *Hollywood's Film Wars with France.* Rochester, NY: University of Rochester Press, 2001.

Newspaper and Journal Articles

Lexis-Nexis (<http://web.lexis-nexis.com/universe/>) can be searched for newspaper articles in French and English relating to the cultural exception and its relationship to French cinema. Many have been published since the early 1990s in both *Le Monde* and *The New York Times,* for example.

Web Sites

UNESCO maintains a site that gives complete information on cultural policy resources and issues on culture and development: <http://portal.unesco.org/culture/en/ev.php@URL_ID=2461& URL_DO=DO_TOPIC&URL_SECTION=201.html> Click on the language (English or French) you wish to read.

Debate on government support for the arts held at the Théâtre de l'Odéon in Paris in 1998, with a number of reports and statements about the cultural exception: <http://www.culture.fr/culture/actualites/ conferen/ami2.htm>

CHAPTER 11

Trouble Down on the Farm: Big Mac Attack

Armed with screwdrivers, crowbars, and chain saws, the festive crowd descended upon a McDonald's restaurant under construction. Taking apart doors, interior walls, part of the roof, and other items, the protesters dumped everything in front of the local site of France's central government before adjourning to nearby cafés and restaurants to celebrate their act of resistance and defiance. The place was the small town of Millau in the Department of Aveyron, in southern France. The date was August 12, 1999.

Several days later, a number of those present at the trashing of the McDonald's were arrested, including José Bové, a local sheep farmer whose droopy moustache bears a purposeful resemblance to that of another famous resister, the *gaulois* cartoon character Astérix. What did this action represent? Why was McDonald's chosen as the target? Why did the action immediately engage not only the French but also many people throughout the world? In order to answer these questions, we must first review the history of French agriculture and examine the conditions that led to a well-conceived and publicized assault upon one of the world's leading symbols of global change in food production and consumption.

Background

The State of French Agriculture

Half of France's population was still on the land or located in small rural towns in 1900. The most usual excursion for the peasant would have been to the nearest market town, just a few kilometers from home, where the local dialect was spoken instead of standard French. Self-sufficient farms were run frugally, with outside repair or purchase serving as a last resort. The peasant's only opening on the world might have been military service, obligatory for males after 1900.

The small farm was the rule. Small farmers represented 38 percent of the total, but they owned only 2.5 percent of the farmland.[1] Most of these farms were not productive, requiring many peasants to hire out as day laborers or farm servants, but official French political culture at the beginning of the twentieth century acknowledged the small farmer as the backbone of society, a source of social equilibrium that might counterbalance the socialist ideas of industrial workers.

When the land could not support all those who lived upon it, rural emigration took place, beginning in the mid-nineteenth century. A rural downturn near the end of the nineteenth century, caused by low farm prices, the phylloxera disease in vineyards, and increased imports, contributed to the decline of the rural population. The low birthrate in the countryside could not keep up with an increasingly aging rural population and the exodus to cities by younger farmworkers. Protectionist government farm policy did not particularly encourage modernization, with the result that the smallest farms had begun to be absorbed by larger ones.[2]

After World War II, France's desire to modernize and to become an exporting nation supported agricultural production. Government intervention provided subsidies, credit banks, and protection of farmlands. Tractors had not been in general use until after 1950, when farm credit became available. Although purchases of modern farm machinery increased production, they also created debt for farmers, something the farmers had traditionally avoided. For their part, farmers unionized in great numbers so as to allow collective communication with Paris. The age of the isolated peasant farmer who negotiated only with local notables was quickly disappearing.[3]

By the 1970s the French government was well entrenched in agriculture as farm subsidies increased. Agriculture became an important mainstay of France's balance of payments in the face of increasing industrial competition from America and the Far East. During the same decade, the European Common Market incorporated new members, starting with Great Britain in 1973. This expansion created the world's second most powerful economy functioning as a free market, but it did not come without the centralized control exercised by the bureaucrats in Brussels, capital of the European Community. This control eventually included the formulation of a common agricultural policy, the *Politique Agricole Commune* or PAC.[4]

Although the 1970s had seen a quintupling of French exports, the 1980s marked a downturn for the agricultural sector. Competition from the United States and other countries like Brazil intensified. Countries like India and China increased the yields of their own agriculture. In addition, the eating habits of Europeans were changing. Now fast-food and specialized products sold in supermarkets were impacting the market. Food processors, in an effort to coax additional spending by consumers, were inventing new products whose processing and marketing required farmers to sign agreements for the production of specific crops.

At the same time, farm subsidies were not keeping pace with debts incurred by farmers as a weak industrial sector absorbed government funds. Agricultural cutbacks, rather than additional subsidies, were required. Internal price supports were removed. Additionally, the United States was demanding, through the General Agreement on Tariffs and Trade (GATT), an end to export subsidies, but countries admitted to the European Economic Community from Europe's southern tier—such as Greece, Spain, and Portugal—required farm subsidies. Agricultural policy was now being made and argued in Brussels or Washington as much as it was in Paris. For the French farmer, globalization had become a reality that was impossible to ignore.

During the Uruguay Round of negotiations of the GATT between 1986 and 1993, an agreement was reached in 1992 concerning subsidies for agriculture. The European Community was to reduce its agricultural subsidies by 36 percent over six years, but resentment ran high in the face of America's Agricultural Adjustment Act of 1993, which permitted restrictions on agricultural imports. French officials ordered limits on agricultural and livestock production in order to keep prices high. Premiums were offered to organic farmers and to those who removed land from production, but French farmers had bought their gains in productivity through the use of advanced farm machinery and especially fertilizers and pesticides purchased through industrial agribusiness. Even then, profits remained modest. As a result, the number of French farmers continued to decrease, with the decades of the 1970s and 1980s registering a 3 to 5 percent decline in the number of those engaged in working the land. Many who remained held part-time jobs off the farm in order to make ends meet.[5]

More Shocks to the System

As researchers and large corporations began to experiment with new methods to increase agricultural production, consumers became more concerned with the possible adverse effects of these techniques, particularly those involving the use of hormones to increase the rate of growth in livestock. Both naturally occurring and synthetic hormones are employed to raise cattle that produce more meat without requiring additional feed. In the 1970s the illegal use of diethylstilbestrol (DES) in veal production in France was found in baby food made from veal. This hormone was a suspect in certain cancers, nerve disorders, and reproductive problems.

More headlines raised consciousness about food safety. In 1990 the U.S. Food and Drug Administration (FDA) found traces of benzene, a petroleum derivative, in Perrier, one of France's most popular bottled waters and a signature export item. The French company absorbed a $40 million recall of 140 million bottles. Within the livestock sector, French beef farmers awoke to a shock in March 1996, when the British revealed cases of bovine spongiform encephalopathy (BSE, or mad cow disease, known in French as *l'encéphalopathie spongiforme bovin*, ESB, or *la maladie de la vache folle*). Variant Creutzfeldt-Jakob disease (CJD), fatal in humans, is acquired by eating beef raised on cattle feed containing body parts of BSE-infected animals. French markets were immediately closed off, but because animal-based feed had already been exported by Great Britain, French herds were affected. As the leading producer of beef in Europe and the home to one-third of its dairy cattle, the French industry was hard hit. Although the government reimbursed farmers for the cattle that had to be slaughtered, the entire industry was affected for several years, showing signs of recovery only in 2000.[6]

On the heels of the mad cow disease scare came the contaminated chicken scandal of spring 1999. A number of Belgian chickens and eggs that had been given feed contaminated with toxic dioxins were eaten or exported to other European countries, including France. Although the Belgian government seems to have known that something was amiss, no warning was given until the affected poultry had already been consumed. Following the chicken scare, Belgian children were affected by nausea and headaches after drinking Coca-Cola products. These soft drinks had also been exported to Holland and France, setting off new worries in those countries.

In response to increasing fears about food additives and purity, actions were being taken on the international scene. In 1988, after eight years of discussion, the European Union banned beef containing growth hormones. Although the United States promised to export only hormone-free beef to Europe, subsequent tests found hormone residues in the meat. Since then, the U.S. position has been that beef raised on hormones is safe for human consumption. The European Union has refused to allow U.S. hormone-treated beef into Europe until it can be proven that the meat is safe, but research over a period of ten years has not produced a final verdict. Finally, the United States lost patience and appealed to the World Trade Organization (WTO), which had supplanted the GATT in 1995. The WTO ruled in favor of the United States, allowing it to impose sanctions on European goods. Subsequently, the United States imposed a 100 percent tariff on a number of products, among which was Roquefort cheese.

The Contemporary Scene

We can now understand one of the reasons for which José Bové and his colleagues dismantled the McDonald's restaurant in Millau in 1999. The American tariffs effectively doubled the price in the United States of the taxed items, including Roquefort cheese. Bové is a small sheep rancher who produces Roquefort from ewes' milk. French farmers immediately called for a boycott of American products. The choice of McDonald's, seen as a symbol of American global reach and dominance, was an easy target that would bring attention to a protest moving rapidly beyond the confines of the cheese war. To say, however, that the action taken against McDonald's was simply another French farmers' protest—the equivalent of yet more imported Italian tomatoes dumped on the highway or truckloads of cheap artichokes spread on the streets—would be to trivialize their concerns.

Comes the (Bio) Revolution

All of these problems—overproduction and resulting low prices, high capital costs, sanitary and health issues, an aging farm population, fewer young producers willing to assume the risks and hard work of farming, general agricultural policy made in Brussels by the European Community, and industrial-style agricultural production for globally market-driven uses (McNuggets, for example)—were brought to a head by the debate over genetically modified organisms (GMOs). Referred to variously as genetically engineered, genetically altered, or transgenic, these living organisms have had the pattern of proteins in their cells manipulated by an altering of their genes. All living organisms have proteins that are manufactured within their cells. The controlling agents of the cell are chromosomes, which themselves are composed of genes, pieces of DNA that are encoded to make particular proteins. The proteins issue instructions to the cells, telling them what to do and when to do it. Scientists have discovered techniques for modifying genes by adding new genes or altering existing ones. The result is a new or different set of instructions issued by the genes such that the organism displays different characteristics. Since the genetic code is replicated in all species, genes taken from one species can operate within another, which is exactly what worries those opposed to GMOs. Many people fear that we have begun to alter nature dangerously, and that we are hastening natural evolutionary development in ways that we cannot foresee.[7]

Genetic manipulation has taken place in two main areas, food sciences and pharmaceutical manufacturing. Because the two have connections and overlaps, many seed companies have been bought by multinational pharmaceutical concerns such as Novartis, AstraZeneca, Schering-Plough, and Pharmacia, which merged with Monsanto, one of the leading developers of GMO seeds. Since the regulatory process is less rigorous in the food sciences domain than in the drug development field, these corporations have poured millions into developing GMO agricultural products that have been quickly adopted by American agriculture. In 1999 about 57 percent of soybeans, 50 percent of cotton, and 40 percent of corn grown in the United States came from genetically modified seeds, while about 60 percent of processed foods in the United States traced their origin to GMOs. The United States produced three-quarters of the world's GMOs in 1999.[8] Five or six major companies own most of the patents on genetically modified crops, with one, Monsanto, dominant in the area of genetically modified seeds and seed licenses.

The United States has used a regulatory approach to GMOs that bases its decisions upon scientific evidence. If sound scientific research is applied, it is believed, then safety concerns should be satisfied. The burden of evidence has to be upon the long-term risks. In the absence of evidence of risk, commercial approval is granted. European regulators have placed more emphasis on risk, which requires more scientific information before making decisions. Permissions to deploy GMOs have been slowed or denied in Europe, annoying American proponents of GMOs. They see them as exaggerated demands for safety that require unrealistic burdens of proof.[9]

José Bové Strikes Again

In January 1998, in an effort to bring attention to the debate over GMOs, José Bové took part in the destruction of transgenic corn stored by Novartis at Nérac in southwest France. He and two others were sentenced to suspended terms of imprisonment of six months. This would not be the last time that José Bové would protest against global agricultural practices through direct action. In fact, he would destroy transgenic rice in June 1999, for which he would be sentenced to four months' imprisonment.

Bové was born in Bordeaux in 1953. His parents were agronomists at INRA, France's national institute for agronomic research. He spent three and a half years in California when his parents moved to the United States to study at Berkeley. He was dismissed from his Catholic high school for having written a disapproved essay on the French "cursed poets" Baudelaire, Verlaine, and Lautréamont. Later, as a conscientious objector to military service, he and his future wife gave up their university studies to establish themselves as squatters on the Larzac Plateau in the south of France in 1973.[10] There he became active in a solidarity movement with the farmers of the region, who refused to be relocated by the French army, which wanted to expand a military base. Bové was sentenced to three weeks in jail for breaking and entering the base, but in 1981 President François Mitterrand put an end to the planned expansion of the installation. Now, 15,000 acres were available, so Bové helped form an organization that would lease the land from the government in order to permit new farming families to establish themselves on the Larzac Plateau.

In 1987 Bernard Lambert, José Bové, and others founded the Peasant Confederation (*la Confédération Paysanne*) as an alternative to the mainstream FNSEA (National Federation of Farmers' Unions, *Fédération Nationale des Syndicats d'Exploitants Agricoles*). They chose as their motto "For peasant agriculture and the protection of its workers" ("*Pour l'agriculture paysanne et la défense de ses travailleurs*"). The *Conféderation Paysanne* stands against industrialized agricultural production (*le productivisme*). This means fighting against the reduction of agriculture to mere production in order to satisfy the specialized, standardized requirements of large food processing corporations. These practices, the *Confédération* claims, ultimately force farm prices down and encourage farmers to use excessive amounts of fertilizer and insecticides or to nourish their livestock and poultry on questionable feed. Productionism also encourages the use of GMOs, which keep the farmer beholden to the large biotech corporations. The *Confédération Paysanne* favors the return to the multiple functions and biodiversity usually found on the small farm, including the promotion of rural social organization and autonomous creation of foodstuffs through advanced but traditional methods free of industrial regimentation.[11]

Opposed to agricultural productionism is what Bové calls peasant agriculture (*l'agriculture paysanne*).[12] By this the *Confédération Paysanne* means responding to society's needs through high-quality, clean foods whose origins are known to everyone; stewardship of rural areas, including ecological equilibrium and biodiversity; promotion of environmentally sound agriculture; promotion of locally managed crops and use of farming techniques that are efficient but that also create products that generate work and encourage repopulation of rural areas; and creation of solidarity among small farmers worldwide.[13] Bové has said, in this context, "Peasant agriculture must permit a maximum number of farmers spread out over the entire region to live decently from their craft by producing, on a human-scale farm, healthy, quality food without threatening tomorrow's natural resources" ("*L'agriculture paysanne doit permettre à un maximum de paysans répartis sur tout le territoire de vivre décemment de leur métier en produisant sur une exploitation à taille humaine une alimentation saine et de qualité, sans remettre en cause les ressources naturelles de demain*").[14]

Bové comes to this position logically. As a young man he was influenced by the civil rights movement in the United States and by

French farmer José Bové raises his fist as he leaves the Villeneuve les Maguelonne jail in the south of France, September 7, 1999. Bové, a leader of a radical farmers' union, was jailed for vandalizing McDonald's restaurant property. (AP/Wide World Photos)

the writings of Dr. Martin Luther King, Jr., and Henry David Thoreau. He read the early anarchists like Pierre-Joseph Proudhon, whose appeals for mutualism and rejection of authoritarianism and whose notion of collectivism—later called worker autonomy (*l'autogestion*)—can be heard in Bové's pronouncements. He also read the Russian anarchists Peter Kropotkin and Mikhail Bakounin, in whom he admired the will to action and the rejection of socialist authoritarianism. Bové's eclectic thought is channeled by affinity with the Catholic theology of liberation. Although Bové does not identify himself with Church causes or religious beliefs, he has stated that he uses Christ's gospel as "a framework for interpreting the world and involvement in it" ("*Une grille de lecture et d'engagement dans le monde*").[15]

As spokesperson for the *Confédération Paysanne*, Bové insists that each country or group of countries should be free to determine its policy for attaining self-sustaining agriculture. Government help to farmers is necessary, but it should not become a disguised subsidy for exports, thus allowing dumping by rich countries on poor countries, a practice that destroys the livelihoods of local small farmers.[16] In answer to questions about food shortages in the developing world, Bové and others say that it is not a question of lack of food. Indeed, they maintain that there is an abundance of food available in the world, but problems of storage, distribution, and the interruption of food supply by wars and political or economic decisions create pockets of plenty as well as areas of want. Nonetheless, critics often call Bové a protectionist. They think him naive because it is neither possible nor wise to stop a globalist trend that is accelerating.[17] Bové's opponents argue that, if a few countries end export subsidies, they will be disadvantaged by the international exporters like the United States, Argentina, and Australia, which will continue to supply world markets.

In response to concerns about food safety, proponents of globalization cite sanitary and health measures now in force that did not exist several decades ago. They blame subsidies and tariff agreements contained in Europe's Common Agricultural Policy that protect European farmers and undercut farmers in developing countries. President George W. Bush has called European policies responsible for prolonging famine in Africa by discouraging use of GMOs.[18] Rebuffed in continuing international discussions, the United States has not signed the UN Cartagena Protocol on Biosafety of January 2000, ratified by the European Union in August 2002. This agreement, which entered into force in September 2003, establishes rules for the international movement of GMO products. It confirms that a country may restrict GMO imports if it has questions about matters of biological diversity or the effect on human health. It also addresses required labeling concerns. (See the Resource Guide for relevant Web addresses.)

Since the action against the McDonald's restaurant in 1999, José Bové's visibility has continued to increase by virtue of his involvement in other protests against globalization. He was prominent as a protester at the WTO meeting in Seattle in 1999 because the *Confédération Paysanne* and groups with similar interests feel that the WTO tends to ignore national and regional regulations on food safety and environmental issues in favor of corporate economic interests. He appeared at the rally against the G8 summit meeting in Évian, France, in June 2003. Bové spent six weeks in jail in 2002 for his role in dismantling the McDonald's restaurant. Shortly thereafter, he was sentenced to prison for his actions in destroying transgenic plants and seeds in 1998 and 1999. In June 2003 French police surrounded his house in the Larzac. They took him to prison to begin a sentence of ten months. In July 2003 President Jacques Chirac reduced his sentence by two months, in addition to the traditional reduction of two months given to all prisoners on Bastille Day. Neither the left, which saw Bové as a political prisoner, nor the right, which interpreted the reduction of sentence as special treatment, was satisfied with the decision. On August 2, 2003, José Bové was freed under a work-release statute. He will be employed part-time by the *Association pour l'Aménagement du Larzac* (APAL) near his home. Bové stated while in prison, "Prison has not destroyed my combativeness nor has it shaken my convictions. It's not by locking up the spokesperson for the *Confédération Paysanne* that the government will succeed in making GMOs and the appropriation by multinational corporations of seeds and agriculture acceptable" ("*La prison n'a pas détruit ma combativité, ni ébranlé mes convictions. Ce n'est pas en enfermant le porte-parole de la Confédération paysanne que le gouvernement réussira à faire accepter les OGM et la mainmise des multinationales sur les semences et l'agriculture*").[19] The issues that Bové concerns himself with are not resolved. With the breakup in discord of the 2003 WTO meeting in Cancún, Mexico, the last of José Bové has not yet been heard.

Discussion

Genetically modified organisms are necessary for the green revolution.

Agree

Genetically modified organisms are the wave of the future and part of the green revolution that has been going on for decades. We should not fear progress in this domain. The increase in world population, the decrease in arable land, and the need to improve the quality and quantity of food crops are important reasons to continue development and distribution of transgenic organisms. The genetic alteration of major crops such as corn and soybeans in order to increase their resistance to destructive insects and herbicides results in decreased requirements for pesticides and herbicides for weed control. Because genes from different species can be transferred, it is possible, for example, to transfer genes from soil bacteria to crops in order to make the crops themselves resistant to predatory insects. Since plants can be modified to gain immunity from broad spectrum herbicides, or to be more efficient users of fertilizers, fewer herbicides and fertilizers will have to be used, thus making for an environmentally friendlier biosphere. Crop yields will increase. Biotechnologies are being developed to engineer more durable and nutritious crops. Biotechnologists are now at work building into plants higher levels of vitamins and improving fatty acid profiles as well as improving flavor. Finally, GMO proponents point to the safety concerns of many national and international regulatory agencies, including the International Food Biotechnology Council, the Food and Agriculture Organization, the World Health Organization, the Organization for Economic Cooperation and Development, the International Life Sciences Institute, and the U.S. Food and Drug Administration. These organizations have concluded that transgenic foods are not less safe than foods developed in traditional ways.[20]

Disagree

The risks in GMOs are as unknown as the potential benefits; the unpredictable nature of long-term outcomes could be extremely dangerous. Problematic areas include dangerous allergenic reactions to foods that contain genes from another species such as peanuts. One of the main worries concerning GMOs is horizontal contamination. This problem occurs when pollen grains from transgenic plants like corn and canola are carried on the wind to nontransgenic plants growing nearby. Genetic pollution ultimately would reduce the biodiversity that provides a natural reservoir of healthy plants. In addition, it is not known if transgenes can ever be bred out of a native plant population once it is affected, thus creating a problem that is permanent. When crop plants such as corn and soybeans are engineered to be pest and herbicide resistant, a new generation of superbugs or superweeds could evolve, endangering not only the genetically modified crops but also traditional or organically grown crops. Tests have proved that some genetically engineered crops are less nutritious than their nontransgenic counterparts as well. Antibiotic resistance is another concern. Genes that provide antibiotic resistance are used as tracers in genetically engineered plants. If the antibiotic-resistant genes are passed on to harmful bacteria, humans will have lost a key treatment for bacterial infections. Finally, the cultural and ethical implications of bioengineered foods should be considered. Food is a key component in culture. Altering food, particularly to introduce new products from the outside by profit-seeking companies, ultimately alters cultural patterns. The speed of biotechnological innovation (decades as opposed to the thousands of years of proven, traditional processes) may be leading us into areas of scientific uncertainty, risk, and liability that could be ruinous.

Biocrops are needed to alleviate world hunger.

Agree

Biocrops will do much to alleviate world hunger. Over a billion people in the world do not have enough food to eat. The poorest nations in the world need to adopt high-yield biocrops in order to head off recurrent famines. Future transgenic plants could resist heat, drought, and poor soil. In addition, the world's population is estimated to reach 8 billion in twenty to thirty years, with the most growth in areas that already overfarm, experience poor crop yields, and show environmental damage. Traditional agriculture will not be sufficient to head off a looming crisis. The attitude of the Europeans on genetically modified food has discouraged many other countries from adopting GMOs, particularly in Africa, where the need is great. They have systematically disregarded scientific evidence that indicates that biocrops are safe. At best, they are dragging their feet, having recently approved only a few applications for new imports of transgenic foods. This is why in 2003 the United States and twelve other countries brought a case against the European Union regarding its ban on biotech foods. If we desire freedom and peace in the world, we must start with the basics. Starving people cannot be expected to believe in democracy.

Disagree

The appeal of genetically modified crops is manipulated by political and economic interests as much as it is motivated by humanitarian interests, so we should naturally be suspicious. American corporations are heavily invested in biotechnology and are the leaders in selling it around the world. They pressure our political leaders to overcome the caution that other countries have displayed by linking biocrops to other political issues, or to use international regulatory bodies where the United States has had favorable rulings, such as the WTO. Other countries have joined the United States in bringing a case to the WTO because they want to leverage free trade agreements with America. The European Union says that it has never blocked food aid to developing countries. In fact, the EU has authorized GMOs in the past, while it continues to process applications for them. The motives of the United States are therefore suspect. America knows that if it has to comply fully with labeling requirements, its genetically modified food products will go unsold. Moreover, there is no science that proves genetically modified foods to be less expensive, more appealing, more nutritious, or safer than traditionally grown foods.

José Bové is a French hero.

Agree

José Bové is admired by many around the world. In a poll taken in 2000 for the large regional newspaper *Ouest-France*, 46 percent of the French thought that José Bové was the person who best defended the interests of farmers. The government's minister of agriculture got only a 27 percent vote of confidence, and the head of the leading farmers' union, the FNSEA, got only a 13 percent favorable vote.[21] That in itself should tell us something. People no longer trust government institutions or the large associations that work hand and glove with them. One of the indications of Bové's effectiveness is reflected in the growing representation of the *Confédération Paysanne* within the *Chambres d'Agriculture* (APCA), the organization that represents French farm interests to government and its agencies. In the elections of 2001 the *Confédération* took 27 percent of the votes, up from 20 percent in 1995.[22] These votes were won at the expense of the FNSEA. José Bové does not benefit from his work for the *Confédération Paysanne*. His salary is about 1,200 euros per month, a little more than $1,400. No wonder people consider him to be a modern Robin Hood, fighting the rich corporations and governments that are motivated by capitalistic, economic concerns at the expense of the little person.

Disagree

Bové is a disingenuous manipulator of the media. At best, he is naive. Under the smiling face, the big Astérix moustache, and the small-farmer façade, one finds a sophisticated thinker who is actually a socialist-anarchist. His conclusions have led him to violent action against property. He is not living under a totalitarian regime, but rather in a country governed by law. As such, there are legal means for the redress of complaints, which Bové has sought to circumvent in order to garner publicity for his cause by playing to the media. He has dressed as a peasant woman (ostensibly a traditional sign of protest) and ridden to jail on a tractor, handcuffed, in order to pander to the camera. In addition to French media, he has been on the front page of the *New York Times,* has been mentioned by *Business Week* as a European star, and has been interviewed for *Sixty Minutes.* One has to remember that the *Confédération Paysanne* only has about 15,000 members, while the FNSEA has 450,000 members. It takes a loud voice and circus antics to get noticed! He cannot really believe that small farms will produce enough food to feed the world's growing population. Moreover, he brushes off the fact that a chain like McDonald's in France, according to its president Denis Hennequin, is a string of small or medium business franchises that employed over 30,000 people in 2000, that invested over 4.5 million euros in French agriculture in the same year, that gave a livelihood to 4,500 farmers, and whose food products are grown or raised in France.[23]

Questions and Activities

1. Form a small group to review the January 2000 Cartagena Protocol on Biosafety (see the Web addresses in the Resource Guide). What does it do, and what are its key provisions? What does it not do? Report to the rest of the class.

2. What is the Convention on Biological Diversity (CBD) of 1992? Do you think the United States should have signed it? Review the text. See <http://www.biodiv.org/>. Report to the class.

3. At his trial in 2002 Bové's lawyers argued that their client's actions were defensible because health risks to the public justified his taking the law into his own hands. Lionel Jospin, France's prime minister at the time, called Bové's fight "just." Resolved: When the

public is in danger, the good citizen must break the law if necessary in order to alert the populace. Debate the question.

4. José Bové indicts globalism. What do you know about the theory of globalism? How does it operate? What does it purport to do? Does it? Agree or disagree with Bové's stance on globalism in an essay based upon your reading and research. Try this site for reading suggestions and point-counterpoint debate: <http://www.aworldconnected.org/>.

5. In a speech delivered in December 1999 in Montreal to the World Civil Society Conference, Kofi Annan, the secretary general of the United Nations, called nongovernmental organizations (NGOs) "the best thing that has happened to the UN in a long time." Do a report on the goals, the influence, and the results obtained by a French NGO (OGN in French). For example, ATTAC (*Association pour une taxation des transactions financiers pour l'aide aux citoyen*) at <http://www.france.attac.org>; *Vía Campesina* at <http://www.viacampesina.org>; Greenpeace at <http:// www.greenpeace.org>; FIDH (*Fédération Internationale des Ligues des Droits de l'Homme*) at <http://www.fidh.org/>; *Médecins sans Frontières* at<http://www.msf.org/>.

6. Examine the ideas of those French philosophers, activists, or movements mentioned in this chapter as having influenced José Bové's thinking. With a partner, choose one of them to explore in more depth in order to inform the class about their key ideas. Be sure to identify the parts of their thought that correspond to what Bové does and says.

7. In spite of spectacular protests against McDonald's restaurants, there are more than nine hundred of them in France. While other fast-food restaurants like Burger King gave up there, McDonald's has proved to be resilient and growing. To what might one attribute this success? Check McDonald's corporate Web site to see how the corporation advertises itself at <http://www.mcdonalds.com/>. You can navigate to the French site at <http://www.mcdonalds.fr/>. How does McDonald's France represent itself, particularly with regard to the quality and origin of its products? You should also check on McDonald's advertising campaign in France in the years following the 1999 Bové incident by researching newspaper stories through Lexis-Nexis. Report your findings to the class.

8. What is the Slow Food movement? Check its Web site at <http://www.slowfood.com/>. Describe its philosophy, positions, and actions to the class. Contrast this group's outlook with that of McDonald's and similar food chains.

9. Carry out a joint project with students in a biology class in your school. Create a bilingual poster in which they illustrate the principles and techniques of genetic modification while you illustrate the pros and cons of the issue.

10. For a research report, choose one genetically modified organism to investigate in depth. For example, golden rice (samples of which were destroyed by Bové in 1999) is a GMO that has been praised for benefiting the farmers who grow it and the people who eat it because it helps thousands who suffer from vitamin A deficiency. The product is not without its detractors, however. Do a case study on this modified organism, which has been both praised and criticized. A Web search under "golden rice" and "responsible biotechnology" will turn up both sides of the question.

11. The *Confédération Paysanne* stands for reform of the European Union's Common Agricultural Policy (*Politique Agricole Commune*, or PAC). What is this policy currently? What is the position of the *Confédération*? Should there be further change? You can consult the site of the PAC at <http://europa.eu.int/pol/agr/index_fr.htm>. You can navigate to the *Confédération Paysanne*'s position on the PAC through its Web site, listed in the Resource Guide of this chapter. Form a team to research this issue, and report to the class after having written your findings.

12. The American Farm Bureau represents itself as the voice of the American farmer. What are its views on the issues presented in this chapter? You may consult its Web site at <http://www.fb.org/>. Its statement on agricultural biotechnology is reproduced at <http://www.molecularfarming.com/fb.html>. You will notice industry statements there as well. How do its views differ from those of the *Confédération Paysanne* or FNSEA? Form a research team to report on each organization in a comparison of their perspectives.

13. Many U.S. corporations like McDonald's, Burger King, KFC, and Wendy's have been hiring scientists and subsidizing research on animal welfare recently. In addition, McDonald's announced that it was requiring its suppliers to reduce antibiotic and growth hormone use. Report to the class on this trend. Do you think that Bové and other activists have contributed to it? As a start, check the article "Animal Welfare's Unexpected Allies," by David Barboza, in *New York Times*, June 25, 2003. See also the best-selling book by Eric Schlosser, noted in the Resource Guide, as counterpoint.

14. The European Parliament approved regulation in 2003 to require very strict labeling for foods for human consumption and animal feeds made with genetically modified ingredients (Regulation (EC)

No 1829/2003 of 22 September 2003). While environmentalists greeted this development favorably, the American farm establishment is against it (search the American Farm Bureau Web site, for example, at http://www.fb.org/news). Form two groups to explore the issue and determine what is at stake. Present your findings in a panel format. As a starting place, check the article by Lizette Alvarez, "Europe Acts to Require Labeling of Genetically Altered Food," *New York Times,* 3 July 2003. The multilingual Web server of the European Parliament is found at <http://www.europarl.eu.int>.

Vocabulary/Vocabulaire

Nouns/Substantifs

agribusiness	l'agroalimentaire (f.)
cloning	le clonage
Common Agricultural Policy (of the European Union)	PAC, Politique agricole commune
Creutzfeldt-Jakob disease (CJD)	la maladie de Creutzfeldt-Jakob (MCJ)
DNA	l'ADN (f.)
farmer	un agriculteur
fertilizer (chemical)	un engrais (chimique)
genetically modified organism (GMO)	un organisme génétiquement modifié (OGM)
genetic engineering	le génie génétique
genetic modification	une modification génétique
genetic transfer	le transfert génétique
globalization	la mondialisation
herbicide	un herbicide
labeling	l'étiquetage (m.)
livestock farmer	un éleveur
mad cow disease	la maladie de la vache folle
multinational corporation	une multinationale
nongovernmental organization (NGO)	une organisation non gouvernmentale (ONG)
patent	un brevet

Trouble Down on the Farm: Big Mac Attack

peasant	un paysan, une paysanne
pesticide	une pesticide
seed	une semence
(scientific) breakthrough	une percée (scientifique)
WTO (World Trade Organization)	l'OMC, Organisation mondiale du commerce

Verbs/Verbes

imbue (with a quality)	(lui) conférer une caractéristique
improve (yields)	améliorer (les rendements)
prevent (rotting)	empêcher (la pourriture)
protest (globalization)	contester (la mondialisation)
sow	semer

Expressions/Expressions

agriculture respectful of the environment	une agriculture respectueuse de l'environnement
antiglobalization movement	le mouvement antimondialiste
biological diversity	la diversité biologique
biotechnical risk	un risque biotechnologique
chicken rancher (or other avian varieties)	un aviculteur
contain a GMO	contenir un OGM
cross-border shipment	le mouvement transfrontière
dioxin-contaminated chicken	le poulet à la dioxine
ecologically friendly farming practices	l'éco-conditionnalité (f.)
environmentally unfriendly measure	une mesure anti-environnementale
food self-sufficiency (opposite of *mondialisation libérale*)	l'autosuffisance alimentaire (f.)
Frankenfood, unhealthy food products	la mal bouffe, la sale bouffe
good, healthy food; opposite of *la mal bouffe*	la bonne bouffe

implant a gene borrowed from another species	introduire un gène emprunté à une autre espèce
keeping fields planted with GMO crops separate (to prevent cross-pollination)	l'isolement des champs (d'OGM)
long-term effects	les effets à long terme
merchandising of life	la marchandisation du vivant
organic farming	l'agriculture biologique
organic vegetable	une légume "bio"
resistant plant	une plante résistante
secrete an insecticide	sécréter un insecticide
security measures concerning the biosphere	la biosécurité
super-resistant plant	une plante hyper résistante
sustainable development	le développement durable
unregulated globalization	la mondialisation libérale
wind barrier hedges	une haie brise-vent

Notes

1. Pierre Miquel, *La France et ses paysans* (Paris: L'Archipel, 2002), 25.
2. Ibid., 36–37.
3. Ibid., 44.
4. Ibid., 283–85.
5. Ibid., 300–302.
6. Ibid., 321–25; as of February 2003 six cases of variant Creutzfeldt-Jakob disease had been registered in France, including one death. Isabelle Capek and Véronique Vaillant, "Les maladies de Creutzteldt-Jakob et les maladies apparentées en France en 2001," Institut de Veille Sanitaire, March 16, 2004.
7. Dan R. Anderson, "Biotechnology Risk Management: The Case of Genetically Modified Organisms (GMOs)," *CPCU Journal* 54, no. 4 (2001): 215–30.
8. Anderson, 218.
9. Les Levidow and Susan Carr, "Sound Science or Ideology?" *Forum for Applied Research and Public Policy* 15, no. 3 (2000): 44–50.

10. Paul Ariès and Christian Terras, *José Bové: La révolte d'un paysan* (Villeurbane, France: Editions Golias, 2000), 6–7.

11. José Bové and François Dufour, *Le Monde n'est pas une marchandise* (Paris: Editions La Découverte, 2000), 104.

12. Bové and his companions can be credited with helping to rehabilitate the word *paysan*. After World War II, when France was modernizing agriculture, the word went out of fashion. Other words like *agriculteur* and *exploitant agricole* were used for *farmer*. The word *paysan* comes from the Latin *paganus*, or countryman, an inhabitant of the *pagus* or countryside, county. Today Bové uses the word with pride to denote an autonomous farmer who acts locally but thinks globally, no longer the isolated peasant of the past. Bové has said, "For the first time, a peasant struggle is becoming a central point in the questioning of society. The word *peasant* is rehabilitated; it is becoming a demand uniting resistance, land and dignity" ("*Pour la première fois, une lutte paysanne devient une lutte centrale de remise en question de la société. Le mot 'paysan' est réhabilité; il devient une revendication alliant résistance, territoire, dignité*"). Giles Luneau and José Bové, *Nous, paysans* (Paris: Hazan, 2000), 17.

13. Bové and Dufour, *Le Monde*, 330–34.

14. Ibid., 328–29.

15. Quoted in Ariès and Terras, *José Bové*, 11.

16. Denis Pingaud, *La Longue marche de José Bové* (Paris: Editions du Seuil, 2002), 222–23.

17. François Bazin and Martine Gilson, "Glavany-Bové: leur premier dialogue," *Le Nouvel Observateur* 1860, 29 June–5 July 2000, 28–30.

18. Kevin A. Hassett and Robert Shapiro, "How Europe Sows Misery in Africa," *Washington Post,* June 22, 2003.

19. <http://www.lemonde.fr/> 8 Aug. 2003; "José Bové est sorti de prison samedi," *Inf OGM,* 5 August 2003, <http://www.infogm.org/breve.php3?id_breve=151> (accessed November 17, 2003).

20. Maureen A. Makey and Charles R. Santerre, "Biotechnology and Our Food Supply," *Nutrition Today* 35, no. 4 (2000): 120–28.

21. <http://www.ifop.com/europe/sondages/opinion/agricult.asp>.

22. <http://www.fnsea.fr/elections/graph.htm>.

23. *Le Nouvel Observateur* 1860, 29 June–5 July 2000, 26.

Bibliography

Anderson, Dan R. "Biotechnology Risk Management: The Case of Genetically Modified Organisms (GMOs)." *CPCU Journal* 54, no. 4 (2001): 215–30.

Ariès, Paul, and Christian Terras. *José Bové: La révolte d'un paysan*. Villeurbane, France: Éditions Golias, 2000.

Bazin, François, and Martine Gilson. "Glavany-Bové: leur premier dialogue." *Le Nouvel Observateur* 1860 (29 juin–5 juillet 2000): 28–30.

Becker, Elizabeth. "Western Farmers Fear Third-World Challenge to Subsidies." *New York Times,* September 9, 2003.

Bové, José, and François Dufour. *Le monde n'est pas une marchandise.* Paris: Éditions La Découverte, 2000.

Gruhier, Fabien. "Cinq questions sur les OGM." *Le Nouvel Observateur* 1819 (16–22 septembre 1999): 43.

Hassett, Kevin A., and Robert Shapiro. "How Europe Sows Misery in Africa." *Washington Post,* June 22, 2003.

Levidow, Les, and Susan Carr. "Sound Science or Ideology?" *Forum for Applied Research and Public Policy* 15, no. 3 (2000): 44–50.

Makey, Maureen A., and Charles R. Santerre. "Biotechnology and Our Food Supply." *Nutrition Today* 35, no. 4 (2000): 120–28.

Miquel, Pierre. *La France et ses paysans.* Paris: L'Archipel, 2001.

Pingaud, Denis. *La Longue marche de José Bové.* Paris: Éditions du Seuil, 2002.

Resource Guide

Further Reading

Benbrook, Charles M. "Sowing Seeds of Destruction." *New York Times,* July 11, 2003.

Borem, Alouizio, et al. *Understanding Biotechnology.* Upper Saddle River, NJ: Prentice Hall PTR, 2003.

Borlaug, Norman E. "The Next Green Revolution." *New York Times,* July 11, 2003.

Charles, Daniel. *Lords of the Harvest: Biotech, Big Money, and the Future of Food.* New York: Perseus Publishing, 2001.

Luneau, Giles, and José Bové. *Nous, paysans.* Paris: Hazan, 2000.

Ministère de l'Écologie; Babusiaux, Christian, et al. *Plantes Transgéniques: l'expérimentation est-elle acceptable?* Paris: La Documentation française, 2003.

"OGM: les vrais dangers." *Le Nouvel Observateur* 2017 (3–9 juillet 2003): 22–29.

Pinstrup-Andersen, Per, and Ebbe Schioler. *Seeds of Contention: World Hunger and the Global Controversy over GM Crops.* Washington, DC: International Food Policy Research Institute, 2001.

Pringle, Peter. *Food, Inc. Mendel to Monsanto—the Promises and Perils of the Biotech Harvest.* New York: Simon & Schuster, 2003.

Rauch, Jonathan. "Will Frankenfood Save the Planet?" *The Atlantic Online.* October, 2003. < http://www.theatlantic.com/issues/2003/10/rauch.htm >.

Schapiro, Mark. "Sowing Disaster?" *The Nation,* October 28, 2002, 11–19.

Schlosser, Eric. *Fast Food Nation: The Dark Side of the All-American Meal.* New York: HarperCollins, 2002.

Soulet, Jean-François. *La Révolte des citoyens de la Guerre des Demoiselles à José Bové.* Toulouse: Privat, 2001.

Stiglitz, Joseph E. *Globalization and Its Discontents.* New York: W.W. Norton, 2002.

Newspaper and Journal Articles

Lexis-Nexis and ProQuest are valuable sources for searching newspaper or journal articles in English or French. Check to see whether the Wilson Select Plus database search engine is available as well in your local public or college/university library. This source is valuable for journal articles. For this topic it is fruitful because it catalogs scientific and environmental journals that may not be available to you locally.

Web Sites

Confédération paysanne:
   < http://www.confederationpaysanne.fr/ >
Information on the Aveyron region of France including the Larzac Plateau:
   <http://www.tourisme-aveyron.com/>
   <http://www.cg12.fr/>
FNSEA, the mainstream French agricultural union:
   <http://www.fnsea.fr/>
World Trade Organization:
   <http://www.wto.org/>
2000 World Economic Forum meeting at Davos, Switzerland, at which Bové protested:
   <http://www.time.com/time/europe/davos2000/davos.html>
Official site of the WEF:
   <http://www.weforum.org/>
Favorable view on biotech applications to agriculture, on the site of Isaaa, the International Service for the Acquisition of Agribiotech Applications:
   <http://www.isaaa.org/>
Fact sheet on the Cartagena Protocol on Biosafety:
   <http://usinfo.state.gov/topical/global/biotech/00021601.htm>
Cartagena Protocol:
   <http://www.biodiv.org/biosafety/default.aspx>
Full text of the Protocol:
   <http://www.biodiv.org/biosafety/protocol.asp>
Circumspect view on biotechnology:
   <http://www.gene-watch.org/>

French agency charged with the dissemination of information about food
    safety: *Agence française de sécurité sanitaire des aliments.*
    <http://www.afssa.fr/>
French public health agency, *Institut de Veille Sanitaire:*
    <http://www.invs.sante.fr>
Effect on developing nations of first-world agricultural subsidies:
    <http://www.nytimes.com/harvestingpoverty/>

Index

Abbé Grégoire, 69–70
Abortion, 176
Académie Française, 69
Acquiring Cross-Cultural Competence (AATF), xiii
Administration and management school (*École Normale d'Administration*), 195
Administrative Tribunal of Paris, 33
Affaire du foulard, 95
Affaire du tchador, 95
Affirmative action (*discrimination positive*); and achieving democratization of higher education, 202–3; Sciences Po, 197–200; vs. parity, 180–81; for women, 177 (*See also* Education; Parity; Sciences Po)
Africa. (*See* Francophone Africa; Algiers)
Afrique Equatoriale Française, 146
Afrique Occidentale Française, 146

Agriculture (*See* French agriculture; Genetically modified organisms [GMOs])
Algiers, 45–64, 100; background of French in, 46–48; Charles de Gaulle and the end of the Algerian War, 51–52; films about, 63; Paul Aussaresses and torture/executions of Algerians, 46, 52–53; war for Algerian independence from France, 48–50; Web sites, 64
Allègre, Claude, 97, 200
Alsace-Lorraine, 105
Amnesty, 52–54
Applied arts school (*Conservatoire National des Arts et Métiers*), 196
Ardennes forest, 26
Ariége, 70
Arkansas River, 118
Assemblée nationale, 123, 175
Assemblée of Quebec, 126

Index

Assimilation, 47–48

Association pour l'Aménagement du Larzac (APAL), 243

Attali, Jacques, *Pour un modèle européen d'enseignement supérieur*, 198

Au pouvoir citoyennes: liberté, egalité, parité (Gaspard, Servan-Schreiber, and Le Gall), 177

Auclert, Hubertine, 175

Aumonerie (chaplain's office), 105

Auschwitz, 27

Aussaresses, Paul, 46, 52–53; photo of, 53; *Special Services: Algeria 1955–57*, 52–53; war crimes and, 52

Autogestion (worker autonomy), 241

Azincourt (Agincourt), battle of, 4

Bac ES (social sciences and economics), 194

Bac L (humanities and literature), 194

Bac S (sciences), 194

Baccalauréat, 193–94, 199; types of, 194

Bakounin, Mikhail, 241

Barbie, Klaus, 27

Barère, Bertrand, 70

Bas Canada (Lower Canada), 119–20

Basque, 70–72, 73

Battle of Algiers, 45, 50

Bayrou, François, 98–99

Beaudricourt, Robert de, 5

Beineix, Jean-Jacques, 217

Belgium, contaminated chicken scandal, 236–37

Bellay, Joachim Du, *Défense et illustration de la langue française* (*Defense and Illustration of the French Language*), 69

Ben Bella, Ahmed, 49

Bertrand, Jean-Jacques, 130

Beti, Mongo, 154

Bilingual education, 68

Biorevolution (*See* Genetically modified organisms [GMOs])

Bishop Cauchon, 9

Bloc Marcoussiste (Marcoussis bloc), 156

Blum, Léon, 219

Blum-Byrnes Agreement, 219–20

Boigny, Félix Houphouët, 149

Bouchard, Lucien, 128

Bourassa, Robert, 124–26, 130

Bourdieu, Pierre, 195, 198–99

Bourges, 4

Bousquet, René, 30

Bové, José, 233, 237; destruction of genetically modified organisms (GMOs), 239–43; as French hero, 246–47; photo of, 241

Bovine spongiform encephalopathy (mad cow disease, *l'encéphalopathie spongiforme bovin* or *la maladie de la vache folle*), 236

Boycotts, 237

Brazzaville, Congo, 147

Breton, 67, 70–73, 76

Bretton Woods, 214

Brevet de technicien supérieur (technical diploma), 194

Brittany, 67–68, 74

Bugeaud, Thomas-Robert, 47

Burgundians (*les Bourguignons*), 4, 5

Burqa, 97

Burrin, Phillipe, 28–29

Bush, George W., 242

Byrnes, James, 219

Calais, 4

Canada (*See* Quebec)

Canadian Confederation, 121, 132

Canonization, of Jeanne D'Arc, 7, 9

Index

CAPES degree, 73
Capetian dynasty (France), 4
Cardinal de Richelieu, 69
Cartier, Jacques, 118
Catalan, 72, 74
Cauchon, Pierre, 6–8
Chambres d'Agriculture, 246
Champlain, Samuel de, 118
Chaplain's office (*aumonerie*), 105
Charest, Jean, 128
Charles VI, 4
Charles VII, 5
Charles X, 46
Charlottetown accords, 127–28
Charte de la langue française (Charter of the French Language), 130
Chenière, Ernest, 93
Cher river, 4
Cherifi, Hanifa, 97
Chevenèment, Jean-Pierre, 95
Chinon, 5
Chirac, Jacques, 33, 76, 101, 103, 178, 243
Christian crosses, 96
Church and state separation, 8 (*See also* Secularism)
Cinema (*See* Cultural exception; Films)
Citizenship (*le Code de la nationalité*), 101
Citoyennes (female citizens), 173
Civil engineering school (*École des Ponts et des Chaussées*), 196
Clerical-nationalism (*le clérico-nationalisme*), 121
Clérico-nationalisme (clerical-nationalism), 121
Clovis, 93
Code de la nationalité (citizenship), 101
Collège Gabriel-Havez, 93–97
Collège Léon Cîrdes, 74

Collèges (middle schools), 69
Colons (settlers), 47
Commission Bélanger-Campeau, 126
Commission Laurendeau-Dunton, 129
Common agricultural policy (*Politique Agricole Commune*), 235
Communautarisme (separate communities), 98
Communauté Financière Africaine (African Financial Community), 148–49
Communauté franco-africaine (Franco-African Community), 148
Compiègne, 5
Concours d'entrée (entrance exam), 195, 197
Confédération Paysanne (Peasant Confederation), 240, 242–43, 246–47
Conseil constitutionnel, 177, 178
Conseil d'État (Council of State), 33, 95–96, 99
Conservatoire National des Arts et Métiers (applied arts school), 196
Constitutional Act (1791), 119
Contamined chicken scandal (Belgium), 236–37
Coopération Franco-Africaine, 149, 156
Corsica, 74, 76–77
Corvée de bois (summary execution), 50
Côte d'Ivoire (Ivory Coast), 149–54
Cour de cassation (French Court of Appeals), 53
Cour européenne des droits de l'homme (European Court of Human Rights), 32–33
Coureur des bois (trapper-hunter), 118
Crécy, 4

Creil affair (headscarfs), 93–97
Crime (*insécurité*), 99
Crimes against humanity, 25, 27–28, 52–53 (*See also* Papon, Maurice [trial of]; War crimes)
"Crisis of universalism," 103
Cross, James Richard, 124
Cultural exception (*l'exception culturelle*), 213–32; Franco-American cinema relations, 218–22; GATT talks and, 213–15, 218, 220–21; *Germinal* and *Jurassic Park*, 215–18; pros and cons of, 222–24; Web sites, 232
Cultural hamburgers (*hamburgers culturels*), 218
Culture heroes, 14–15
Culture "texts," 13–15
Curé (village priest), 92

D'Arc, Jeanne, 3–23; background, 3–4; birthdate (1411 or 1412), 3; birthplace (Domrémy), 3; burned at the stake, 7; canonization of, 7; as cultural hero, 14–15; divine inspiration and, 4, 15–16; *Front National* (Jean-Marie Le Pen's right-wing party) and, 11–13; military action, 5; role in Hundred Years War, 4; trial of, 6–7; Voltaire and, 7–8
Darc (probable last name of Jeanne D'Arc), 4
Dauphin, 4–5
Death camps, French Jews and, 27–31
Debré, Jean-Louis, 101
Déclaration des droits de l'homme et du citoyen (Declaration of the Rights of Man and of the Citizen), 173

Déclaration d'indépendance du Bas-Canada, 120
Decolonization, 148; pros and cons, 157–58
Decree of 2 Thermidor, 71
Défense et illustration de la langue française (Du Bellay), 69
de Gaulle, Charles, 26–27, 147; and end of the Algerian war, 51–52; visit to Quebec, 123
Delors, Jacques, 213
Democracy: affirmative action and, 202–3; parity and, 181–83
Dépêche de Toulouse (Jaurès), 72
Descoings, Richard, 199
Dey of Algiers, 46
Dictionnaire philosphique (Voltaire), 69
Diethylstilbestrol (DES), 236
Dion, Léon, 131
Discrimination positive (*See* Affirmative action)
Divine inspiration, Jeanne D'Arc and, 4, 15–16
Divorce, 176
Diwan *école maternelle* (Diwan kindergarten), 73
Diwan schools, 68, 76
Drancy, 27–28
Dreyfus, Alfred, 11
Droit du sol (territorial right), 101
Droit à la différence (right to be different), 97, 99
Dunkirk, 26
Durham, John George, 120

École des hautes études commerciales (School of Advanced Business Studies), 122
École des Ponts et des Chaussées (civil engineering school), 196
École libre (private school), 106, 194

École Nationale d'Administration (administration and management school), 195

École Normale Supérieure (prestigious teaching and humanities school), 195

ECOWAS, 150–51, 156

Edict of Villers-Cotterêts, 68

Education, 193–209; affirmative action and democratization of higher education, 202–3; *grandes écoles,* 193, 196–98; higher education and social privilege, 195–96; Sciences Po affirmative action plan, 197–200; secondary and postsecondary, 194–95; testing and merit pros and cons, 200–202; Web sites, 209 (*See also* Affirmative action)

Égalité, 175

el-Kader, Abd, 47

Electric torture (*la gégène*), 50

Enlightenment, 7–8

Entrance exam (*concours d'entrée*), 195, 197

Equal Opportunity Observatory (*Observatoire de la parité*), 178

European Charter on Regional and Minority Languages, 75–77, 79–80

European Commission, 75, 213

European Community, 235

European Convention on the Rights of Man, 32

European Court of Human Rights (*la Cour européenne des droits de l'homme*), 32–33

European Economic Community, 235

European Parliament, 176, 178, 179

European Union, 75, 181, 242; ban on U.S. hormone-treated beef, 237

Europe's Common Agricultural Policy, 242

Euskara, 73

Fanon, Frantz, *The Wretched of the Earth,* 157

Fédération Nationale des Syndicats d'Exploitants Agricoles (National Federation of Farmers' Unions), 240

Fellahs (peasants), 48

Female citizens (*citoyennes*), 173 (*See also* Parity)

Ferry, Jules, laws, 92

Feudal idioms, 71

Fifth Republic, 76, 177

Fifty-fifty representation (*une sur deux*), 180

Films: 1940–1944 occupation of France, 42; Algiers, 63; Francophone Africa, 168; Jeanne D'Arc, 22 (*See also* Cultural exception)

Fitzpatrick, Marjorie A., vii

FNSEA (French farmers' union), 246–47

Food and Drug Administration (FDA), 236

Food safety, 237–38, 242 (*See also* Genetically modified organisms [GMOs])

Franc Zone, 148

France, Anatole, 8

Francisation (Frenchification), 71

Franco-African Community (*communauté franco-africaine*), 148

Franco-American cinema relations, 218–22 (*See also* Cultural exception)

Franco-Prussian war, 47, 105

Francophone Africa, 145–69; background, 146–49; countries, 146;

decolonization through violent upheaval (pros and cons), 157–58; films and videos, 168; Ivory Coast crisis (2002), 149–54; language and culture in, 154–57; maintaining French language in (pros and cons), 158–59; Web sites, 169

Francophone Summit (*Sommet francophone*), 154

Francophonie, 121, 148, 154–55

Fraternité, 175

Fratriarchy, 175

Free French Forces, 27, 49, 147

French agriculture: background, 234–36; contemporary, 237; food safety, 236–37; genetically modified organisms (GMOs) and, 238–43; Web sites, 255–56

French born in Algeria (*les pieds noirs*), 48–49, 51

French cinema (*See* Cultural exception)

French Court of Appeals (*la Cour de cassation*), 53

French feminist movement (*See* Parity)

French Republic, 25

French Resistance, 28–30

French Revolution, 70, 92, 174, 176

French Union, 148

French women and politics (*See* Parity)

Frenchification (*francisation*), 71

Front de libération du Quebec (Front for the Liberation of Quebec), 123–24

Front de Libération Nationale (National Liberation Front), 49–50

Front National (Jean-Marie Le Pen's party), 11–13

Front Populaire, 48

Fur traders, 118

Gandhi, Mahatma, 16

Garne, Kheira, 45

Garne, Mohammed, 45

Gaspard, Françoise, Claude Servan-Schreiber and Anne Le Gall, *Au pouvoir citoyennes: liberté, egalité, parité*, 177

GATT (*See* General Agreement on Tariffs and Trade; Uruguay Round negotiations of the General Agreement on Tariffs and Trade)

Gbagbo, Laurent Koudou, 149

Gégène (electric torture), 50

Gendron Commission, 130

General Agreement on Tariffs and Trade (GATT), 235 (*See also* Uruguay Round negotiations of the General Agreement on Tariffs and Trade)

Genetically modified organisms (GMOs), 238–56; green revolution and, 243–45; José Bové's destruction of in France, 239–43; in U.S., 238–39

German, 70

Germany; Nazi Germany, 29–31; occupation of France, 25–27 (*See also* Papon, Maurice [trial of])

Germinal (French film), 215–18 (*See also* Cultural exception)

Germinal (Zola), 215

Giordan report, 73

Globalization (*See* Cultural exception; French agriculture; Genetically modified organisms [GMOs])

Gouges, Olympe de, 173

Gouverneurs des colonies, 147

Gouverneurs généraux, 146–47

Grandes écoles, 193, 195–98 (*See also* Education; Sciences Po)

Green Party (*les Verts*), 178

Green revolution, 243–45 (*See also* Genetically modified organisms [GMOs])
Groulx, Lionel, 122, 123
Guyenne, 4

Habitations à loyer modéré (housing projects), 100
Halimi, Gisèle, 178
Hamburgers culturels (cultural hamburgers), 218
Haut Canada (Upper Canada), 119
Headscarves in schools, 91–116; consequences, 98–100; Creil affair, 93–97; incidents, 97–98; newspaper and journal articles, 115–16 (*See also* Secularism)
Hélias, Pierre-Jakez, *The Horse of Pride*, 72
Henry V, 4
Henry VI, 4
Herr, Lucien, 10
Hidjeb (scarf), 96
High-speed train (*train à grande vitesse, TGV*), 216
Hitler's Final Solution, 31
Hollywood (*See* Cultural exception)
Hormones: and meat production, 236–37 (*See also* Genetically modified organisms [GMOs])
Horse of Pride, The (Hélias), 72
Housing projects (*habitations à loyer modéré*), 100
Hudson Bay Company, 118
Hundred Years War, 4
Hurons, 118

Ighilahriz, Louisette, 45
Ikastola schools, 73
Indigénat, 147
Industrialized agricultural production (*le productivisme*), 240
Insécurité (crime), 99

Institute of agronomic research (INRA, France), 239
Instituts universitaries de Technologie (technical schools), 195
Integration, 48
Iroquois, 118
Italian, 70
Ivoirité (cultural discrimination), 151–54
Ivory Coast (*Côte d'Ivoire*), 149–54

Jaures, Jean, *Dépêche de Toulouse*, 72
Jaurès, Jean, 10
Jews, in France during World War II, 26–31
Joliet, Louis, 118
Jospin, Lionel, 76, 95
Jurassic Park (American film), 215–18 (*See also* Cultural exception)

Kantor, Mickey, 220–21
Kindergarten (*la maternelle*), 68, 73
King, Jr., Martin Luther, 16, 241
Kippa, 96
Kropotkin, Peter, 241

Laïcité (*See* Secularism)
L'agriculture paysanne (peasant agriculture), 240
Lake Meech accords, 125–27
Lambert, Bernard, 240
Landry, Bernard, 128
Language (*See* Francophone Africa; Quebec; Regional languages)
Laporte, Pierre, 124
Larzac Plateau, 239
LaSalle, René, 118
Latin, 68–69, 72
Law 22, 130
Law 63, 130
Law 101, 130–31
Law 178, 130

Laye, Camara, *L'Enfant noir,* 154
Le Nouvel Observateur, 98
Le Pen, Jean-Marie, 11–13
Le rapatriement de la Constitution
    (patriation), 125
Legislation, parity and, 183–84
L'encéphalopathie spongiforme bovin
    (mad cow disease), 236
L'Enfant noir (Laye), 154
Les Beurs (second generation
    Maghrebi immigrants), 91, 93,
    99–102
Les Bourguignons (Burgundians),
    4, 5
Les pieds noirs (French born in
    Algeria), 48–49, 51
Lesage, Jean, 122
Lévesque, René, 123–125, 128, 130
L'exception culturelle (*See* Cultural
    exception)
L'Express, 177
Liberal Party (*Parti Libéral*), 122
Libération, 217
Liberté, 175
L'Idée d'indépendance au Quebec
    (Séguin), 123
Linas-Marcoussis, 150
Lingua franca (shared language), 71
Linguicide, 69–71
Linguistic policies (*See* Regional
    languages)
Loi Cadre, 148
Loi Deixonne, 72
Loi Falloux, 71
Loi Guigou, 101
Loi Haby, 73
Loi Méhaignerie, 101
Loi Roudy, 180
Loi Toubon, 73
Loire River, 4
Loire Valley, 5
Louis X, 174
Louis XIII, 69
Louis XIV, 118

Louis-Philippe, 47
Louisiana, 118
Lower Canada (*le Bas Canada*),
    119–20
Luftwaffe, 25
Lycées, 95

McDonald's, 233
Mad cow disease, 236
Maid of Orléans, The (Voltaire), 8
Maladie de la vache folle (mad cow
    disease), 236
*Manifeste des 577 pour une
    démocratie paritaire* (*Le
    Monde*), 177
Marcoussis bloc (*le bloc
    Marcoussiste*), 156
Marquette, Jacques, 118
Maternelle (kindergarten), 68, 73, 75
May Day, 12
Mendès-France, Pierre, 49
Merovingian royal dynasty, 93
Michelet, Jules, 9–10
Ministre des colonies, 146
Ministry of Education, 194
Minority languages in France (*See*
    Regional languages)
Mitterand, François, 49, 73, 93,
    194, 216, 221–22, 239
Moncornet, 26
Monsanto, 238–39
Montcalm, Louis-Joseph de, 119
Morocco, 100
Motherland (*la patrie*), 10
*Mouvement contre le racisme et pour
    l'amitié entre les peuples*
    (MRAP), 95
Mulroney, Brian, 126, 127
Muslims: Algeria and, 48–49;
    headscarves in schools and,
    91–116

Napoléon III, 47
National Assembly, 26, 50, 75

Index

National Convention, 69

National Federation of Farmers'
Unions (*Fédération Nationale
des Syndicats d'Exploitants
Agricoles*), 240

National Liberation Front (*Front de
Libération Nationale,* the FLN),
49–50

Nazi Germany, 29–31

Négres blancs d'Amerique
(Vallières), 129

New France (*La Nouvelle
France*), 118

92 Resolutions, 120

Norman, 71

Normandy, 4

North African immigrants, 91, 93,
99–102

North American Free Trade
Agreement (NAFTA), 133

Nouvelle France (New France), 118

Nuremberg Tribunal, 31

*Nuremberg War Crimes Trial
Proceedings,* 27–28

Oberg, Karl, 30

Observatoire de la parité (Equal
Opportunity Observatory),
178, 179

Occitan, 70, 72, 74

Ohio River, 118

Ohio Valley, 118–19

Oise river, 26

Organisation de l'armée secrète, 51

Orléans, 4

Ottoman Empire, 46

Papineau, Louis-Joseph, 119–20

Papon, Maurice (trial of), 25–43;
appropriateness of the case,
34–35; background, 25–27;
the indictment, 27–28; photo
of Papon, 32; reexamination of
the past, 34; the trial, 28–31;

the verdict, 31–33; verdict
aftermath, 31–33; Vichy,
26–27

Parity (*la parite*), 173–91; achieving
parity, 176–80; French women
and politics, 174–76; necessity
of legislation, 183–84; parity
and democracy, 181–83; parity
vs. affirmative action, 180–81;
Web sites, 191

Parizeau, Jacques, 127–28

Parti Libéral, 122, 128

Parti Québécois (PQ), 123–25,
128, 130

Passeron, Jean-Claude, 195, 198–99

Patois, 67, 70–71

Patriation (*le rapatriement de la
Constitution*), 125

Patrie (motherland), 10

Patrimony, 3

Pearson, Lester, 129

Peasant agriculture (*l'agriculture
paysanne*), 240

Peasant Confederation
(*Confédération Paysanne*), 240,
242–43, 246–47

Peasants (*fellahs*), 48

Péguy, Charles, 10

Perrier water, 236

Pétain, Marshal Philippe, 26

Philippe le Bon, 5

Philippe V, 174

Place du Vieux-Marché, 7

Plains of Abraham, 119

Plantagenet dynasty (England), 4

Poitiers, 4

Politique Agricole Commune
(common agricultural
policy), 235

Polytechnique (engineering school),
195, 196

Pope Benedict XV, 7

Pope Calixtus II, 9

Popular Front, 92

Postsecondary education in France
(*See* Education)
*Pour un modèle européen
d'enseignement supérieur*
(Attali), 198
Prefecture of the Gironde, 27, 30
Préparatoire (*prépa*), 195
Priority education zones (*Zones
d'éducation prioritaire*), 197
Private school (*école libre*), 106, 194
Productivisme (industrialized
agricultural production), 240
Project républicain, 95
Proudhon, Pierre-Joseph, 241
Provençal, 71
Public schools, 194
Pucelle (maiden), 5

Quebec, 117–44; in the eighteenth
and nineteenth centuries,
119–21; in the twentieth
century, 121–22; Canadian
Confederation (pros and cons),
132; the Charlottetown
accords, 127–28; the
Constitutional debate (1982),
125; early history of, 118–19;
the Lake Meech accords,
125–27; language and identity,
129–31; the October Crisis,
123–24; post-Charlottetown,
128–29; the Quiet Revolution,
122–23; separation from
Canada (pros and cons),
133–35; Web sites, 143
Quebec Act (1774), 119
Queen Victoria, 121
Quiet Revolution (*la Révolution
tranquille*), 122–23
Quotas, 176–77, 180 (*See also*
Affirmative action; Parity)
Ratonnades (raids), 50
Razzia, 47
Rebellion des Patriotes, 120

Regional cultural programming,
74–75
Regional languages, 67–90;
European Charter on Regional
and Minority Languages,
75–77, 79–80; percent spoken,
74; post-World War II and
linguistic policies, 72–75;
pros and cons of teaching,
77–79; revolution and
linguicide, 69–71; the Third
Republic, 71–72; under
monarchy, 68–69; Web sites
for, 81–83, 90
Révolution tranquille (Quiet
Revolution), 122–23
Right to be different (*le droit a la
différence*), 97, 99
Right-wing partisan causes, Jeanne
D'Arc and, 11–13
Rotterdam, Holland, 25–26
Roudy, Yvette, 180
Rouen, 6–7

Saint Lawrence River, 118
Salic law, 174
Scarf (*hidjeb*), 96
School of Advanced Business
Studies (*École des hautes études
commerciales*), 122
Sciences Po, 197–200 (*See also*
Affirmative action; Education)
Second Republic, 47
Secondary education in France (*See*
Education)
Secularism (*laïcité*), 91–116;
background, 92–93; pros and
cons of tolerance of differences,
104–6; Web sites, 116 (*See also*
Headscarves in schools)
Séguin, Maurice, *L'Idée
d'independance au Quebec,* 123
Separation of church and state (*See*
Secularism)

Index

Serments de Strasbourg, 68

Sétif, 48

Settlers (*colons*), 47

Shared language (*lingua franca*), 71

Signum, 72

Sommet francophone (Francophone Summit), 154

Special Services: Algeria 1955–57 (Aussaresses), 52–53

Standards for Foreign Language in Learning in the 21st Century, xiii

Stasi commission, 102–3

Suffrage: French women, 174 (*See also* Parity)

Summary execution (*la corvée de bois*), 50

Tariffs, 237

Teacher education institutions (*Instituts universitaires de formation de maîtres*), 195

Teaching school (École Normale Supérieure), 195

Technical diploma (*brevet de technicien supérieur*), 194

Technical schools (*Instituts universitaries de Technologie*), 195

Terminale (last year of high school), 194, 200

Territorial right (*le droit du sol*), 101

Terror tactics, for and against, 54–55

Testing: merit and, 200–202 (*See also Concours d'entrée;* Education)

Third Reich, 29–31

Third Republic, 47, 174; Jules Ferry laws, 92; regional languages and, 71–72

Thoreau, Henry David, 241

Thorez, Maurice, 220

Tirailleurs Sénégalais, 147

Torture: for and against, 55–56; in Algiers by French, 45–46, 50

Touvier, Paul, 27

Train à grande vitesse, TGV (high-speed train), 216

Trapper-hunter (*coureur des bois* or *voyageur*), 118

Treaty of Maastricht, 73

Treaty of Paris, 119, 123

Treaty of Troyes, 4

Trials: Jeanne D'Arc, 6–7; Maurice Papon, 28–31

Trudeau, Pierre Elliott, 124–25, 129

Tunisia, 100

UN Cartagena Protocol on Biosafety, 242

Une sur deux (fifty-fifty representation), 180

UNESCO (*See* United Nations Educational, Scientific and Cultural Organization)

Union Act (1841), 120

United Nations Educational, Scientific and Cultural Organization (UNESCO), 214–15

Upper Canada (*le Haut Canada*), 119

Uruguay Round negotiations of the General Agreement on Tariffs and Trade (GATT), 213–15, 218, 220–21, 235 (*See also* Cultural exception)

Valenti, Jack, 221–23

Vallières, Pierre, *Négres blancs d'Amérique,* 129

Vaucouleurs, 5

Verts, les (Green Party), 178

Vichy state, 25–27, 72 (*See also* Papon, Maurice [trial of])

Village priest (*curé*), 92

Villepin, Dominique de, 150

Voltaire, 7–8; *Dictionnaire philosphique* (Philosophical

Dictionary), 69; *La Pucelle* (The Maid of Orleans), 8
Voyageur (trapper-hunter), 118

War crimes, 52–53 (*See also* Crimes against humanity; Papon, Maurice [trial of])
Web sites, 255–56; Algeria, 64; cultural exception, 23; Francophone Africa, 169; French agriculture, 255–56; French education, 209; genetically modified organisms, 255–56; headscarves, 116; immigration, 116; Jeanne D'Arc, 23; newspapers, 43;

Papon trial, 43; parity for French women, 191; Quebec, 143; regional languages, 81–83, 90; secularism, 116; World War II, 43
Wolfe, James, 119
Worker autonomy (*l'autogestion*), 241
World hunger, biocrops and, 245–46
World Trade Organization, 221, 237
Wretched of the Earth (Fanon), 157

Yarmulke, 96, 103, 105, 106

Zola, Emile, *Germinal*, 215
Zones d'éducation prioritaire (priority education zones), 197

About the Authors

MICHAEL B. KLINE is Professor of French at Dickinson College.
NANCY C. MELLERSKI is Professor of French at Dickinson College.